Theodor Geiger

ON SOCIAL ORDER

AND MASS SOCIETY

THE HERITAGE OF SOCIOLOGY

A Series Edited by Morris Janowitz

Theodor Geiger

ON SOCIAL ORDER
AND MASS SOCIETY

Selected Papers

Edited and with an Introduction by
RENATE MAYNTZ

Translations by Robert E. Peck

THE UNIVERSITY OF CHICAGO PRESS

CHICAGO AND LONDON

Library of Congress Catalog Card Number: 69–19157

THE UNIVERSITY OF CHICAGO PRESS, CHICAGO 60637
The University of Chicago Press, Ltd., London W.C. 1

Contents

Preface

THEODOR GEIGER (1891–1952), who was born in Germany and emigrated to Denmark after Hitler's rise to power, has been an important figure in German as well as in Scandinavian sociology. In contrast, among the English-speaking public Geiger is very little known, in spite of the fact that he did important and often pioneering work in many areas of sociology that have enjoyed sustained interest in the United States. Moreover, there is a great affinity between Geiger's general outlook and that which characterizes much of American sociology. Had he published his major works in English, Geiger would almost certainly have won wide acclaim and renown in the United States during his lifetime. However, none of his major works has so far been translated into English. Geiger was a prolific writer. A recent bibliography counts 164 titles, of which 92 are in German, 50 in one of the Scandinavian languages, mainly Danish, 17 in English, and 5 in other languages. The English titles include only articles and some proposals and outlines written together with David Glass for the subcommittee on stratification and mobility of the International Sociological Association.[1]

[1] See the bibliography contained in the volume edited by Paul Trappe, *59*, which also includes all existing translations. The selective bibliography compiled for this book is based on Trappe's and contains all 17 items in the English language. In the following, references to Geiger's works will be made by citing in italic type the corresponding number in the bibliography at the end of this book.

Throughout his life as a sociologist, Geiger combined theoretical with empirical interests. If he rejected all speculation without a factual basis, he showed an equally strong disdain for empiricism without a theoretical foundation. The topics he dealt with include the nature and basic approach of sociology; fundamental concepts; education, including adult education; industrial organization; class structure, stratification, and mobility; the history, social origin, and functions of the intelligentsia; the sociology of law; the tactics of propaganda; ideology; the nature of modern "mass society" and democracy.

Although many of these topics are interrelated, an attempt to offer a representative cross section from Geiger's lifework would have produced a book of necessarily fragmented appearance. In such a cross-sectional anthology it would be impossible to present Geiger's views on any one subject fully enough to demonstrate the level of sophistication he achieved. Empirical studies in particular do not easily lend themselves to excerpting. Besides, there has been appreciable progress in sociological analysis in a number of the areas Geiger had dealt with, so that today some of his publications can no longer command the same interest as at the time of their first appearance. For these reasons it was decided to limit the translation to selections from three books which, at least in the opinion of this editor, have fully retained their intrinsic interest.[2] These selections present major parts of Geiger's writings on the sociology of law and the social order, on ideology, and on the nature of modern society. The selections were arranged in such a way as to bring out the train of thought that links them into one comprehensive and coherent argument. However, the reader need not follow the suggested sequence but may start with the second or third part of the translation. The introductory chapter which follows may help the reader to decide which of the three parts of the translation is of the greatest interest to him.

The three books on which the translation is based belong to Geiger's later works; two of them were published only after his

[2]   *27, 48, 58.*

death. But all three books incorporate and elaborate on topics with which Geiger had been concerned for a long time. In all of them, it is Geiger the theorist and political thinker who is speaking, not the careful researcher and analyst of empirical data. To counteract somewhat the bias inherent in this selection, the introductory chapter will briefly describe Geiger's work in the areas not documented in this translation.

To present Geiger's major arguments as fully as possible it was decided not to translate a few chapters from each book in full, omitting the rest, but rather to choose smaller sections from a wider range of chapters in such a way that a coherent work results. To make it easier for those readers who wish to locate the translated sections in the original German texts, the following rules were adopted. German chapter headings were translated as literally as possible, unless specifically stated otherwise in a footnote. However, owing to the omission of whole chapters, the chapters in the translation may have different numbers than in the original books. In the *Sociology of Law*, where Geiger makes use of subsection headings, these were also translated as literally as possible. In the few cases where a paragraph in a chapter or subsection of the translation was actually taken from one differently entitled in the original, this is indicated in a footnote. The original sequence of chapters, subsections, and paragraphs was retained unaltered. The structuring of the text by paragraphs corresponds by and large to that in the original sources, though occasionally smaller parts taken from several paragraphs were combined into one paragraph. No special indication is given where whole chapters or (in chapters of the *Sociology of Law* only) subsections preceding the first translated subsection have been omitted. The subsequent omission of subsections, however, as well as the omission of paragraphs, sentences, or parts of a sentence, is indicated by the usual omission sign.

Inevitably, there were occasional conflicts between producing a smooth translation and keeping scrupulously to Geiger's sometimes involved formulations. In a number of such cases this conflict was resolved in favor of readability. However, this does not mean that liberties have been taken with the German text. A correct rendering of meaning always had absolute priority, but this does not exclude some polishing. Such polishing includes the occasional verbalization of a symbol or formula in the *Sociology of Law*. It might also be mentioned here that Geiger's symbols were used rather than the first letters of the English words for which they now stand.

The translator and I have occasionally added notes to the translated matter. These are distinguished from Geiger's notes by the abbreviation *Ed.* or *Trans.* following the note.

To render thanks is the editor's final and most pleasant duty, though a difficult one where so many persons have contributed. Morris Janowitz, convinced many years ago that to make Geiger's work better known was a worthwhile task, is to be thanked for making the arrangements necessary for the realization of the project. Frank Benseler of Luchterhand Verlag has helped solve a difficult problem which arose with respect to the copyright for one of the books chosen for translation. Uta Gerhardt has offered advice on the selections to be made. Robert Peck, the translator, has performed his often difficult task with great care and devotion, making cooperation with him a pleasant experience for the editor. Both the translator and the editor have profited from the advice of many persons on difficult translation problems. Dr. Rehbinder especially is to be thanked for frequent help with a number of legal terms used in the *Sociology of Law*. Gertrud Winkler helped with proofreading and the adaptation of footnotes. Last but not least, I want to thank Gisela Fischer for the arduous labor of typing the final version of the manuscript. It goes without saying that ultimate responsibility for any shortcomings of the book rests with the editor.

Renate Mayntz

Introduction

THEODOR GEIGER: THE MAN AND HIS WORK

Biography[1]

THEODOR GEIGER was born in 1891 into the family of a German gymnasium professor. He grew up in Bavaria. As a schoolboy he developed an interest in Scandinavian languages, and his parents rewarded him with a trip to Norway when he graduated from the gymnasium. Later on he studied law in Munich and Würzburg. The First World War broke out after he had completed his first juridical state examination. Geiger volunteered for military service and was wounded in Russia. After the war he finished his studies and got his doctorate in law. His first major publication, which dealt with the legal position and social situation of illegitimate children, shows his developing sociological interests. During this time, he was a social democrat by political orientation. In 1918 he had joined the Social Democratic Party, which he left again in 1932. Although clearly influenced by socialist thinking, Geiger was never an orthodox Marxist, nor did he find it easy to subscribe to party doctrine and submit to party discipline.

In 1920 Geiger moved to Berlin, where he subsequently worked as a journalist, in adult education, and in the national Bureau of Statistics. From 1924 to 1928 he taught at the Institute of Adult Education (*Volkshochschule*) in Berlin. By the end of this period, Geiger had developed into a full-fledged

[1]   The following is based on Paul Trappe's introduction to *59*.

1

sociologist and had published several sociological works. In 1928 he was called to a chair of sociology at the Politechnic (*Technische Hochschule*) in Braunschweig. His early social democratic convictions and his critical attitude towards ideologies brought him under attack when the Nazis came to power, and although he tried to ward off the imminent danger of being dismissed by pointing to his patriotism and lack of Marxist orthodoxy,[2] the pressure brought on him made him emigrate to Denmark before the end of 1933.

At first Geiger lived in Copenhagen. He received a research fellowship from the Rockefeller Foundation and worked at the Institute of History and Economics, also giving guest lectures at the University of Copenhagen. In 1938 he was given a full professorship at the University of Aarhus. In 1940 when German troops occupied Denmark, Geiger had to leave Aarhus and sought refuge with his parents-in-law in Odense, where he continued to write. From the beginning he was under police surveillance, and life became increasingly difficult until in 1943 he had to flee. He went to Sweden, where he was later joined by his wife and children. For the next two years Geiger lived in Stockholm, teaching there as well as in Uppsala and Lund. During this time the contact with the Uppsala school of philosophy had a stimulating influence on his work, especially with respect to value philosophy and ideology.

After the war, Geiger returned to Aarhus and joined the university again. There he founded and directed a social research institute which was the first Scandinavian institute devoted to sociological research. With several Scandinavian colleagues he started a publication series which later developed into the journal *Acta Sociologica*. Geiger also belonged to the founders of the International Sociological Association. This active and productive life came to a sudden end when he unexpectedly died in 1952 aboard the ship bringing him back to Denmark after spending a year as visiting professor in Toronto, Canada.

[2]   In a letter written to the Rektor of the Technische Hochschule on September 1, 1933, partly quoted by Paul Trappe in *59*.

Methodological Position, General Approach, and Basic Concepts

Geiger's methodological position has always been fundamentally a positivistic one. But he developed this position explicitly only in his later writings, those he worked on after his emigration and especially after he had been involved in the debate with the Uppsala school of philosophy.[3] Geiger strongly advocated the principle of the methodological unity of all empirical sciences. He saw no essential, qualitative difference between natural and social sciences: there is only one kind of science, and its fundamental method consists in establishing laws.[4] Sociology, in other words, is a nomothetic discipline and has attained the status of a true science only after overcoming the speculative and normative approaches which characterized its early phase. This view implies a rejection of the idiographic approach; Geiger's arguments in this connection are the ones familiarly advanced by the analytical (or neo-positivistic) theory of science. Sociology should investigate, not the unique, but that which recurs or is common to a plurality of persons or groups, and formulate it in statements of covariance. This presupposes the use of general rather than individualizing concepts, and of measurement.

It is consonant with this view that Geiger put a strong emphasis on empirical sociology, which proceeds by inductive generalization to formulate testable propositions whose objective validity depends on their agreement with observation. However, the laws that sociology may discover are in Geiger's opinion covariances which in most cases must be expressed in probabilistic terms. Geiger rejected the ontological concept of cause and acknowledged the arguments against a deterministic

---

[3]   See Part II of this book, and especially the introduction to Part II; see also the three previously unpublished items in the collection published by Paul Trappe, *59*, pp. 45–55, 75–84, 97–99.

[4]   This view is expressed in *46*, where Geiger also discusses the special problems in sociology of achieving precision, due to the constant historical changes in the phenomena under discussion and the difficulty of gaining access to them.

understanding of causality. His modified conception of causality substitutes probabilistic for deterministic relations. But he did not ask whether probabilistic statements may not—at least in many cases—merely reflect the joint operation of several deterministic relationships which we have as yet failed to isolate. Nor did he, in the context of his methodological considerations, discuss the question of the nature of uniformities in the social realm. Correspondingly he did not distinguish between mere empirical regularities (observed correlations) and social laws. This reflects a still widely prevalent hiatus between methodological statements of principle and substantive considerations about the nature of "social laws."

By defining empirical sociology as *conceptually structured* quantitative investigation of social phenomena,[5] Geiger explicitly rejected a theoretically uninformed empiricism. He repeatedly stressed the importance of conceptual analysis as a means to develop clear concepts which provide the frame of reference necessary to guide and structure an investigation. Such concepts are to be descriptive (that is, not normative) and to have precise empirical referents; they are to be developed from observational data and experience. This does not mean, however, that Geiger adhered to the doctrine of operationalism. Nor was he a behaviorist in the sense of rejecting introspection and reference to subjective factors which cannot be observed directly. Geiger paid due attention to subjective factors while being fully aware of the technical and methodological difficulties involved in making valid inferences about them. He accepted the use of introspection, mainly to formulate hypotheses where phenomena are not directly accessible to observation.

Geiger's methodological position implies the acceptance of the maxim of value freedom, that is, the assumption of a clear distinction between fact and value and the restriction of science to making only statements of fact, but no value judgments. The epistemological rationale for this restriction is that the criterion of truth in the sense of an agreement with reality is applicable only to statements of fact. The preference for the criterion of

[5]   See *59*, p. 79.

truth over other possible criteria which might be used to define the goal of a science is itself a value decision, as Geiger realized very well.[6] In the later years of his life his passionate engagement on behalf of this value became ever more clearly pronounced. In the form of a strict and uncompromising rationalism it pervades his writings on ideology and still more his last book.[7]

It seems that Geiger was always of a critical bent of mind. But in the different phases of his life the objects of his criticism changed. If he directed himself against irrationalism, ideology, and the confusion of facts with value in his later years, his early criticism was of a more pragmatic nature. If in his later years he stressed the values of truth and rationality, his earlier devotion was more to social values such as justice, equality, and the emancipation of the underprivileged. This socially committed attitude also expressed itself in Geiger's membership in the Social Democratic Party.

The joint influence of socialist thought and a socially committed attitude is visible in Geiger's early concern—both practical and as a writer[8]—with adult education. Adult education at that time was especially directed at the working class. Geiger saw it not simply as a "cultural mission"; he also focused on the political and social consequences of adult education. He pointed out that lack of appropriate education makes for ideological susceptibility and demanded that adult education should attempt to promote intellectual capabilities instead of merely giving the worker access to the nation's "culture." He advocated reforms in the organization and curriculum of the existing institutions of adult education. But his views implied a reformist rather than a revolutionary attitude, and he stressed the adaptive and integrative functions of education.

Since Geiger was interested in the subject of education throughout his life, the way in which he dealt with it reflects

6   See Part II below, p. 164.
7   See *58*, and Part III of the translation.
8   These writings consist of a series of journal articles listed in the bibliography in *59*.

quite well certain shifts in his basic approach. At first his interest in education was of a practical nature. Later he became more interested in a systematic and analytical treatment of the subject. Though he never devoted a major work to this topic, he did discuss briefly the relationship between sociology and education as two scientific disciplines and also outlined a program for the sociological investigation of education, both as an institution and as a major social function.[9] Still later, in a third phase, Geiger dealt with education in connection with his demand for intellectualization and the development of nonideological, value-free thinking. This can be seen in Part III of the translation.

During the first stage of his career, which was characterized by a more active engagement on behalf of social values and social reforms, Geiger's writings frequently had both a polemical and a normative flavor. If he later insisted on strictly distinguishing between the factual and the normative, he himself did not always conform to this rule in his early years. But Geiger never advocated a complete abstinence from values for the scientist. As pointed out in the introduction to Part II, he emphasized that the choice of questions for scientific investigation may quite legitimately be determined by subjectively held values. But it is not clear whether he realized that every question about reality inevitably implies some value premises by the mere fact of its necessary selectivity, its singling out of certain phenomena, aspects, or relationships in preference to other equally possible ones.[10] The same selectivity is of course implied in the formation of the concepts in which a question is formulated. By virtue of this fact the results obtained in answer to some question, even though empirically correct, can never be value-indifferent, that is, the results will have a selective significance in terms of the interest which guided the question. A similar argument can be made with respect to the "facts" with which social scientists work, and

[9]   See 8; this article is reprinted in 59, pp. 293–315.
[10]   At least in one place such a realization may be implied; see p. 149 below and reference to this in the introduction to Part II.

which Geiger held to be clearly distinguishable from values. If facts are recognized as constructs resulting from selective perception, the very possibility of strictly separating facts from values becomes doubtful. Geiger obviously had a vested interest in the assumption of such a dichotomy, because it is basic to his later theory about ideology and the social consequences of the objectivation of values. It follows that Geiger would certainly have rejected the dialectical conception of social science as inherently critical of reality, that is, as able to make objectively founded value judgments. This latter view is based on the fundamental premise of the unity of fact and value, and among its adherents Geiger is likely to find his most outspoken critics.

As briefly mentioned above, the second phase in Geiger's work and thinking is characterized by the development of a more systematic and analytical sociological approach. This development started while he was still in Berlin, and two publications from the second half of the 1920's reflect it especially: *Die Gruppe und die Kategorien Gemeinschaft und Gesellschaft* (The group and the concepts of "Gemeinschaft" and "Gesellschaft"), 1927, and *Die Gestalten der Gesellung* (The forms of sociation), 1928.[11] These publications also attest to the influence which the so-called school of formal sociology (e.g., Simmel, Tönnies, Vierkandt) had on Geiger. He emphasized, as did Simmel, that sociology as a science is not defined by an object of cognition all its own, but rather by its method and cognitive intention. Again like Simmel he stressed that social phenomena are not static substances, but events and processes. Accordingly, Geiger demanded that dynamic conceptual models be used. And whereas his later works are no longer characterized by the formalistic approach, he retained the emphasis on processual analysis throughout his life, as can be seen later in his treatment of mobility.

In the two publications mentioned above, Geiger attempted to develop analytical dimensions and basic categories to describe and classify forms of social association. He starts from

[11]   See 5 and 6.

the notion that "I" and "We," individual and group life, are two fundamental and inseparable modes of human existence. His concept of group is developed in a critical discussion of Vierkandt and Tönnies. With respect to the latter he criticizes especially the tendency to conceive of "Gemeinschaft" and "Gesellschaft" as a dichotomy of real types of groups; these concepts, Geiger argues, rather refer to principles of social organization which can be found in varying proportions to characterize all groups. In addition to groups, Geiger also analyzes other forms of association, among them the pair and the social stratum. While it is pointless to describe Geiger's analytical system in detail, it should at least be mentioned that much of his later work of a more substantive nature is an elaboration of ideas already contained in these early publications. This holds for parts of the *Sociology of Law* (e.g., the historical sequence of custom, mores, habitual or common law, and formal law, which he developed there), as well as for the distinction of forms of social association which he made in his later analysis of mass society. Thus there have been significant developments, but never a radical break in the work of Theodor Geiger.

Class Society, Stratification, and Mobility

Some of Geiger's most widely read publications are devoted to the problems of class structure, stratification, and social mobility. His interest in this area dates back to the late 1920's and his views at that time still reflected his socialist orientation. This interest can also be seen in two essays about industrial sociology published in 1929 and 1930,[12] where he stressed that the industrial firm is shaped in important respects by the type of society in which it exists. Subscribing to a dichotomic view of class structure at the time, Geiger saw the existing class antagonism reflected in the social organization of the factory and criticized the notion of the firm's being a co-operative community (*Werkgemeinschaft*) as an ideology which masks the real conflicts of interest.

[12]   See 7 and 11.

At that time the Marxist concept of class and class structure was a major point of reference for most European sociologists dealing with this topic—whether they accepted, rejected, or modified it. This is also true of Geiger, who at first used the term *class* in the Marxist sense. However, even in his first publication on the subject, *Zur Theorie des Klassenbegriffs und der proletarischen Klasse* (On the theory of the class concept and the proletarian class), 1930,[13] Geiger rejected the Marxist doctrine of the perennial and exclusive predominance of a class structure based on the ownership of the means of production. Based on a rather elaborate analysis of different class concepts, Geiger's conclusion is that the Marxist concept of class society is a type concept which describes the prevalent tendency (*Tendenztypus*), but not necessarily all of reality. He argued that, in principle, there may be other relevant criteria of stratification, although at that time the Marxist class concept still seemed to him to capture adequately the predominant features of contemporary society.

Geiger's approach to the subject attests to his conception of society as essentially dynamic. His focus is on processes of historical change. Thus the then prevalent class structure is seen as having superseded the earlier, corporate structure of estate society, which increasingly recedes into the background with the growing importance of productive relations for the shaping of the social structure. But he still finds recognizable residues of the old estate order within class society, and he predicts that after a period of increasing class antagonism, class society may in turn undergo a change in a yet unknown direction. In this process of development, he sees the classes as passing through different stages, from being mere statistical categories to assuming the characteristics of social groups. This recalls Marx's distinction between classes *an sich* and *für sich*, though Geiger phrases this difference in terms of his own formal categories.

Using the class concept to describe a particular historical configuration, Geiger subsumed it under the more general con-

---

[13]   See *12*.

cept of stratification—a terminological decision to which he held through his later writings on the subject. The concept of stratum means more to him than a mere statistical class based on some objective criterion. Rather it is a group in the sociological sense, a concept which refers to a real phenomenon. However, he distinguishes clearly between subjective and objective aspects of social class, pointing out that there is no necessary coincidence, that is, no deterministic relationship between objective social position and class consciousness.

In view of Geiger's subsequent revisions of earlier opinions, it is of interest to note his treatment of the middle class in *Zur Theorie des Klassenbegriffs.* Geiger points out that the middle class is heterogeneous in composition, partly characterized by residual elements of estatelike grouping and the corresponding corporate ideology, and cannot therefore be unambiguously assigned to either of the two large, opposing classes. Geiger saw no positive, integrative function for the middle class but rather held that, speaking in terms of a general tendency, it would be ground to pieces by the developing class society. Although the picture of a society composed of three rather than two classes may be correct as a static snapshot, the dichotomous class model, in his opinion, more truly describes the predominant tendency of development.

In a study published two years later and based on statistical data, *Die soziale Schichtung des deutschen Volkes* (Social stratification in Germany),[14] Geiger sought to isolate the socioeconomic strata that act as collective forces in economic life and that share a similar mentality. For this purpose, the economically active population was classified into five groups. The classification modifies the simple dichotomous distinction between capitalists and proletarians by taking into account such additional criteria as size of enterprise, being independent but not an employer, and degree of qualification (for employed persons). It is not assumed that everyone who, by the objective criteria used, belongs to one particular stratum necessarily

[14]   See *15.*

shares its mentality; rather the objective strata circumscribe the potential sphere of expansion of a given mentality.

In his analysis of the five strata, Geiger distinguishes two middle class groups: the "old" middle class of artisans, merchants, and farmers, characterized by a defensive mentality and the struggle to retain their threatened prestige, and the "new" middle class of highly qualified employees and professionals, characterized by a pervasive ideological insecurity. The middle class as a whole, because of its orientational insecurity and defensive attitude, is held to be highly susceptible to some new ideologies, including the Nazi ideology of *Volksgemeinschaft*. In a noteworthy revision of his earlier view, Geiger now thinks that the increasing importance of the new salaried middle class—which has a nonproletarian mentality even though by the objective criterion of position within the productive system, it should be called for the most part proletarian—may foreshadow the ascendancy of a new principle of stratification, rather than being doomed to disappear in a growing class antagonism. But what this new principle would be Geiger could not yet say.

This idea was developed further in *Die Klassengesellschaft im Schmelztiegel* (Class society in the melting pot), written after World War II.[15] By this time Geiger had become convinced that Marxist class theory, while correctly describing major tendencies of development in an earlier phase of capitalist society, can no longer be fruitfully applied to modern industrial society. While defending the Marxist class concept against polemical attacks which do no justice to its intended meaning, he points out that a number of predictions made by class theory have been proven false by the course of development. His criticism is especially directed against the predictions of increasing immiserization of the proletariat, a polarization of the classes, and heightened class antagonism. In particular, Geiger points to the rising standard of living of the working class, the

---

[15]   This book was first published in Danish and one year later in German; see *28* and *32*.

decrease in working class consciousness and militancy, the institutionalization of class conflict through bargaining procedures between legitimate collective organizations, and above all to the increasing differentiation within the large group of salaried employees. There is now no question of a threat that the middle class will disappear through absorption into one of the formerly predominant classes. Professional experts, intellectuals, and civil servants have come to constitute new and important strata, and Geiger even sees the position of the "old" middle class as economically improved, in spite of progressing industrialization. Thus the class structure is being crosscut by a variety of new stratification principles, and class position in the traditional Marxist sense seems to Geiger no longer to be of prevalent importance. He emphasizes especially the increasing importance of income as a criterion of stratification, pointing out that this criterion makes for a status continuum rather than for the emergence of bounded social classes.

In this book, Geiger also discusses the possibility for a managerial ruling class to develop. He modifies Burnham's hypothesis by emphasizing the expansion of state bureaucracy, which to Geiger will most likely provide the new ruling group. In this connection he envisages a reversion in the relationship which Marxist theory held to obtain between the economic basis, the class structure, and the political superstructure: the economic system can be, and increasingly is, shaped and changed by political decisions made by a ruling group which no longer represents predominantly or even exclusively the capitalists, so that the political system becomes the determining agent. In this matter, Marxist theory seems to Geiger to have been based on the implicit assumption of a liberalistic economy, which has a historically limited validity.

The last book to be mentioned in the context of this section is Geiger's monograph on mobility and changes in social stratification in the city of Aarhus.[16] The study is based upon census data for nearly 40,000 men living in Aarhus in 1949, providing

[16]   See *39;* there are also a number of articles on the subject of mobility, see *47* and *52;* see also the five papers, *41* through *45.*

information about their present occupation, their father's and —where applicable—their father-in-law's occupations. The analysis of these data produced what can probably be called Geiger's best empirical study, a pioneer work in the field of mobility both by virtue of its conceptual approach and the techniques of evaluation used.

True to his emphasis on a dynamic perspective, Geiger thought it insufficient simply to describe a status distribution or even to establish the movement of individuals within a given stratification system used as a static frame of reference. He therefore turned his attention to the changes within the stratification system produced by fluctuations (aggregate mobility) which change the relative size as well as the social rank of strata. But it is not vertical mobility along a dimension of social status which Geiger investigated. He argues that—at least with the data available to him—no vertical system of clearly bounded and unambiguously ranked strata can be established. Therefore he used eighteen occupational categories (occasionally combined into five more comprehensive ones) to chart intergenerational mobility. To take the time dimension into account, there is also a comparative analysis of mobility tables for different age groups in the sample. Furthermore the study extends to relations of intermarriage, which are shown to approximate somewhat more to statistical randomness than does the choice of occupation.

Geiger performed an elaborate statistical analysis on his data, using as points of reference the three ideal states of a complete lack of mobility, total fluctuation, and a statistically perfect (i.e., completely proportional) distribution of the men with different social origins over the occupational groups. He used a number of statistical measures for his analysis, and it may be noted that he in fact developed what corresponds to the now well-known index of association, though he neither gave it this name nor actually used it in his evaluation.[17]

---

[17]   To be more precise: the two indices of representation which Geiger used to analyze the diagonal cells of the mobility tables, if combined into one formula, correspond to the association index now in use.

To report Geiger's findings would consume too much space, and even then it would hardly be possible to show how carefully and with what painstaking attention to factual details Geiger went about his task of data analysis and interpretation. Throughout he took into account the many factors which impinge upon the reliability of the data and the validity of the inferences made from them. However, this also had the effect of inhibiting conclusions of larger theoretical significance, conclusions going beyond the empirical generalizations derived from the data. As many before and after him, Geiger faced the difficulty of combining high empirical exactness with high theoretical significance. The intrinsic limitations of his data in terms of the area and period covered assigns the status of hypothesis to those general explanations of his findings that he did offer. The most important of these refers to the observation that the rate of mobility tends to decrease towards the present. Geiger suggests that this may be partly due to the fact that after a period of transition between different types of stratification, there is now following a period of consolidation and greater stability. In addition, the tendency toward socioeconomic leveling connected with democratization may, he argues, decrease the subjective desire for upward mobility as a means to escape from an underprivileged position. These suggested explanations show impressively how much Geiger's conception of the contemporary social structure had changed by this time from his earlier view of a dichotomized class society.

The Intelligentsia

Geiger's scientific interest in the intelligentsia is related to his interest in ideology and his growing concern with the problems of rationalization and modern mass society. During his exile in Sweden in 1943, Geiger gave a series of lectures on the topic of the intelligentsia in Uppsala. *Intelligentsen*, a book published in Stockholm in 1944, is based on these lectures.[18] A revised German translation of this book was pub-

[18]   See *23*.

lished in 1949 under the title *Aufgaben und Stellung der Intelligenz in der Gesellschaft* (Functions and position of the intelligentsia within society).[19] After his return to Denmark, Geiger continued to be interested in the subject and conducted an empirical study on the origins and structure of the Danish intelligentsia, based on the evaluation of the *Danish Dictionary of Biography*.[20] Owing in part to the limitation of his data, this study is largely descriptive. The theoretical frame of reference for this work is contained in his earlier book.

In *Intelligentsen*, Geiger uses a variety of approaches: historical-descriptive, analytic-classificatory, functional, and normative. While often stimulating, this mixture does not make for a high degree of systematic coherence. The guess may also be hazarded that if Geiger had attempted to do an empirical investigation on the subject before or at the time when he developed his theoretical approach, there would have been less ambiguity about the empirical referents of a number of his concepts.

The definition of the intelligentsia which Geiger uses is a functional one: the intelligentsia are those who create the objects of representative culture ("objects" should not be taken too literally, since for Geiger this also includes the performing arts and, under certain conditions, the activity of teaching). This group is distinguished from the educated (*Gebildete*), who participate in but do not create culture, and from the academics (*Akademiker*), who apply theory in practical work. Obviously, these groups are not mutually exclusive, nor can it be said that any one of them wholly comprises the other two. Geiger further makes a distinction between the intelligentsia and the intellectuals. The latter constitute the larger category, but they are not defined in terms of a specific function. Geiger feels that "intellectual" is more a sociopsychological concept, referring to those who are occupied with spiritual, immaterial work without necessarily being creative.

Discussing the emergence of the modern intelligentsia and

[19]   See *31*.
[20]   See *30;* brief summaries of the study can be found in *35* and *36*.

its historical predecessors, Geiger shows how the substantive content of the intelligentsia's creative work depends largely on the type of society and its position within it. The modern intelligentsia developed only after the dissolution of estate society and the growth of future-oriented rationality with the Enlightenment. In this context, the intelligentsia has the functions of sustaining the dynamics of progress, of spiritualizing life through the creation of works of art and of knowledge as an end in itself, of rationalizing life through the development of science bent on application, and of criticizing and thus checking power. This last function is of course partly destructive rather than constructive, as Geiger himself points out. But he apparently did not feel compelled to solve the resulting contradiction with his initial definition of the intelligentsia.

It is the critical function of the intelligentsia which Geiger emphasizes most, and his discussion of it manifests his passionate engagement on behalf of truth and rationality and his deep concern with the evil potentialities of unbridled power. His treatment of the subject becomes normative rather than descriptive at this point. Critique is for him one of the four analytically developed types of relationship between the intelligentsia and the ruling power: the intelligentsia can dominate it, can be completely subservient to it, can perform instrumental services for the rulers without necessarily supporting their goals, and finally can serve as critics. The first relationship Geiger considers to be illusionary, the second a betrayal of the intelligentsia's true function, the third as a legitimate possibility, but only the fourth as essential. This, however, does not prescribe a revolutionary role to the intelligentsia, which is supposed to be critical not only of existing but also of aspiring rulers since there is a fundamental conflict between power and the intelligentsia's need for freedom in fulfilling its creative functions.

Among the critical tasks which Geiger discusses in detail, the destruction of ideological justifications and rationalizations figures prominently. It is empirically true, Geiger admits, that the intelligentsia not only destroys but also creates ideologies, but the latter he considers to be an illegitimate activity in view of the intelligentsia's social function. The intelligentsia may develop and claim truth for empirically confirmed scientific statements, or it may present creations of imagination as art or metaphysics, but it is illegitimate for it to claim objective truth for the latter and thus put forth an ideology. This argument contains *in nuce* Geiger's theory of ideology. At the same time, his view of the legitimate functions of the intelligentsia points to an important, maybe even the major, problem connected with the approach that Geiger developed more fully in the later years of his life.

This problem is briefly the following: though not limited to the destruction of ideologies, the critical function as well as the creative function of the intelligentsia does not include policy formation or goal-setting. It is true that among the critical functions Geiger also includes the criticism of specific policy measures and of shortcomings of the social order itself. But in the first case, this criticism is in reference to the stated intentions of the policy measures in question, and in the second case criticism is actually limited to making statements about causal relations—for example, between capitalism and periodic unemployment—which account for effects whose undesirability is taken for granted. The definition and justification of policy goals is excluded in both cases. Nor could Geiger have argued otherwise, since goal-setting on the group level is a prescriptive, even normative, activity and hence in Geiger's view without any objective justification. As will be seen in Parts II and III of the translation, Geiger accepted as legitimate only subjective value decisions which claim no objective validity, no obligation for others. His fatefully restricted concept of rationality thus excludes the goals of human action from that to which rational argument can be applied. But if reason cannot be applied to the choice of goals, even the critical functions of the intelligentsia are severely restricted: it can only operate within a given set of value premises, but it cannot challenge these premises themselves since this can be done only on the basis of some contrary value standard. The consequence of this seems to be that when the intelligentsia restricts itself to what in Geiger's opinion are its legitimate functions, the setting of social goals must be left to the irrational forces of arbitrary power. Needless to say, Geiger himself does not formulate any such conclusion. Rather he fashions his argument in terms of an objection to Mannheim's claim of a political leadership role for the intelligentsia and his related view that the free-floating intelligentsia can achieve truth through a synthesis of viewpoints.

Geiger implicitly recognizes the normative character of his understanding of the intelligentsia's critical function when he points out later on that as a matter of fact, the intelligentsia does not always and in all its subgroups manifest a critical attitude but rather displays the full range of attitudes between political indifference and political engagement. Characterizing subgroups of the intelligentsia in terms of their prevalent attitude, he finds a connection between the specific type of activity engaged in, the greater or smaller political vulnerability of that activity, and the attitude displayed. For instance, the work of natural scientists or engineers, being of an apolitical nature, can be carried on within almost any political system and hence such professionals are mostly indifferent in political attitude. In contrast, the social scientist is quickly faced with the choice between martyrdom and morally self-destructive subjugation if power comes to dominate spirit, and hence can afford least of all to let power go unchecked. With this example, Geiger obviously draws on personal experience.

Geiger rounds out his analysis by considering the intelligentsia's social position and class alignment, its economic situation, and how it is perceived and judged by other social groups. This discussion is often perceptive and differentiates well between various social contexts and between subgroups of the intelligentsia, thus avoiding sweeping generalizations. Geiger shows that though there are historical variations, the intelligentsia as a whole does not belong to any one social class, neither in terms of objective position nor in terms of subjective identification. But he argues against Mannheim that the intelligentsia is not free-floating either, the different subgroups being usually aligned with some specific social group. Thus he describes four types of intelligentsia—gentry, bourgeois, proletarian, and democratic—in terms of social origin or position or both, the two-dimensionality of this structural classification making for some ambiguity, which is compounded by the historical dimension also implied. The typology used to structure the discussion of the intelligentsia's economic situation, with source of income as basic differentiating criterion, is more helpful in this respect. Geiger's analysis of the employed intelligentsia and of that group which lives from production for a competitive market—two of the types he discusses—anticipates arguments currently familiar from the sociology of professions.

Sociology of Law and the Social Order

Turning now to Geiger's treatment of the three major topics represented in this translation, an attempt will be made to sketch in those parts of the argument that were omitted from the translation and to draw attention to certain points of special importance or lasting interest. Some of these are of a controversial nature, and if this is pointed out rather than passed over, it is done in the conviction that esteem for a scientist's contribution is better expressed by arguing with him than by acknowledging his views and thus disposing of them.

The earliest evidence of Geiger's developing sociological perspective came very soon after he obtained a doctorate in law, with the publication of his study on illegitimate children in 1920, a legal treatise with sociological overtones.[21] In the course of outlining his views on the forms of sociation eight years later,[22] Geiger briefly returned to the subject of law from a more systematic perspective. He distinguished between the substantive and the formal analysis of law. The first of these, in the form of a cultural sociology of law, would deal with the content of legal norms, the social conditions of their creation, the internal structure of the system of laws, and the influence of specific legal norms on social life. The formal sociology of law

[21]   See 2.
[22]   See 6; the relevant parts are reprinted in 59, pp. 357–63.

as then envisaged by Geiger would consider law as a type of social order and investigate its distinguishing characteristics, the mode of its operation, and its relation to a specific social structure.

The *Vorstudien zu einer Soziologie des Rechts* (Preliminary studies on the sociology of law) which Geiger published nearly twenty years later[23] is characterized by the second rather than the first approach. At this time, however, Geiger thought no longer explicitly in terms of a form-content dichotomy, nor did he present his perspective as that of formal sociology. Moreover, his substantive views had been influenced by his contact with the Uppsala school of legal and moral philosophy. It was this contact which rekindled his interest in the subject of law.

Axel Hägerström, founder and most important representative of the Uppsala school, advocated a realistic, value-free treatment of law, cleansed of all elements of speculation and metaphysics. Geiger basically agreed with this intention, and his investigation of law as a social phenomenon was similarly aimed against the metaphysical notion of a moral obligation being intrinsic to law. Nevertheless, Geiger disagreed with the teachings of the Uppsala school in a number of points and conducted a heated and often polemical debate with its representatives.[24] He called it a mistaken realism to restrict an empirical approach to law to observable regularities of behavior, norms being in the opinion of the Uppsala school mere ideas and hence unreal. The concept of norm, Geiger argued, does refer to a real phenomenon. Thus his sociology of law begins with the attempt to clarify the empirical content of the concept of norm.

Geiger's analysis of norms achieves a higher degree of

23   See *27;* after having been out of print for some time, it was published again in 1964 by Luchterhand Verlag as volume 20 in the series *Soziologische Texte*, with an introduction and bibliography by Paul Trappe. This is the edition on which the translation is based.
24   This debate found expression in several publications, of which *25* is probably the most important. It is also much in evidence in the *Vorstudien;* these sections, however, have been mostly omitted from the translation.

conceptual clarity than most attempts in this field. But this makes it also relatively easy to recognize the problematical aspects of his elaborate and highly systematic conceptualization. Geiger does not follow the idealistic tradition of defining norms as behavioral expectations (with the implication that such expectations involve an element of duty or obligation), but neither does he share the extreme behavioristic view which would reduce norms to de facto regularities of behavior. The rejection of the first viewpoint, however, seems to be of greater importance for Geiger's own concept of norm. Finding the binding nature of a norm to rest ultimately in the chance that deviations will be sanctioned, Geiger advocates a concept of norm which implies neither subjective feelings of obligation nor the notion of value. He realizes, of course, that feelings of obligation and institutionalized values are part of empirical reality; especially when he turns from conceptual analysis to the description of the developmental process leading from a social order based on habit, through the stage of mores, to the final differentiation between morality and law. But in Geiger's opinion (which is elaborated in Part III of the translation), modern society is characterized by a prevailing dissensus on basic moral issues, which produces insoluble normative conflicts. These conflicts are emotionally charged, precisely because behavioral norms are infused with a claim to some binding value. Thus the conflict becomes socially disruptive. Since feelings of internal obligation attached to norms are only harmful under these conditions, Geiger advocates a general renunciation of moral claims for social norms; this is his program of value nihilism. Thus it seems in the end that Geiger's engagement on behalf of value nihilism influenced his concept of norm, which eliminates from the definition precisely those elements which Geiger would have purged from social reality.

It is clear that Geiger here stands in sharp contrast to the structural-functional school of thinking with its emphasis on the value system. If values can no longer serve as the ordering mechanism, there must be some other basis of social order for modern society. Geiger believes that the value nihilist may conform to norms out of the rational insight that some kind of order is prerequisite to social life. But it seems that the value nihilist would be faced with a problem similar to that of the intelligentsia—being deprived of any standards with which to challenge or justify specific substantive norms. Even the "social usefulness" of a norm cannot be discussed without reference to values, so that what is left in the end is some sort of enlightened self-interest, a cost-benefit calculation in terms of subjective individual utilities. It is a question whether a viable social order could in fact be based, even hypothetically, upon such a principle. However, Geiger did not discuss this as an empirical question.

The repeated emphasis which Geiger put on the fact that man by definition lives in society, that is, within the framework of some social order, may have prevented him from seeing the relation between individual and society, between motives and social norms as problematical. This seems to be connected with the fact that in contrast to structural-functional theory, Geiger did not make a systematic analytical distinction between cultural, social, and personality systems, which may in turn explain the conspicuous absence in his treatment of norms, of the concept of internalization and of a theory of socialization. Instead he has recourse to a psychological theory which sociologists today would hardly subscribe to and uses it to explain habit formation in terms which recall behavioristic theories of learning through selective reinforcement. He seems to assume in chapter 2 that the genesis of a specific social order could be explained if first the formation of individual and collective habits could be explained, and subsequently the elevation of certain collective habits to a normative status. But though to all outward appearances Geiger uses a genetic perspective at this point, he might really have had in mind a more analytical distinction.

Geiger does not offer a substantive theory about the selective mechanism through which certain customs attain the status of norms. Instead he convincingly rejects some explanations that have been offered, notably the view that it is socially useful customs which become norms. His criticism of this functional argument is the more impressive if one considers the time at which it was written. In fact, Geiger did not even phrase his critique in the terminology of functionalism; he spoke of *Nützlichkeit* (usefulness, utility) rather than of functionality.[25] Also, his conception of utility has a more rationalistic flavor than is true of the concept of function in the context of contemporary system theory; there seems to be an implication in Geiger's conception that utility *could* be objectively established, which would provide for an alternative to value standards in guiding social action.

Further it is noteworthy that Geiger makes no reference to power processes in his treatment of the genesis of social order. Enforceable requests or orders may, however, be a much more important source of norms than habits (individual and collective), and even in the origin of habits, repeated demands made by a powerful interaction partner may play a significant role. In chapter 1 Geiger does recognize that norms can originate from explicitly voiced expectations as well as evolving out of habit, but he applies this mainly to legal norms and does not follow it up in chapter 2. Nevertheless it would be quite wrong to say that Geiger neglected power phenomena generally. Rather it seems that the impression of a harmonic-evolutionary perspective is often conveyed where Geiger uses a formal, analytical approach instead of a processual and more historical one. Thus in the framework of a formal analysis Geiger may speak of a central authority as coming into being when the social aggregate increases beyond a given size (see p. 74); but when he later turns to the genetic aspect of this process, Geiger points out that in the case of an exogenous origin of the central authority (the historically prevalent form according to him), coercion, subjugation, and power relations play a dominant role.

In fact, Geiger devotes a whole chapter to the relationship between law and power in the original German text. This has not been included in the translation because the discussion is

[25]   In the translation, however, the term *function* is occasionally used where this does justice to the intended meaning of a phrase.

largely phrased in terms of a long and polemical debate with certain authors from the Uppsala school who accused Geiger of "sociological positivism," attributing to him the view that law is established by the volition of a ruler or central authority. Designating his own position as "legal realism," Geiger counters that he has never maintained that the ruling powers at any given time operate within a legal order which they themselves have established. He does hold, however, that power precedes law *in general*, both historically and functionally. First, power is involved in every social order. The legal order in particular, presupposing a central authority, is based on power. Second, the specific content of the legal order is also determined by power factors, and changes in the legal order follow upon changes in the power system. Although eventually the legal order will not contain any norms which run counter to the interests of groups with sufficient power to effect changes in it, this must be seen as a process occurring over time and within a structural setting that cannot be conceived of in terms of a simple dichotomy between rulers and ruled. As Geiger puts it, the central authority *manifests* an often very complicated power constellation rather than simply being identical with "the rulers," and the content of the legal norms at any given time has largely originated at an earlier period and provides a framework (though one that can be changed) within which the central authority must operate.

Geiger has also been called a legal positivist, one who defines as law that which has been enacted as such. Quite correctly he argues against this that his position should rather be designated as positivistic empiricism, since not mere enactment but actual enforcement is for him the decisive criterion of a legal norm. This defense is made in the context of chapter 5 of *Vorstudien*, but has not been included in the translation since the major point is already evident from the preceding discussion and is repeated in the brief section on "real" and "ideal" law with which chapter 5 in this translation opens. This section is of crucial importance because it clearly expresses the main direction of Geiger's criticism: not legal positivism, but metaphysical notions of law. This deserves emphasis because the full extent of Geiger's criticism of such notions cannot be perceived from the translation, which omits a number of sections where he criticizes concepts of legal science from the sociological point of view with the intention of isolating their nonempirical elements. To one of these concepts—"legal consciousness" conceived of as a constitutive factor of law—he even devotes an entire chapter, the eighth and last in the German text. This concept, important in legal philosophy, is criticized on empirical grounds as a hypothetical construct devoid of explanatory power in a sociological perspective. Even if here also, Geiger engages in a debate with the Uppsala school, it is in sections such as this that his basic agreement with the antimetaphysical orientation of the same school is most in evidence. It is clear that Geiger's positivistic empiricism does not supply a standard on which a substantive critique of specific legal norms could be based, but then such an undertaking would have been considered as unscientific by him.

There is no need to point out the many insights and stimulating ideas presented by Geiger in his analysis of law, since the reader will see that for himself. Certainly Geiger is one of the few sociologists ever to deal systematically with this topic, and the fact that he does so within the framework of a discussion about norms and social order in general is a particularly fruitful aspect of his approach. Conversely, it is surprising that the phenomenon of law should have been so neglected by other theories which are concerned with the problem of social order at the societal level, like structural-functionalism. In fact, this neglect and the concomitant failure to distinguish systematically between legal and nonlegal components of social order seem related to the conception of society as a "natural system model," characterized by processes of spontaneous adjustment and by control through internalized norms. The implications of harmony and consensus in such a conception have often been noted by critics of structural-functionalism. But if Geiger did not share this perspective, neither did he fully subscribe to the opposite view, the so-called conflict and power model of society where order rests largely on external control. Geiger rejects both internalized control (morality) and coercion as the basis of the legal order and of the social order of modern society in general, pointing out that although the fear of sanctions is certainly an important factor, it is but one of the motives making for conformity, and more important for voluntary than for forced compliance at that. Thus, to the two alternatives of emphasizing either internal or external control as the main foundation of social order Geiger adds a third. This third alternative is maybe most clearly stated where he describes the "calculation of obligation" as basis of the individual's decision to conform (see pp. 93–94). Such a calculation presupposes a rational orientation, and this—rational insight combined with a pragmatic, even utilitarian action orientation —is indeed Geiger's third alternative. But at this point the previously noted normative element enters into his analysis: less visibly than the value nihilism which Geiger advocates, the calculation of obligation is a prescription more than an empirically descriptive statement.

Inevitably, Geiger's sociology of law raises more questions than he can answer in empirical terms, which is why with realistic modesty he calls his study preliminary. Some of the main areas for future investigation would refer to the interweaving of law and other forms of social order, the cross-cultural comparison of the objects of legal regulation, the genesis of specific legal norms and the general principles underlying the process, and finally, the institutional or organizational aspects of the legal order—a topic which Geiger treats only in analytic and highly abstract terms. For Geiger's study to raise all these questions is additional evidence of its fruitfulness.

Ideology

Geiger's theory of ideology is the connecting link between his sociology of law and his last published book, *Demokratie ohne Dogma* (Democracy without dogma), from which Part III of the translation has been taken. Speaking about law and morality, Geiger argued that under modern conditions of social life the infusion of norms with value judgments has a socially disruptive effect. This theme is not only elaborated upon, but significantly expanded in *Demokratie ohne Dogma*, which culminates, as does the translation from the *Sociology of Law*, in a plea for practical value nihilism, that is, abstention from making value judgments. Value judgments are for Geiger ideology in pure form—not the only type of ideological statements, but a particularly important one. This is why his theory of ideology has been chosen for Part II of the translation.

The small volume entitled *Ideologie und Wahrheit* (Ideology and truth), published posthumously,[26] is part of an unfinished monograph which Geiger planned to write on the sociology of thought.[27] The other parts of the incomplete manuscript were published, also after his death, under the titles *Befreiung aus dem Ideologiebann* (Liberation from the spell of ideology) and *Bemerkungen zur Soziologie des Denkens* (Remarks on the sociology of thought).[28] In addition, Geiger wrote an essay entitled *Kritische Bemerkungen zum Begriffe der Ideologie* (Critical remarks on the concept of ideology) which he contributed to a volume celebrating the eightieth birthday of Alfred Vierkandt,[29] and finally there is an article on "Evaluational Nihilism" by Geiger in the first volume of *Acta Sociologica*[30] which roughly corresponds in content to the first chapter in our translation of *Ideologie und Wahrheit*. Aside from these publications devoted specifically to the topic of ideology, there are occasional remarks on the subject in many of Geiger's other works. The several writings on ideology overlap in content, but the argument is developed most fully in *Ideologie und Wahrheit*. However, since Part II presents only a selection from this book, it seemed necessary to summarize some important points which either have been omitted in the translation or which need under-

---

[26]   See *48*.
[27]   This is mentioned by Trappe in his introduction to *59*.
[28]   See *59*, pp. 431–459, and *57*.
[29]   See *33*.
[30]   See *51*.

scoring because they are treated only very briefly. Since the full scope of Geiger's theory of ideology can only be grasped if these points are taken into consideration, it was thought better to present this summary as an introduction to Part II, where it becomes immediately relevant, rather than to include it in the present discussion. The following will therefore be limited to a few more general remarks.

As will be evident from Part II, Geiger's concept of ideology is related to Mannheim's concept of partial ideology, though Geiger prefers to emphasize the differences rather than the similarities in viewpoint between Mannheim and himself. It may be less evident that there is also a connection between Geiger's concept of ideology and Pareto's concept of derivations, seen as rationalizations of nonlogical actions.[31] Derivations manifest a need for logic by justifying and in effect camouflaging nonlogical actions in terms of logical or pseudo-logical arguments. Similarly, Geiger's concept of ideology refers to a theoretical justification of vital engagements, or put differently: ideology consists in a misjudgment of reality under the influence of some subjective involvement with the object or relationship to it. Clearly discernible additional influences on Geiger's theory of ideology are Max Weber's ideas on value freedom, and the teachings of the antimetaphysical Uppsala school—although in the latter case Geiger again prefers to emphasize where he parts company with this school rather than where he agrees with it.

In a certain sense, Geiger's concept of ideology is an epistemological rather than a sociological one. A reason for this might be found in the fact that his theory of ideology was to form part of a projected treatise on the sociology of thought, but in fact much more than this is involved in his choice of perspective. Even more clearly than in the case of the concept of norm, Geiger's definitional choice reflects a certain selective interest or value orientation. In dealing with ideology, Geiger was not so much interested in the positive social func-

---

[31]   This is pointed out by Kurt Lenk in his introduction to *Ideologie*, Soziologische Texte Vol. 4, Neuwied, Berlin, 1961.

tions of idea systems which interpret social situations and provide guidelines for action, as he was concerned with the dangers inherent in a departure from rational thinking, a violation of the criterion of truth. Thus his explicitly made and admittedly subjective value decision in favor of rational thinking guided only by the criterion of truth, becomes the reference point for his definition of ideology as being essentially a violation of this value. It follows from this that Geiger's evaluation of the phenomenon he calls ideology is wholly and unremittingly negative —not only because it violates the value of truth (which would be a subjective evaluation) but more importantly because in his opinion this violation has potentially disastrous social consequences: violent social strife characterized by the readiness to coerce, terrorize, subjugate and even kill other human beings in the name of some value–idea or "cause." This part of the argument involves an empirical proposition which warrants serious consideration. Geiger's fears about the consequences of ideological thinking—the ultimate basis of his passionate rationalism—are of course founded in personal experience; indeed he often mentions the terrors of the Nazi regime as an example in this particular context. It might be debated whether Geiger's firm conviction that there is no other way to safeguard against the repetition of such events except by making a radical distinction between facts and values and abstaining from value judgments is wholly justified (leaving aside the problem of how to realize this prescription in case it could be shown to be potentially efficacious). But there can be no doubt that what Geiger was trying to prevent is still as real a danger at this particular moment of history as it was ever before, and this gives an undiminished actuality to his writings on the subject.

Mass Society

A good part of the themes developed in *Demokratie ohne Dogma*, the book on which Part III of the translation is based, had already been formulated elsewhere by Geiger. In this book, which was ready for publication in 1950 but appeared in print for the first time only in 1960,[32] Geiger draws the conclusion from his analysis of the nature of modern society, from his theory of ideology, and from his views on the implications of value philosophy. But the intention of the book is political, as he says himself in the "Open Letter to the Reader" which prefaces the German text. He underlines this intention by stating that the conclusions which he draws are not logically necessary and that they will probably meet with objections. Yet he pleads with the reader to consider them well before rejecting them. The "Open Letter" concludes with these words: "In the sixteen years which have passed since I last published in German,[33] I have been much preoccupied with questions of ideology, propaganda, value philosophy, and the sociology of cognition. From this resulted the unorthodox views which I will present in this book. By today instigating rebellion against publicly approved beliefs, I admit, repent, and atone for the sins of my own past. Maybe you, my reader, will feel that behind much of what will sound harsh and cold to you there lies my deep concern with the destiny of man, that eternally downtrodden, tormented, and violated creature. Has the time not finally come to release him from the bondage of the various . . . isms and systems and to let him live?"[34]

What Geiger means by this bondage is elaborated with reference to historical events of the recent past in an introductory chapter to *Demokratie ohne Dogma*, which is not included in the translation. With special reference to the period between the two world wars Geiger analyzes the implications and effects of certain trends of thought, in particular Spengler's philosophy of history and the ideology of the German *Jugendbewegung*. Their popularity reflects for him a widely shared feeling of anxiety and impotence which, though especially characteristic

[32]   Published in the Humanities Series of Acta Jutlandica in Denmark, the book bore the title *Gesellschaft zwischen Pathos und Nüchternheit* (Society between pathos and rationality); see *58*. It was republished as *Demokratie ohne Dogma* by Szczesny Verlag in 1963.
[33]   This was written in 1950 when Geiger in fact expected that this would be his first postwar publication in German.
[34]   *58*, p. 8.

of the period after 1918, has its roots already in the last decade of the nineteenth century. The urge towards mysticism, the emotionalism and romanticism of the youth movement, the popular cultural criticism of modern technology and the large city, and the cult of "Gemeinschaft," manifest for Geiger the failure to meet the challenge of life in modern, industrial society. He states: "With the slogan of 'Gemeinschaft' a generation which was unable to cope with a mass society based on the principles of rationality and efficiency set up as the counter-image of a better world the emotional exuberance and immaturity of puberty."[35] In this way, Geiger thinks, the ground was prepared for Fascism and Nazism. He is careful enough not to assert an immediate and direct causal relationship between the emergence of these regimes and the trends of thought which he analyzes, especially since there are also certain contradictions between the two. As Geiger put it, Mussolini and Hitler invented an ideological crossbreed of affective community with regimented mass mobilization—a monstrous creation of a sick imagination.[36] But the danger has not passed with the destruction of these regimes. Geiger finds indications that the cultural criticism and feeling of impotence in the face of modern society still persists, and so does its aggressive and socially disruptive potential. It is to ward off these dangers that Geiger wishes to point out the fallacy of all attempts to recapture the emotional warmth of communal life in modern mass society, and to show the attitude which alone is appropriate for life in such a society.

Geiger developed his analysis of modern mass society in critical opposition to the meaning with which this term was then used by popular cultural criticism. A briefer statement of his critique is contained in an article aptly entitled *Die Legende von der Massengesellschaft* (The myth of mass society),[37] which was published in 1951 and preceded most of the now familiar sociological thinking on the subject. The contemporary view

[35]   *58*, p. 16.
[36]   *58*, p. 21.
[37]   See *40*.

is essentially in agreement with Geiger's statement that the mass element of modern society does not consist in a lack of structure, but rather in a significant structural change through the ascendance of large-scale formal organizations and the separation between the private and public spheres of life.

To argue thus meant for Geiger a change in perspective from his earlier conception of the nature of the mass. In 1926 he had already published a book entitled *Die Masse und ihre Aktion—Ein Beitrag zur Soziologie der Revolution* (The mass and its action—a contribution to the sociology of revolution).[38] Defining the mass as a special type of social association, Geiger conceived of it as a historical phenomenon which is indicative of social disorganization and follows from the dissolution of value community and the attendant loss of legitimacy on the part of the rulers. Where these conditions are present, the mass exists in latent form. Under the influence of certain external stimuli it manifests itself in collective acts, a localized phenomenon of short duration which generally does not include the whole latent mass. Geiger thought that the mass is mainly recruited from the proletariat, but it is something quite distinct from a revolutionary mass movement which has constructive as well as destructive intentions. The mass is characterized by an emotional and wholly negative orientation, its intentions are destructive, but in an expressive rather than an instrumental way.

Though Geiger later used the term mass to refer to certain structural features of modern society rather than to indicate expressive crowd action, there is an important link between this early book and the main theme of *Demokratie ohne Dogma*. The manifest mass—or mass in action—is described by Geiger in terms which he later uses to characterize the belligerent community of pathos (a result rather than defining criterion of mass society) as an affective community of destructive intention, a community in negation. However, in the later book Geiger sees that such an affective community can also take the form of organized mass movements and can even infuse cer-

[38]   See *4*.

tain formal organizations instead of becoming manifest merely as "mass in action."

When Geiger said that he expected his views in *Demokratie ohne Dogma* to meet with criticism, he probably thought primarily of his argument for rationality and against affection and morality as a basis for social order and a guiding principle of social action. Some of the objections which might be raised with reference to this argument have already been touched upon, and only one further point for debate shall here be mentioned. Though Geiger emphasizes certain structural features of modern society, he locates the source of the dangers with which he is concerned not in the social structure itself but rather in the individual's adaptation to it. This becomes evident already where he argues that the feeling of impotence often said to characterize "mass" existence does not so much express a realistic assessment of the effects of structural changes in society, but is mainly due to the heightened individual consciousness of being dependent on external forces, combined with intellectual capacities insufficiently developed for the grasp of a complex society. It may be felt that not more than a shift in emphasis is involved in stressing the one or the other, but the consequence is that in the first case the fault is found with the society and in the second with the individual, which leads to different prescriptions for remedial action. This is evident in Geiger's emphasis on the need for intellectualization, which is linked with a neglect of questions of structural change—not only as an alternative but even as a precondition for the realization of the attitude changes which he advocates.

More clearly than in Part III of the translation this selective emphasis comes out in the original German book, where Geiger elaborates in detail his program for the completion of the interrupted process of enlightenment, as he calls it. This program consists of making systematic use of the criticism of ideologies, eliminating all metaphysics from the guiding principles of social action, practicing value nihilism, and avoiding propaganda. These prescriptions do not apply only to the individual citizen; Geiger also wishes them to be heeded and acted upon by the mass media, the educational system, and politicians. But this too refers to action orientations and not to changes in the structure of institutions.

The same perspective characterizes Geiger's discussion of the problems of modern mass democracy in the final chapter of the book, also omitted from the translation. Although at this stage of his life Geiger no longer held strong convictions about the preferability of a certain economic order, either capitalistic or socialistic, he was not at all neutral with respect to the political system; he preferred democracy to all others because it guarantees the freedom of dissent. But he refused to express this in terms of a generalized value judgment. In a statement which reflects very well his skeptical realism, he called democracy "a modus vivendi for those who disagree among each other, but nothing to sing hallelujah about or wave flags for. Stated with sober simplicity, democracy is that one among all the political forms as yet developed and tried out which makes the coercion unavoidably exercised by the collectivity over the individual, the pressure of social interdependence, relatively most bearable for most people. This is the best that can be said of any political system."[39] But even this relative advantage, Geiger feels, is threatened at present. As policy-making requires increasingly more expert knowledge, the chances of effective control exercised by the electorate are lessened, and the politicians have become accustomed to mobilize support not by rational argument but by an appeal to emotions. The conclusion which Geiger draws from this analysis is again in terms of a change of attitude rather than in terms of any structural changes: rational enlightenment is to increase the control chances of the population and will both force and enable the politician to convince rather than to persuade, to argue for his policy proposals rather than propagandizing them.

In view of the emphasis which even social scientists in the Western world have recently come to put again on planned social change, Geiger's recommendations which put the burden of adaptation on the individual have certain conservative im-

[39]   *58*, p. 253.

plications. But to point out that Geiger's analysis is character-ized by a selective emphasis does not mean to say that it is mistaken as far as it goes. In fact, his critique of ideology and call to reason may gain in relevance and appeal at a time when another upsurge of belligerent communities of pathos threatens, while little of his program for intellectualization has yet been realized.

The main reason for Geiger's lack of emphasis on questions of structural reform doubtlessly lies in his skeptical aversion against all political programs for radical change which, based on some ideology, mercilessly extort a high price in human suffering in the name of something which, as likely as not, is a utopia. Needless to say, this aversion does not make him a con-servative; if he was not a revolutionary at heart, Geiger certainly was in favor of pragmatic reforms and always critical of the status quo. But this normatively based option for value-free science puts a serious restraint on the possibility to advocate and justify major policy decisions on any but admittedly sub-jective grounds. This problem continues to trouble social scien-tists today and becomes more pressing as they are increasingly expected to provide social guidance. The dilemma assumes critical proportions as we experience a new urgency of solving massive sociopolitical problems precisely at the time when the legitimacy of decision-making comes to rest more than ever on objective knowledge. That Geiger confronts us with this issue gives a pointed actuality to his work.

Renate Mayntz

I. Sociology of Law

1

THE SOCIAL ORDER

Social Order as Behavioral Coordination

SOCIETY AS a way of life is the opposite of solitude. The concept of "society" implies interrelationship and interdependence between a number of individuals, a community life which involves an infinite chain of actions and reactions. In order to live together, people must be able to predict with reasonable certainty how others will behave in recurrent typical situations. These predictions then become the basis for the conjectural disposition of our own conduct. The behavior of other members of a social group, especially their reactions to my conduct, must to a certain extent be predictable. Only then can an M_1 within a group Σ adjust his actions to coordinate with the expected reactions of $M_{2,3...x}$, and only under this condition can M_1 relate his own existence to that of $M_{2,3...x}$. I call this mutual dependence of action between members of a group MM_Σ the *coordination of behavior*. It is the essence of group order. . . .

Behavior Model (Gebarens-Modell) and Behavior Expectation

Social order is based on the principle that, in a hypothetical aggregate Σ, a specific stable relationship exists between certain typical situations *s* and the corresponding typical modes of behavior *g*. I call the aggregate in which such an order is pres-

Translated from *Vorstudien zu einer Soziologie des Rechts* (Neuwied am Rhein: Luchterhand Verlag, 1964), pp. 48–336, and printed here by permission of the publisher.

ent the *order-bearing group*. When someone is confronted with situation *s*, then behavior *g* is usually the result. This connection between a given situation and a given behavior is expressed by the formula $s \rightarrow g$, the arrow indicating that *g* follows *s*. Every social order can be conceived as a system of correlations following the pattern $s \rightarrow g$.

The psychological processes by which such correlations originate will for the time being be postulated without further explanation. Every time *s* occurs, its perception induces the idea of *g* in the observer, so that *g* appears as the appropriate "response" of the acting person to *s*. In other words, $s \rightarrow g$ represents a model or pattern: for the actor as an *example* for his behavior in *s*, for the observer as an *expectation* of certain behavior on the part of the actor.

For the sake of thoroughness we should note here that there is one other type of correlation. $s \rightarrow g$ says that a given behavior *g* is associated with a given situation *s*. In other cases, however, it is expected that a given behavior will be avoided. If we designate the nonexpected behavior as *t* (= taboo), the corresponding formula is $s \rightarrow \bar{t}$: non-*t* usually occurs in *s*, that is, any kind of behavior with the exception of *t*. In the following discussion, the reader should remember that in certain cases $g = \bar{t}$. Only when something holds true exclusively for $s \rightarrow \bar{t}$ will this formula be explicitly used.

It is by no means the case that given a certain set of circumstances observers will expect the *same* behavior from all members of the given group or that a certain M_x will expect the same behavior from M_y that he, M_x, would display in the same situation. Decisive in such cases is that the actual behavior of M_x agree with the expectations—based on previous experience— of $M_{1, 2, 3 \ldots}$, but not that the behavior of M_x be the *same* as that of $M_{1, 2, 3 \ldots}$. The predictability of action requisite for social interdependence is, in other words, based not necessarily on *identity of behavior* for everyone, but rather on the *consistency of behavior* on the part of individuals and the coordination of their behavior with that of others. Identical behavior on the part of many individuals is mutually expected only when they all occupy the same position within the order-bearing Σ. Only to the degree that equality exists between $M_{1,2,3...}$ is their behavior coordinated by virtue of its sameness. If M_x and M_y are unequal, then their conduct will correspondingly differ in a given situation. M_x does not expect M_y to behave in the same manner as he behaves, but he *does* expect M_y to behave the way people like M_y usually behave in a given s.

Coordination of behavior based upon *inequality* is, moreover, the general rule. This does not necessarily mean "social inequality" in the usual sense, i.e., status or class differences resulting in unequal rights. Not only do peasants, nobility, and bourgeois in an estate society behave differently under the same circumstances, but men and women, adults and children, etc., also behave according to dissimilar behavioral models in every society, regardless of its structure. Behavioral coordination is achieved when someone who is implicated in s and the general public entertain a justified expectation that the acting party will behave in a certain way, even if it be other than what is customary for other members of the group in the same given situation.

This may be expressed more exactly by reducing the factor s to its constituent elements. An s consists of a set of external circumstances u and one or more persons, namely, at least the actor H himself and possibly also B, someone implicated in s and affected by the acts of H. If $H_1 \neq H_2$, then for a given u the formula is: $u\dfrac{H_1}{B_1} \neq u\dfrac{H_2}{B_2}$. The symbols above and below the line here and in the following indicate that an active party (above) and a passive party (below) are involved. Two situations, even when formally represented as the same, are in reality dissimilar if the persons involved in each are dissimilar. If H_1 occupies another position in Σ than H_2, then H_1 can never be involved in quite the same s as H_2, even when confronted with the same set of circumstances. Hence no one expects that kind of behavior from him which H_2 would display in the same situation. . . .

If it is considered the general rule in a Σ for H_1 and H_2 to conduct themselves differently under the same given circumstances, or for *H* under the same given external circumstances to conduct himself differently toward B_1 and B_2, this indicates that a special kind of order is involved. Such specific inequalities are obviously only possible as *regular* phenomena if the existence of different categories of *MM* within the order-bearing Σ is generally accepted. Every category of members will then occupy a special place within the structured Σ and different behavioral patterns will obtain for them corresponding to their "places" or positions. Categorical differences within the membership of Σ, in themselves the manifestation of an order, are a prerequisite for the differences in patterned behavior.[1]

Regularity and Social Order

Social order manifests itself externally as perceptible regularity in the processes of group life. This does not mean, however, that *all* perceptible regularities in group life are manifestations of the social order. The rhythms of social life resulting from natural causes and regularities in the behavior of the *MM*'s based upon purely physiological conditions are not manifestations of order in the strict sense of the term, even though in the primitive stage they may become points of departure for the emergence of certain forms of social order. When birds instinctively build nests at a certain time of year it is not social order but a natural law. If however the rhythm of life resulting from the change of seasons becomes ritualized in religious ceremony, it must then be regarded as part of the social order of the Σ.

Hence statistically observable regularities of the type $s \rightarrow g$ may possibly *indicate* a socially ordered pattern, while not themselves *being* phenomena of social order. We can thus distinguish between regularity and normality, that is, between processes in which a rule can be *recognized* and those which *follow* a rule. Social order begins where the rule of natural law ends. In order to describe a regular activity as a manifestation of the social order it must be hypothetically possible for the individual—

---

[1]   In the original German text, this paragraph belongs to another section, entitled *Handelns- und Zustandsordnung.*—Ed.

instead of $s \rightarrow g$—to act according to $s \rightarrow x$, $s \rightarrow y$, or more generally, $s \rightarrow \bar{g}$ "if he wished." Social order is present only in so-called acts of will. . . .

Order and Norm

The expression "social order" makes one immediately think of a complex of established norms or rules by which life is regulated in a Σ where the members "conform to the norms." Legal science, which considered norms (legal rules) as its proper object of study and regarded their elucidation as its main purpose, was formerly dominated by a normative viewpoint. Sociology necessarily has a different point of view. Its object of study is social reality and it centers its attention on the entire mechanism of the social order, whereby the first and most important fact is that the course of events in a Σ runs in ordered channels. Sociology has as its object of study this ordering mechanism in its entirety, and norms have meaning only as components of this mechanism, that is, only insofar as they actually influence the course of life in Σ.

This point of view became current around 1900 as a characteristic of a special branch of jurisprudence (*Rechtssoziologismus*). Various later legal philosophers exaggerated it to a point, however, where the norm concept became etherealized and was denied all substance of reality. This is not the place for a polemic discussion of this would-be legal realism. Without for the moment going into this theory, I will here distinguish between the effective or *real order* and the *system of norms* and show that both of these, together with social control, constitute the total ordering mechanism. One must further distinguish between the norm itself and its form of verbal expression. I will therefore speak of norm in the actual sense or *subsistent norm* and of the normative maxim (*Normsatz*) or *verbal norm*.

The organization and activities of an association are ordered by a body of rules or verbal norms, a constitution or bylaws. It provides for general meetings, establishes a governing body and officers, and defines the limits of their duties (structural order). In addition it establishes the duties and privileges of the members, regulates election and voting procedure, and possibly provides for fines or punishments for the violation of certain regulations (action or conduct order). As long as the activities of the association proceed along the lines thus prescribed, the real order is created by the enactment of normative maxims. The order is secondary; the maxims are primary.

This however is not always the case. Otherwise there could never be a regulated group life without a system of norms set down in words. A contrary example is presented by the family, consisting of the parents and several children. The structure of the family and the relationships between its members are regulated in general terms by law; but we may ignore that here. Within the general institutional framework one will find in the life of every individual family certain patterns resulting neither from statutory law nor from the rules explicitly laid down by the head of the family. Certain correlations of the type $s \rightarrow g$ have become habitual through constant practice. It might appear as if this real order did not correspond to any system of norms. That such a complex does exist, however, becomes evident the moment some member of the family deviates from the model $s \rightarrow g$ or prepares to do so. On the part of the actor there will be that inner uncertainty which we usually call a "bad conscience." But if in spite of the warnings of his conscience he acts in violation of $s \rightarrow g$, the others will disapprove. This indicates that the actors as well as the spectators regard g as the mode of behavior appropriate to s, which means that $s \rightarrow g$ is an active normative principle. Still, the norm need not necessarily be expressed in words. The real order is here primary, while the corresponding subsistent norm comes about as the result of previous actions. The model $s \rightarrow g$ first becomes established as an actual regularity in the process of family life and assumes in the course of repetition the character of a norm in the minds of the family members. The model is perceived and experienced as "correct."

A third example: since earliest times it has been customary in a certain tribe for a traveler and his horse to help themselves to what food and fodder is available along the way, as long as they consume it on the spot. This behavior model is a part of the real order and acts as a subsistent norm. It would appear unseemly if the traveler would take more than he could use at the moment or if the owner would not allow him to eat his fill. This custom eventually found expression in the rule: "Three are free." Thus the subsistent norm was expressed and reinforced in a normative maxim. The subsistent norm is not created by the verbal norm, but is only confirmed by it. The verbal norm simply states the fact that $s \rightarrow g$ is an established model of behavior. It does not decree that from now on $s \rightarrow g$ must be considered a binding norm. Legal science distinguishes between "custom" and "statute" as sources of legal norms; more generally, one can speak of an habitual order in the one case and of a statutory order in the other.

In one case the real order has *grown* out of life in the Σ habitually reinforced as a subsistent norm and then expressed in a normative maxim. In the other case the real order is *introduced* or enacted by the normative maxim; the normative maxim proclaims the subsistent norm. I will therefore call the verbal norm in the first case *declarative*, in the second case *proclamative*.

Viewed in terms of their origin, the primary real order, evolving from habits, represents the earliest form. Long before anyone could have thought of establishing correlations of the type $s \rightarrow g$ or $s \rightarrow \bar{t}$ as imperatives or as prohibitions for future action, they must have considered these familiar, habitual behavior models as binding and conducted themselves accordingly. But this evolutionary aspect will be discussed more extensively below (chapter 2).

Habitual Order—Unreflective Behavior

. . . There is no necessary connection between the origin of normative substance[2] (models)—habitual or statutory—on the one hand and the relationship of the individual to the norma-

---

[2]   Substance is used in this context in the sense of "content," in contradistinction to "form."—Trans.

tively sanctioned model $s \rightarrow g$ on the other. The new member M_n may well come to follow the habitually generated model $s \rightarrow g$ simply through the routine of example and imitation, without ever becoming conscious that $s \rightarrow g$ is the substance of a norm. But in exactly the same way M_n can also get used to acting according to a model $s \rightarrow g$ which was first established purposely by a normative maxim. On the other hand, an $s \rightarrow g$ which has evolved through habitual practice, once it has finally been formulated in a normative maxim, can then be perpetuated verbally. Others then communicate the norm to M_n in this form and enjoin him to act accordingly. He thus gains knowledge of the norm and an idea of its binding nature, even before he finds himself in the given s or has had the opportunity of observing the g-response of others to the s—in other words, before he could become used to responding with g to s without conscious reflection. . . .

Norm and Normative Maxim—The Nature of the Norm

The formula $s \rightarrow g$ states only that in a given Σ, g usually occurs in the case of s. This state of affairs has been described as the "real order." A norm is given when the model $s \rightarrow g$ is reinforced by a binding obligation (v)—it being irrelevant for the moment what "binding" actually means. The formula $(s \rightarrow g)_v$ hence describes a norm whose substance is the model $s \rightarrow g$. The norm is not universally binding, however, but only in reference to a specific circle of persons, whom I call norm-addressees (AA). The formula for the norm is then $(s \rightarrow g)_{vAA}$. Further, it may be that $s \rightarrow g$ is only v for AA with respect to another specific category of persons, whom I call norm-beneficiaries (BB), those who benefit from the norm. The relationship between active and passive parties was represented above by means of a fraction symbol. "Parents are obliged to care for their dependent children in accordance with their means" is a norm which could be written as follows: $(s \rightarrow g)_{v\frac{AA}{BB}}$, where AA are "all persons who have dependent children" and *BB* are "all dependent children." If I state the norm, "Educated people don't talk slang," there is no category of beneficiary. Since a prohibition is here involved, the norm would look thus: $(s \rightarrow \bar{t})_v{}^{AA}$. But in order to include both possibilities in one formula I shall write: $(s \rightarrow g)_v\frac{AA}{\div}$, where $\div$ means that *AA* may possibly have obligations toward certain *BB*'s. Where *BB* are given and identified I shall write as above $(s \rightarrow g)_v\frac{AA}{BB}$. The subsistent norm hence consists of three or four elements: (1) the nucleus (*Normkern*) $s \rightarrow g$, (2) the stigma (*Normstigma*) v, (3) the addressees *AA*, and finally (4) (in certain cases) the beneficiaries *BB*.

Thus is the subsistent norm determined. The normative maxim expresses this relationship in words. If we call the verbal expression w, then the verbal norm or the normative maxim is given by the formula $w[(s \rightarrow g)_v\frac{AA}{\div}]$, which means "it has been stated in words that certain persons (with respect to certain other persons) are bound to respond to a certain situation with a certain behavior." Normative maxims are: the written paragraphs of the law, the articles in the bylaws of an association, the verbal directives of an official authority to its subordinates, or the orally transmitted formulae in which an existing moral custom finds expression.

Such combinations of words as such are not however automatically norms, but only their verbal shells. It is a norm that "cyclists" $(-AA)$ "may" $(= v)$ "ride only with their lights on" $(= g)$ "after dark" $(= s)$. The sentence, "Cyclists may ride only with their lights on after dark," expresses this subsistent norm in words.

This strict distinction between subsistent norm and normative maxim is by no means irrelevant. Frequently a normative maxim is mistakenly or at least inaccurately described as a norm, whereas the norm itself may even exist without the verbal shell of a maxim. Nor does every statement with the grammatical form of a normative maxim have a corresponding subsistent norm. If $s \rightarrow g$ is a moral custom in the milieu Σ, this model is then binding for $MM = AA$ without its binding nature having to be expressed in a special normative maxim. If the idea of a binding obligation for $s \to g$ then leads to $(s \to g)_v\frac{AA}{\div}$ being formulated in the normative maxim $w[(s \to g)_v\frac{AA}{\div}]$—and in all probability this will sooner or later be the case—the only result is that the subsistent norm becomes fixed so that it can be communicated *in abstracto*. But the subsistent norm whose nucleus is $s \to g$ was already in existence before its verbal formulation took place and continues to exist unchanged afterwards. The extent to which the verbal form may nevertheless influence the operation of previously habitual norms will be discussed in a later context.

On the other hand, not every maxim in the form of a verbal norm really contains a norm. The normative maxim is merely a language unit and has only the meaning which the speaker or writer imparts to it and which the listener or reader derives from it. "It is forbidden to fly to the moon" is a normative sentence in the best form, but it cannot be interpreted as having a binding obligation, inasmuch as committing the "forbidden" act is presently impossible. The speaker himself cannot mean his sentence to be the expression of a binding norm. "It is forbidden to eat beans" expresses an idea which 2,000 years ago was a norm in a certain Σ but which, since the Pythagorean sect no longer exists, no living person feels to be binding. An act of legislation which the public for any reason ignores and which the authorities make no effort to enforce is a normative maxim, but it lacks the binding character of a norm. The authors meant it to be binding, but no one takes it seriously and it is only valid on paper. Neither the public nor the state regard it, any longer, as obligatory.

It might therefore appear as if the normative maxim were without any real meaning and that one need only to take the subsistent norm into consideration. But, as we have said, there are various possible relationships between the normative maxim and the subsistent norm. If the normative nucleus has grown out of the habitual practices of life in Σ, so that its origin cannot be attributed to a certain person or a legislative act, then the norm is itself habitual and merely the manifestation of an actually operating real order. The normative maxim, on the other hand, assuming that the subsistent norm has been set down in words at all, remains nothing but a post-factum normative shell. It expresses the norm, affirms its existence, and is therefore purely declarative. In other cases $s \rightarrow g$ neither previously existed as a real order within Σ nor was $s \rightarrow g$ endowed with a v-stigma (i.e., it had not been raised to the status of a subsistent norm) before $w[(s \rightarrow g)_{v\frac{AA}{\div}}]$ was proclaimed. Here the norm itself has been enacted by a corresponding, proclamative normative maxim.

. . . Both kinds of norms—those originating in habit and later set down in words and those originating in a proclamative maxim—contain an expectation on the part of the Σ of how the AA's will behave. The normative maxim consequently expresses the idea that the Σ expects the AA's to observe the model $s \rightarrow g$. And behind this programmatic manifesto stands the Σ as guarantor of the order with sanctionary powers over the MM's, including the AA's.[3] . . .

The Reality of the Norm Is its Potential Efficacy

. . . If v has a *real* substance, then obviously we must look for it within the *real* order. That would be simple enough if $s \rightarrow g$ were a consistent rule for the course of events within the Σ and if it could be proven that $(s \rightarrow g)_{v\frac{AA}{\div}}$ were the cause of this regularity. But apparently $(s \rightarrow g)_{v\frac{AA}{\div}}$ does not necessarily result in almost every A responding with g in almost every case of s; otherwise the factor v would not have any function. In such a case the course of events would follow the pattern of a natural law and could simply be written: $s\frac{A}{\div} \rightarrow g\frac{A}{\div}$. "When A confronts someone else in s, he treats him according to g." The formula $(s \rightarrow g)_{v\frac{AA}{\div}}$ does not say however that AA in s *actually* act according to g, but only that they are *bound* to do

---

[3]   In the original German text, this paragraph belongs to another section, entitled *Die Norm ist kein Befehl oder Imperativ.*—Ed.

so. Although the v-stigma is affixed to the model $s \to g$, it is not seldom that $s \to \bar{g}$ also comes to pass. If the real substance of v is to be found in the fact that g follows s, then one must either conclude: "AA often deviate from $s \to g$, hence the norm is not binding," or else "The norm is only binding in cases where g really follows s." But to say that the norm is only binding for those who wish to conform to it would be sheer nonsense. By the "obligation" of a norm we mean that it is binding on all MM_Σ belonging to category AA: all officials, all women, all homeowners, etc. "All" means those persons having the characteristics which constitute the category AA, regardless of their inner respect for or compliance to the norm. If A acts according to $s \to \bar{g}$, then he is told that he "should" have acted according to $s \to g$, i.e., he is reminded that he is bound by the norm. Nonobservance of the norm does not make it any less binding.

If, therefore, the AA's generally put the normative nucleus into practice, in spite of every individual being able to deviate from the norm and some actually doing so, then we must either give up looking for a real substance behind v or else look for it elsewhere than in the realization of the nucleus $s \to g$. The solution is to be found by considering what happens if A, instead of fulfilling $s \to g$, acts according to $s \to \bar{g}$. The result is a reaction on the part of the social environment, Σ. What kind of reaction and who does the reacting will be discussed later. For the moment I will give the reacting party the general designation of "group-public Ω" or simply Ω.

Every A involved in s must choose between two possibilities: either he responds with g, putting the normative nucleus into practice and thus fulfilling the norm and satisfying Ω, or else he acts contrary to the norm and in opposition to the general expectation of $s \to g$, in which case Ω reacts in a way which is unpleasant or harmful for him.

We now have a new correlation model. Behavior in violation of a norm creates a secondary, typical situation consisting of two elements: (1) the fact that all AA's should act according to the norm $s \to g$, and (2) the fact that a "criminal" A_c acted in a contrary manner, $s \to \bar{g}$. . . . This is regularly followed by a reaction r on the part of Ω against the A_c. The new, secondary correlation model has the formula: $[(s \rightarrow g)_v\frac{AA}{\div} + (s \rightarrow \bar{g})\frac{A_c}{\div}] \rightarrow r\frac{\Omega}{A_c}$. According to this model, every A in Σ who becomes involved in s must face the alternative of either putting the model $s \rightarrow g$ into practice or else of exposing himself to r by acting according to $s \rightarrow \bar{g}$.

These alternative courses of action constitute the substantial reality of v. This may be expressed by the equation:

$$v = s \rightarrow \begin{cases} \rightarrow g\dfrac{A}{\div} \\ \\ \rightarrow \bar{g}\dfrac{A_c}{\div} \rightarrow r\dfrac{\Omega}{A_c} \end{cases}$$

or simply: $v = s \rightarrow \begin{cases} \rightarrow g \\ \rightarrow c \end{cases} \rightarrow r$. The symbol $\rightarrow \begin{cases} \rightarrow \\ \rightarrow \end{cases}$ represents

"either-or" and c stands for "offense" (*crimen*).

The efficacy of the norm is thus determined disjunctively. It exists *either* in the realization of the normative nucleus *or* in deviate behavior with a social reaction as the consequence. On the other hand v, the idea of binding obligation, is not disjunctive but unitary; v is neither the one alternative nor the other. It is the *either-or* per se—the alternative facing the AA's —which constitutes the substance of v.

It is, however, not absolutely certain that a c results in an r under all circumstances and in every particular case. The offense of A_c may go undiscovered; the beneficiary in s may not bother to object to the $\bar{g}$ of A_c; the group-public may be remiss in the application of its sanctions; or A_c may be cunning enough to avoid the sanctions. If the substantive reality of the norm were therefore to be defined without qualification as its alternative effects, it would mean that in the exceptional cases mentioned and in similar other cases the norm was "not binding," since there is neither a fulfillment of the norms nor a reaction against nonfulfillment. A norm which is generally binding, but now and then not binding, would be a conceptual monstrosity. The determination of the substance of v therefore requires a modification. A_c, by committing $(s \rightarrow \bar{g})\frac{A_c}{\div}$, exposes himself to the danger of incurring $r\frac{\Omega}{A_c}$. His *risk* corresponds to the potential efficacy of the norm. The *probability* of this alternative can be expressed as a proportion of the total number of s-cases: $(s \rightarrow bg) + [(s \rightarrow c\bar{g}) \rightarrow r] = e$, where b is a numerical expression for the number of cases in which the normative nucleus is fulfilled (g-act), c is a numerical expression for the number of cases in which the normative nucleus is violated ($\bar{g}$-act), and e means "efficacy coefficient." Further: $s - [b + (c \rightarrow r)] = i$, where i represents the "coefficient of inefficacy" of the norm, e and i being complementary with respect to s, that is, $s = e + i$.

The obligation v has a relative numerical quantity $v = {}^e/_s$, where e is the number of cases in which the norm proved effective, i.e., was either followed by a reaction or else its violation resulted in one, and s the total number of cases in which the norm-addressees were actually involved in the typical situations specified by the norm. The degree of intensity of v is determined by the relationship between these two quantities. This does not mean that in cases of e the norm is v and that in cases of i the norm is $\bar{v}$. The norm is v in every single case of s, but in such a way that in each of these cases v has a quantified intensity given by the relationship ${}^e/_s$. . . .

Who Is Ω?

. . . Ω reacts to $s \rightarrow \bar{g}$. But who is Ω? This quantity is only tenuously described by the term "group-public." Here we must first establish that Ω consists schematically and *theoretically* of all MM_Σ, not only the AA's. If a *universal* norm is involved, which is directed without distinction at all members of the group, then $AA \equiv MM$, that is, they are identical. If however the norm is *partial* and directed only at a certain category of persons, then $AA < MM$. In this case also, Ω stands for MM, since it is clear that not only the remaining norm-addressees, but all members of the Σ bearing the partial norm will take offense at $(s \rightarrow \bar{g}) \frac{A_c}{\div}$.

In every case, therefore, Ω is schematically and theoretically equal to MM. But if we imagine a concrete case in which an A_c has been subjected to an r because of an $s \rightarrow \bar{g}$, we can hardly maintain that MM was the instigator of r. A_c also belongs to MM, but we can scarcely imagine him reacting punitively against himself. In any concrete practical case, therefore, we must consider Ω as $MM - A_c$, regardless of whether $MM = AA$ (universal norm) or $MM > AA$ (partial norm). In other words: Ω is always "the others." . . .

Even with this qualification the subject of r is still described purely schematically. When $(s \rightarrow \bar{g}) \frac{A_c}{\div}$ occurs, there will not always be an active response on the part of $MM - A_c$. The following cases are hypothetically conceivable: (1) The active r is actually initiated by all $MM - A_c$, for example, A_c has incurred general disapproval and gets a cold shoulder from everyone. (2) A limited part of $MM - A_c$ personally observed $(s \rightarrow \bar{g}) \frac{A_c}{\div}$ or was informed of it and actively responds against A_c. (3) B, directly affected by $(s \rightarrow \bar{g})\frac{A_c}{B}$ is the first to react, and his r is approved and supported by all $MM - (A_c + B)$ or by a representative part of them. In this case two reactions are present, one physical, the other psychological—under certain conditions the latter being more painful for A_c than the former. (4) A direct r is instigated by a party charged with actively responding in behalf of the Σ ("judge" $= \Delta$), while $MM - (A_c + \Delta)$ as "public opinion" approve and support the official r. . . .

2

THE GENESIS OF THE
SOCIAL ORDER

From the Behavior Model to the Subsistent Norm

. . . As LONG as a hypothetical H habitually and unre-flectively responds to s every single time with g, a norm is not involved. The model $s \rightarrow g$ is not endowed with a v-stigma; it is in fact a regular occurrence and deviations from it are incon-ceivable. The first time H acts according to $s \rightarrow \bar{g}$, however, the indignation of B, and the understanding which the nonpar-ticipant $MM_{\bar{B}}$ show for B's indignation, implies approval of the contrary model, $s \rightarrow g$. "H should have acted this way" is the earliest form in which the v-stigma makes its appearance. The model $s \rightarrow g$ thus becomes the nucleus of a norm. It is not the conscious idea of a norm which causes $\bar{g}$ to be declared non-acceptable behavior; rather the first deviation from a previously habitual model $s \rightarrow g$ results in this model becoming the sub-stance of a norm. The offense is prior to the prohibition.

From this moment on one is conscious that a certain be-havior is not only expected of someone in s, namely the habitual g, but is in fact demanded. A morally and legally neutral custom has been transformed into mores,[1] a subsistent norm based upon

---

[1]   Geiger here uses the word *Sitte*, and subsequently also its synonym *Gesittung* and the corresponding adjective *sittlich*. In German these words designate phenomena distinct from custom (*Brauch*) on the one hand, and morality (*Moral*) on the other hand. For lack of English terms exactly equivalent to these shades of meaning, *Sitte*, *Gesittung*, and *sittlich* have been translated as "mores," "morality," and "moral." This somewhat obscures the distinction Geiger makes with the introduction of

habitual practice. From now on $\bar{g}$ is not only a deviation from a previously de facto regularity, but an offense against the normality which society demands.

Latent Norm—Potential Reaction

To be completely accurate, we must be more careful in our formulations. According to what we have said, it may appear as if the subsistent norm originates with the first deviation from the model $s \rightarrow g$ and the consequent reaction (public indignation). That would be saying too much. The act $s \rightarrow \bar{g}$ will someday lead to the realization that $s \rightarrow g$ is provided with v-stigma within a Σ, and the public reaction is only a manifestation of this fact. But no one is in a position to know for how long this was already the case before $s \rightarrow \bar{g}$ occurred. . . . It hence appears that under certain circumstances we are dealing with a *latent norm*. . . . The latent norm corresponds to the *reaction potential* of Ω in the case of a breach of norm.

The subsistent norm is prerequisite for the performance of $r;$ the norm itself however is predicated on Ω's willingness to react.

Hence the somewhat surprising conclusion that the normative character of a norm which is followed without exception is latent. The fact of its alternative effects cannot be established as long as one of the two alternative cases has never materialized. Not until r has been performed or omitted after $s \rightarrow \bar{g}$ occurred can one know for certain whether at the time of the action $s \rightarrow g$ was endowed with a v-stigma (a normative nucleus) or whether it was only a general habit (a custom). As long as it is not put to the test, the social significance of $s \rightarrow g$ must necessarily remain indeterminate, even if there are often numerous indications given for Ω's attitude toward $\bar{g}$ if it were ever to occur (i.e., calculation of obligation). A critical dis-

---

the German terms *Moral* and *moralisch* in chapter 6. *Moral* and *Sitte* (*Gesittung*) are both nonlegal, but whereas *Moral* refers more to internalized norms, the latter is conceived of as supported both internally and externally.—Ed.

cussion of the axiom, *"nulla poena sine lege poenali,"* would find its starting point here. In addition the concept of normative latency is of general significance for practical jurisprudence. . . .

Selection of Habitual Behavior Models— The Problem

Under the following headings we will consider the question: How does it happen that within a given Σ the v-stigma is applied to some modes of behavior and not to others? What factors govern the selection? To be exact, we are concerned with a selection in three phases:

1. Certain modes of action, performed at least once by a given individual H, become steady habits, whereas others are dropped. Why?

2. The MM's of a Σ that function as HH's are able to observe each other. There are a great variety of possible modes of action to imitate. Some of these, having been performed one or more times by a certain H, are generally imitated and become a collective practice, whereas other modes of action of other HH's do not. Why?

3. Certain general practices are endowed with v-stigma, thus becoming the substance of subsistent norms, while others remain noncompulsory habits. Why?

First, however, a word concerning how these questions are meant if they are to serve a scientific purpose. They are not meant, for instance, as an attempt to explain "custom" and "subsistent norm" *a prima origine*. We must remember that the social order is only one facet of social life, whereas the concept of society is inherent in the concept of man. Thus any attempt to explain the genesis of the primeval social order must necessarily be an attempt to explain the origin of mankind. No matter how much philosophers of evolution may speculate about such a question, there can be no scientifically founded answer. What might be possible to investigate, however, is not the presocietal genesis of *the* custom and *the* subsistent norm, but the development of this or that practice, this or that norm, within a given social context—that is, on the basis of existing customs, mores, and social institutions controlling behavior. But even so formulated the question remains an extremely difficult one. Perhaps it would be possible, with the help of methods not yet developed, to trace step by step the origin of an habitual model of behavior in contemporary society—a tedious job, since it involves extremely slow-moving processes. The task can only be attempted on the basis of a direct observation of the complete process from beginning to end. Historical sources give only scanty information or none at all in this connection. . . .

The Myth of Functionality

The more hopeless the possibility of finding empirical answers, the more zealous are the efforts of the know-it-alls to propound their universal explanations. One example thereof is the theory of functionalism, which maintains that the usefulness of behavior is the determining factor for the general acceptance of various modes of action and for their attaining the status of social norms. This dogma has its origin in the trite rationalism of the later Enlightenment and in social Darwinism. It is still current today, however, most recently as the basic concept in Malinowski's *The Foundation of Faith and Morals* (1936) and in Mannheim's *Man and Society in an Age of Reconstruction* (1946; first German edition 1935). Even an opponent of metaphysical words and concepts such as Hägerström considers himself free from any obligation to provide evidence for his mistaken thesis of a "general sociological law" that "only those things endure in the general struggle for survival which are useful for the continuation of society."[2] If social utility were the deciding selective factor in the shaping of social institutions, then we would have to expect irrational elements to play a rather subordinate role in human society. But instead we behold what tremendous efforts have been necessary in the

[2]   "Om sociala vidskepelser," *Socialfilosofiska uppsatser* (Stockholm, 1939), p. 188.

course of the preceding centuries, and are still necessary, to introduce principles of reason and utility—even in modest proportions—into Western society. The theoretical rationalists are actually the most dangerous promoters and guardians of social irrationality: by constantly discovering the latent functions of institutions, they inspire a distrust of systematic efforts to rationalize, at least to some degree, the course of social life. Compared with the alleged inherent functionality of traditional social processes, attempts at artificial planning appear to be shortsighted, bungling, and opposed to the "higher reason" of natural evolution. But it should be noted that it is possible for utility to act in two different ways as principle of selection.

1. The development of habits, customs, and norms is *motivated* by ideas of utility. Where individual persons are concerned, conceptions of purpose undoubtedly play a certain role in decision-making. Nor is there any evidence to suggest that this is less the case in primitive communities than in civilized ones, although rational calculation may be somewhat defective in the former. It is certain, however, that instrumental considerations guide our actions only to a limited extent. That has been sufficiently confirmed by the more recent findings of psychology. Especially in the process of habit-forming, the idea of usefulness appears to have very little influence. On the contrary, age-old habits often prove to be the most formidable obstacles to the spread of useful innovations. "Habit is, by definition, thoughtless."[3] But if the individual is influenced only to a limited extent by instrumental motives, we can expect this to be even less true in the case of collective activity, as in the emergence of customs and mores through the selection of certain imitated modes of action. . . .

2. Under the influence of the Hegelian idea of the "cunning of reason," reinforced by the sociological application of the Darwinian dogma of selection, belief arose in the triumph of utility in the affairs of the objective world. One senses the after effects of Enlightenment metaphysics, whereby Reason, moving

[3]   H. Finer, *The Future of Government* (London, 1946), pp. 139–40.

into God's place, takes over the world-guiding function of Divine Providence. As irrational as human motives are, and social institutions appear to be, they are supposedly governed nonetheless by a secret reasonable purpose which has only to be discovered. And the discoverers leave no stone unturned in their attempts to prove their proposition. Only the results are deficient to such an extent that such efforts are completely wasted.

a) It is not difficult to find in ethnological literature a number of primitive customs which, with a bit of good will, can be interpreted as useful. By carefully picking and choosing it is possible to construct a highly impressive picture—as long as one ignores the discarded material. In order to prove that pragmatic selection of customs and mores occurs spontaneously, it is necessary to show that they consistently fulfill a useful function. This is not achieved by citing a collection of well-chosen examples. Is it useful to slit the lower lips of small children and force a wooden disk into the wound? Is it useful for the Indians to permit holy cattle to consume half the grain crop and to trample down the rest? And not to forget the present: is it more useful to greet someone by removing your hat than in some other way? Or more useful to reward certain services by tipping than by paying a stipulated fee?

b) When attempts at a direct explanation in terms of usefulness fail, recourse is taken to a conception of functionality relative to the specific circumstances of the time and place, that is, with respect to the entire social structure of the Σ. If bride-stealing is a general practice, then it may be useful to keep your daughter behind locked doors. But is the custom of bride-stealing itself useful? If not, then why isn't it done away with? Indeed, how did it originate in the first place? Strangely enough, the utility of a practice is judged in relationship to the total social structure, the latter however is accepted uncritically as given. In this way, moving in a circle from one thing to the other, one believes that he has explained each phenomenon as useful in relation to the others, although in reality he has proven nothing but that there is a certain inner harmony in the rhymelessness, a method in the madness. If the relative usefulness of a practice is seen in its adjustment to irrational social conditions, then the principle of utility cannot have guided the formation of society in former times, which led to the development of these irrational conditions. The primacy of utility in social life would have resulted in resistance to the irrationally constituted environment, not adjustment to it.

c) If worst comes to worst, and neither an absolute nor a relative functionality can be discovered, one may nevertheless assume on the basis of general experience that the irrational and hence inexplicable usage must be the surviving remnant of a long since transcended stage of society, in which it once served some useful purpose. The ends are forgotten but the means have survived. There is a leap from the empirical confirmation of an hypothesis to an appeal to first principles. What a remarkable lack of consistency in the argument! An anachronistic practice, firmly established as a habit, resists the new demands of reason. In other words, the origin of collective behavior models is supposedly determined by pragmatic selection, but not their modification or disappearance!

d) Finally, the whole theory of utility is based on a fallacy. What does "useful" mean? There is hardly any conceivable kind of act which could not serve some postulated purpose or other, and hence *everything* can be interpreted as useful as long as one does not attempt to analyze the rationality of the subjective purposes. . . .

"Ignoramus"

The fact is, the actual causes for the formation of a given habitual order are unknown, and will for the time being remain so.

The modes of action of individuals in isolated cases are apparently the result of manifold combinations of a large number of causal factors; they are accidental, in the sense that the basic, highly multi-causal relationship has not been clarified.

When *H* responds to *s* with *g*, the engraphic-ecphoric mechanism[4] goes into operation, leading to the formation of a habit.

The engraphic-ecphoric law is, however, only a general, formal rule stating that *H*, if he has once responded to *s* with *g*, is disposed to respond again with *g* in case *s* is repeated. In view of this rule we must now ask why it is that in certain cases the formation of habits does not come to pass—according to what principles does the negative selection or the elimination process take place. In reply we can only make surmises, some of which however have a high degree of probability.

1. One such cause for the failure of habits to develop is that *s* seldom occurs in the life of *H*. This is implied in the idea of "habit." The longer the interval between the successive instances of *s*, the more doubtful will it be whether the recollection of $s \rightarrow g$ will remain intact until the next time. In the course of time it can become blurred or forgotten. The intensity of the engram $s \rightarrow g$ is therefore a function of the frequency of *s*.

2. On the other hand it will also depend on the intensity of the first impression. If the first occasion of *s* was of vital importance to *H*, or if it were brought into sharp relief by the surrounding circumstances, then it will have left on *H* a much deeper impression. Then the engram is deep enough from the very beginning to withstand a longer lapse of time than one left by a less poignant *s*. The intensity of the engram is hence a function of the depth with which it was first experienced.

3. The lapse of time may also play another kind of role. If there has been a long interval between successive occurrences of *s*, changes in the environment may cause *s*, in view of the altered circumstances, to take on a new aspect. It is also possible

---

4   In a previous section, omitted in this translation, Geiger mentions the mnemic theory of R. Semon, according to which *engraphy* occurs when a psychic experience leaves a lasting trace, or *engram*, on the memory. When the impression consists of more than one element, the result is an *engram-complex*. $s \rightarrow g$, once enacted, produces such an engram-complex. Repetition of a single element of the original experience may elicit recall of the entire complex, this process being called *ecphory* (triggering).—Ed.

that certain features of the new environment will act upon H as additional factors in the motivation of decisions determining his behavior in s. A given s represents an entirely different "pragmatic problem" in the environment and total social context today than at the time of the first s, long since past.

4. At this point, by the way, we must mention a fact which may otherwise become blurred by our schematic approach. Until now we have hypothetically assumed that a certain kind of s is an objectively given entity, determined by a set of external circumstances and involving one or more persons. But no two real sets of circumstances are completely similar. What appears to X to be a repetition of the same s_1 may be perceived by Y as a somewhat differently constituted s_2. It remains an unsolved puzzle what laws determine how the various elements of perception are combined by the individual to form the complex conception of a situation, which then becomes the remembered image. Which of the separate impressions are regarded as basic to the complex situation and which are irrelevant or merely accidental? We are operating with the s-concept, therefore, as if it referred to an objectively measurable entity, although we are forced to admit that we don't even know what constitutes the substantial nature of a certain s in the minds of given individuals. Hence it can very well be that an observer will get the impression that H is involved in the same s_1 as before, whereas H regards himself as being in an entirely new s_2.

5. The practical realization of ecphory can be cancelled by counter-effects. H responded to s the first time with g. This resulted in an event k ($=$ consequence) which made H feel uncomfortable. If s occurs again, the ecphoric effect of the previous experience is indeed $s \rightarrow g$, but g is not put into effect because of its unpleasant associations. "A burned child is twice shy." We are actually dealing here with a further engram-complex: $g \rightarrow -k$. The negative nature of k is then transferred to g itself. Here motives of utility, among other things, act as a brake; or more simply, the motive of inutility. In the first instance of s, g proved to be "harmful." The idea of g is indeed

ecphorized when *s* is repeated, but it is not realized because *g* is "not useful." Among the experiences which would cause an aversion to the engram *s* → *g*—and of particular importance in this context—is the possible unfriendly reception of *g* on the part of others with whom one is living in social interdependence. In order to avoid a repeated reaction of disapproval, the next time *s* occurs *H* substitutes another form of action for the ecphorized *g* ("burned child").

6. Considerations of utility were mentioned in the preceding paragraph as counter-motives for the realization of ecphorically determined behavior models. It is generally known, however, that habit can be stronger than reason. An engram complex *s* → *g* becomes deeply rooted as a result of frequent repetition over a long period of time. But it can come to pass that a change of circumstances in the general environment makes *g* impractical, or an advance in knowledge reveals that *g* has always been impractical. Nevertheless, it is possible that *H* will persist in the habit *s* → *g*, which is still stronger than the conflicting incentives.

Those are only a few of the possible conditions for the formation of habits, i.e., the selection of once-performed modes of behavior for future constant repetition.

Similar considerations obtain for the formation of customs, i.e., the general adoption of forms of behavior originally practiced only by individuals. Here we must consider two questions: (1) For which situations do customs originate? (2) Which of several behavioral responses to an *s* becomes elevated to a custom?

The first question has already been answered in passing. The formation of a custom can only occur—and always *will* occur—with respect to an *s* which typically appears within the Σ-milieu, so that every single M_Σ or all members of a certain limited category of MM_Σ must at all times be prepared to meet the hypothetical *s*. The more primitive the level of social development and the less differentiated the organization and living conditions of the Σ, the greater will be the role played by the (in this sense) typical *ss* in the life of each individual M_Σ. The more uniform the conditions for existence are for all, the more will customs determine the behavior of the MM_Σ.

To the question, which of several possible g-responses for a typical s is selected and elevated to a collective custom, we can only give answers as vague as those for the preceding question on the laws determining the habit-forming process of an individual. In fact much the same process is involved in both cases, the former being the interrelative equivalent of the latter, solitary condition. This process can also be formally "explained" in terms of the engraphic-ecphoric mechanism. Under primitive conditions and in relatively small Σ's the individual MM's have each other under close mutual observation. The knowledge that H_1 responded to an s with g leaves the spectators with the same engram-complex as H_1 himself. The difference between personal experience and detached observation can therefore hardly constitute more than a difference of degree in the intensity of the impression. If s has ever occurred, whether it involved the present H or any other H, and whether it drew the response g from the present H or from some other H, then in the present new instance of s, a response with g is, *ceteris paribus*, more obvious than any other mode of action. The regular performance of a habit has been called "self imitation" by some, thus emphasizing the basic similarity between imitating others and the repetition of our own behavior. The process of imitation is in fact one of the ways in which the engraphic-ecphoric mechanism operates.

We know no more and no less about why some examples are generally followed and others are not than we know about the selection of modes of action in the formation of personal habits. The six conditions listed above, *mutatis mutandis*, also apply here. Irrespective of these general conditions, there is one special condition involved in the formation of customs: the prestige of the person setting the example provides an incentive for imitation. This prestige may be categorical (based upon the social status of the individual) or personal (determined by outstanding individual characteristics). Even in the most primitive societies, when a categorical status system is completely lacking, one can always find "style-setting" individuals.

And now we finally come to the question of how it happens that in a given Σ some customs (i.e., general habits) have attained the status of norms while others have not. The difference is, as we have said, that noncustomary behavior arouses curiosity but it does not provoke the intervention of Ω. A moral norm, on the other hand, is a rule of conduct whose violation Ω is prepared to meet with an r. But we cannot make any more concrete statements about the various facets of this selection process than we could about the two phases discussed above.

Why does the disappointment of an ecphoric expectation cause the observers to only shake their heads wonderingly in one case and to react with angry disapproval in another? This question is not answered, but only avoided, by the explanation that an r is provoked by nonobservance of those behavior models whose maintenance is necessary for the preservation and cohesion of the Σ. Where can we find the criterion for this necessity? Apparently only in the judgment of the public opinion current in Σ.

If we again consider the idea that social life demands a certain predictability in the behavior of the "others," this is only a general observation which does not tell us (1) with respect to which typical situations obligatory behavior models are given or (2) which particular behavior models are obligatory with respect to these situations. Nor can these questions be answered by alluding to the vital interests of the individual or the collective interest of the Σ.

1. The defensive needs of the individual cannot be a standard of selection. Assuming that $s \rightarrow g$ is customary and that g is an act affecting the interests of B: $(s \rightarrow \bar{g})\dfrac{H}{B}$ hence puts an end to B's plans and he reacts with resentment. What is essential, however, is not B's reaction, but that of Ω, so that the major question is: Does B have Ω's support in his indignation? Does Ω confirm B's feelings of resentment? Or, put another

way: Does Ω regard B's indignation as "justified" by recognizing his interest in $(s \rightarrow g)\frac{H}{B}$ as legitimate? In any case we know this much: it is possible for various other members of B's group to perform acts which are unpleasant for him and injurious to his real or presumed interests without Ω finding cause to intervene in his behalf. Of course we can assume that B will have Ω on his side if H's behavior is contrary to custom. By virtue of the engraphic-ecphoric mechanism, $s \rightarrow \bar{g}$ also strikes bystanders as at least strange, if not reprehensible. But why is $s \rightarrow g$ an established custom? (See above!) That social life necessitates the defense of certain given interests of the individuals in their relation to one another is at any rate a long since obsolete postulate of natural law. . . .

2. Nor can the needs of the Σ itself determine which behavior models will be provided with the ν-stigma. The ethnographers can tell of many customs among primitive peoples which are rigidly upheld to the detriment of the prosperity and continued existence of the Σ. Which modes of behavior are obligatory for the sake of the group and which are incompatible with the common interest depends on the current public opinion. But of what explanatory value is it when we state that the conception of the public interest prevailing within a given Σ determines which typical situations the social order tries to deal with and which modes of behavior are then enforced by social pressure? Obviously none at all. The reaction of Ω to $\bar{g}$ is our only clue to whether or not the public within the Σ is interested in g. Often enough a mode of behavior appears to be upheld as obligatory only because it has been customary for such a long time. But *why* is it customary? (See above!)

Social life demands that people display a certain predictability of behavior in certain typical situations. It is however an arbitrary postulate of natural law that life and property must be secure and agreements respected in order for a society to exist. It is necessary for the sake of collective existence that there be a certain stability to the order, specifically with respect to the *certainty* of the members concerning the content of the order (that is, knowledge of rules) as well as to their *security* through the enforcement of that order. However, it is not of great consequence *which* regularities one can be certain of. It is not the "security of life" that is necessary, but rather the certainty of knowing under what circumstances one is in danger of being killed. Not the "security of property" (what is "property"?) is necessary, but the certainty of knowing under what conditions I must be prepared for others to appropriate what I have managed to scrape together. And if I have to reckon with a promise being broken, I must learn to take the precaution of a formal pledge. There is even in these cases a certainty and a security in the mutual relationships between the MM_Σ's, making it possible for each individual to plan ahead, though under conditions quite remote from what *we* are used to considering a secure order. . . .

The absence of a norm likewise provides certainty in regard to a given s: H knows that he may act as he pleases and without any risk, while B knows that he must be prepared for any kind of behavior on the part of H. Even if he considers himself injured by this behavior, B cannot expect any redress through Ω and would even expose himself to the retributions of Ω if he were to attempt a reprisal against H on his own. The norm therefore assures B a relatively high probability that H will commit or omit certain acts, whereas the absence of a norm assures H a relatively great freedom from risk for his arbitrary actions. In both cases there is certainty of order in typical situations.

Regarding the questions discussed under this heading, we can only say: People practice certain modes of action until they become habits. In groups certain modes of behavior become fixed in custom. In societies certain habitual behavior models are provided with v-stigma, that is, they are elevated to the status of norms. Why, in specific cases, does this occur for one mode of behavior and not for another? *Ignoramus.*

3

LAW AS A TYPE OF ORDER

Law as a Special Kind of Social Order

IF WE now attempt to distinguish law in the usual sense from other types of social order our conclusions are not to be taken too dogmatically. There are no mystic powers that give the word *law* the right to "mean" one particular thing and nothing else. What it *ought* to mean is purely a matter of definition, and definitions are the crutches of knowledge. . . .

One thing must be emphasized from the beginning: there is no obviously clear-cut boundary between law and other orders in the sense that every concrete manifestation of order is either legal or nonlegal. That much is already inherent in the idea of law as the product of social evolution. If the law grows out of a former prelegal system, we can expect transitional phases in which the current order is not yet quite legal but already more than merely prelegal. And since the law is distinguished by various characteristics, it may well be that here and there a particular characteristic is still missing. We must therefore be prepared to encounter a central region in which the phenomena are without doubt legal in the fullest sense of the word and concept, surrounded by a zone of other phenomena which are more or less—but not entirely—legal. In this case I will speak of *imperfect law*.

Among the conceptions which are associated with the idea of (positive) law is, first of all, that of the *state*. Law is thought of as a social order valid for a nation-state, which, if not devised by the state, is at least maintained by state guarantees. . . .

A "Central Authority"

It is not sufficient to conjoin the law to the state as the law-bearing social aggregate. To define law as "the social order supported by the state" would be inadequate. By defining law in terms of the state and the state in terms of the law, there is a danger that our statements will contain no more information about either than the usual glib commonplaces.

What do we mean by "state"? The usual definitions are not especially satisfying. . . . To avoid even the appearance of wanting to trespass on the domains of the political scientist, I shall here call the law-bearing social aggregate (the Σ in which the law obtains), not "state" but simply the "legal community." It is then a moot question whether or not this is the same as the "state," or whether we may postulate the existence of a law prior to the state—or perhaps even a prelegal state.

According to our conception, the legal community is internally differentiated and contains a number of diverse groups over whose nonlegal orders the law is superimposed as a uniform network. Only in a figurative sense, for instance, can we attribute a legal order to a fully isolated primitive horde. The idea is always implicit that within the all-embracing "legal system" there is always more or less room for individual "autonomous" orders. What we mean can be represented with reservations by the well-known antithesis "state and society"— ignoring, of course, the liberal postulate which was once identified with this dichotomy. A unified legal society is spanned across a multitude of "free associations." Hence we only speak of a legal order when *a superordinated central authority has been constituted within a social milieu consisting of separate coexistent or interlocking groups*. This is the most general and neutral expression for the idea of a "nation with an organized supreme authority." . . .

The Establishing of Apparatus and Organs

With respect to the structure of the ordering mechanism, the legal order may be distinguished from the prelegal by the presence of a special apparatus for the administration of the order and the consequent establishment of various organs for this purpose.

In the stage of development where the social order is still exclusively moral, the controlling mechanism functions spontaneously in the manner described above: the Ω insures that the norms are observed, this Ω in each particular case being embodied by the respective "others." . . . In the legal order the maintenance of the norms and the administration of the retributive reactions is no longer left up to spontaneous action on the part of the "others," but is entrusted to especially created organs. This is one—and the most conspicuous—of the facts by which the *institutionalization* of the order becomes apparent.

The function is transferred from Ω as such to an instance acting in the name of the Σ, which we will hereafter refer to as Δ ($\delta\iota\kappa\alpha\sigma\tau\dot{\eta}s$ = judge). In this context Δ will not only stand for the function of passing legal judgments (in the strict sense), but will include the enforcement of sentences and preventive vigilance, that is, the police function. . . .

The transfer of control of the order to special Δ-instances results in the structure becoming an external power with respect to the individual M. In the stage of spontaneous reactions on the part of Ω the delinquent is, of course, also in a passive position in relation to the Ω. The "others," acting in concert and "from outside," exert a pressure on him. Here, however, viewing the structure as a whole, the passive role of this exposure is compensated and offset, inasmuch as the same individual is called upon in other cases as a member of Ω to take active measures against other offenders. Sometimes he is subjected to the norm and at other times he enforces it. This alternation of roles ceases with the transfer of the r-function to an instance Δ. The control mechanism of the social order, established as an impersonal institution, is then located firmly and exclusively in certain hands. This mechanism and its organs emerge as an objective force external to the persons involved.

The essence of this process of institutionalization can be reduced to a general expression. Social interdependence asserts itself in the mechanism of social order. In groups with a pre-legal structure, adjustment, conformity, and social pressure on the part of one's neighbors are manifested in diffuse and spontaneous actions. *In the legally ordered society social interdependence is institutionalized and monopolized.* It is concentrated in a central authority and administered by organs of this authority.

Law is, therefore, an order-mechanism monopolized by a central authority.

The Legal Relationship as a Social Type

The foregoing discussion of the institutionalization process may now be supplemented by some observations concerning the social structures typically corresponding to legal orders. G. Gurvitch[1] distinguishes between *droit social* and *droit individuel* as two kinds of law, corresponding respectively to a social atmosphere of trust and of distrust. His description of these elementary social relationships at once reminds one of Tönnies's antithesis of *Gemeinschaft* and *Gesellschaft*. When considering Gurvitch's typology, we must take into account that he has adopted a broad, ethnological concept of law. According to the terminology of the present exposition, the so-called "law of a trusting atmosphere" is not law at all, but rather a prelegal phenomenon. The law appears to me to be a type of order belonging specifically to a social atmosphere of distrust. One could say, with reservations, that its very presence is an expression of distrust, a sign of "lost social innocence."

The spontaneous mechanisms of adjustment, conformity, and retribution alone can guarantee the maintenance of the social order only when a number of requisite conditions have been fulfilled:

1. The integration of the individual M_Σ into the Σ is extremely intensive. That means that his entire intellectual life is governed to the maximum by the collective body, and that —to use a modern expression analogously—he is united with

[1]   *Elements de la Sociologie juridique* (Paris, 1940), pp. 156 ff.

the others in a tight and unconditional "value community." The fact of social interdependence exercises such a direct influence on his actions that the probability of voluntary conformity is exceptionally high.

2. As a corollary to this intensity of the collective way of life there is a low degree of personal emancipation. Free development of the personality appears to be closely related to the individual's being located at the intersection of several social circles. By constantly changing roles between his various social circles, the individual gains a certain distance to them all, increasing his consciousness of being an independent person. Hence the intensity of social interdependence is a function of the homogeneity of the total social environment. The degree of social differentiation within a given milieu is inversely proportional to the efficacy of social interdependence as an immediate determinant of behavior.

3. The spontaneous action of the control mechanisms, in regard to vigilance as well as to retribution, is predicated on a certain intimacy in the living arrangements. This, on the other hand, will be most evident in a relatively homogeneous, undifferentiated milieu. Intimacy as a general characteristic of a given Σ implies, firstly, that the individual lives his life for the most part before the eyes of the public; secondly, that this public is not anonymous, but known (composed mainly of persons with whom the individual is personally acquainted); and thirdly, that personal interest and concern for the affairs of others is the general rule. Under these circumstances the individual, as a potential norm violator, feels himself under constant public surveillance and moral censorship; his inner subservience to the opinion of the onlookers acts as a moralizing force. On the other hand the spontaneous occurrence of r in case of a norm violation is almost inevitable. Of course a B who considered himself injured would naturally react in any kind of social atmosphere. But the salient point is that the r of Ω, supporting B in his indignation, may only be expected with certainty if the remaining MM_Σ are interested in the person of B and his affairs.

The social environment characteristic of a legal order is different. Law exists where there is a differentiated society, united by a central authority. The legal society comprises a number of differentiated, if frequently interrelated, subgroups. The variety of competing group milieus leads to variations in value concepts, thus undermining the "value community," which may even disintegrate in the face of resulting value antagonisms. The individual gains in internal and external independence, but social interdependence remains unimpaired. In fact, in a society with division of labor and technical apparatus for the control of nature, social interdependence is actually increased: the isolated individual in an advanced civilization is far more helpless than the isolated savage. But social interdependence no longer functions as a direct impetus, but is counterbalanced by heightened individualism. A differentiated legal community, moreover, must be of a considerable size, simply in terms of numbers. Instead of the intimate way of life in the small group, we find larger societies characterized by a reserved coolness in interpersonal relationships. People maintain interest in individuals and their affairs within their own circle of friends, relatives, and neighbors, but it is not extended to include the whole of the legal community. In such an atmosphere of general anonymity a spontaneously functioning control mechanism is no longer feasible. In these great social conglomerations whose boundaries exceed the limits of personal experience, the individual is not essentially at one with the others, even though his existence is shackled to theirs. The desire grows to evade social interdependence if it becomes uncomfortable, while the inclination of onlookers to intervene on behalf of victims of norm violations becomes lukewarm. Vierkandt attempted to characterize this difference in social relationships with the types "communal relationship" and "acknowledgment relationship." Instead of intimate solidarity there is a loyal respect for others; instinctive unity is replaced by rational reciprocity.

In an atmosphere of personal alienation, "distrust" is the natural attitude. By distrust in this context we hardly mean that everyone is permanently suspicious of everyone else on principle. The situation could be described more accurately as a "lack of trust." The enforcement of the order (that is, security; cf. page 66 f.) necessary for collective existence can only be guaranteed by a centrally administered, impersonal control apparatus. . . .

Changes in Reaction Caused by Instance Δ

When the order-bearing Σ increases beyond the limits possible for an intimate way of life, a central authority, Π (= πολιτικὸν κράτος), comes into being, in which the social interdependence is concentrated. Generally speaking, social interdependence then no longer functions on the basis of instinct (that is, by virtue of affective solidarity within a limited, perceptible circle), but rather in part because of conscious recognition of the vital necessity of fitting into the social whole and in part because of the actual or threatened use of organized coercion on the part of the Π and its organs. The special function of social interdependence which lies in the maintenance of order by reacting to norm violations becomes institutionalized and its administration is delegated to the instance Δ. . . . The social order takes on a specifically legal character, the mechanism of spontaneous reaction is succeeded by the apparatus of legal procedure and its enforcement, and the administration of the reactive function becomes an institutionally differentiated task and eventually a professional or official occupation.

1. A concomitant and direct result of the institutional specialization of the administration of justice as a specific social function-complex is the creation of systematic procedures. Not until the reaction has become a delimited functional area within the whole of vital social processes do such concepts as "lawsuit" or "litigation" come into being. . . .

2. Such procedural norms regulate the position of the various persons involved in their relationships to one another: judge, jury, bailiff, plaintiff, defendant, witness, counsel, etc. They also govern the course of the proceedings, especially

through the rules of evidence. Under certain conditions this leads to an extensive formalization of the reactive function. It is not sufficient grounds for the infliction of a reaction that instance Δ is—in a general, logical sense—convinced on the basis of available facts that a breach of norm has taken place. The reaction must be dependent on the presentation of evidence *in accordance with the given rules. . . .*

3. We shall now discuss in greater detail the reaction monopoly exercised by Π. We must first distinguish between the monopoly of passing a sentence and the monopoly of enforcing it.

The *sentencing monopoly* is the specific prerogative of instance Δ. A norm is then "legal" when the spontaneous r of B and/or Ω is succeeded by the r of Δ. Without a judgment there can be no legal reaction, and without the complicity of instance Δ there can be no judgment. Δ alone decides in the legal order whether or not there are grounds for an r, and any action against the accused which has not been legitimized by a formal judgment is itself a norm violation. The $r\dfrac{B}{A_c}$ without the benefit of a judgment is an illegal act of vengeance and as such must be countered by $r\dfrac{\Delta}{B_c}$. The spontaneous $r\dfrac{\Omega}{A_c}$ which is not the execution of a formal sentence is lynch law, i.e., a so-called collective crime which must be prosecuted by $r\dfrac{\Omega}{MM}$.

This of course only means that spontaneous reactions of a particular kind must be eliminated, namely those which "under usual circumstances" are contrary to the norms. If someone who has been robbed or physically attacked breaks off all social contact with the thief or assailant, discriminating against him in personal relationships, it is—inasmuch as no general legal norms are violated by this behavior—strictly the private concern of the victim and has nothing to do with the reaction monopoly of Δ. And if the public withdraws its confidence from someone who is suspected of fraud or convicted of it, or if the public displays open contempt for a father who abuses his children, etc., these are not legal, but moral, reactions and likewise do not prejudice the reaction monopoly of Δ. It may be, however, that the legal order will set express limits to these spontaneous, extralegal reactions, for example, by the prohibition of boycotts or of slander; it is punishable to call a thief a thief or to refer to an ex-convict as a jailbird.

The sentencing monopoly does not necessarily include the *enforcement monopoly*. On the contrary, archaic justice often seems to have been limited to the sentencing monopoly. The judgment of instance Δ simply established that a norm had been violated and that a reaction against the A_c was called for. In the case of norm violations of the type $(s \rightarrow g)_{v\frac{AA}{BB}}$, for example, instance Δ declares that B has a "claim" to compensation or retaliation and then turns the execution over to B (and his faction) to be carried out privately. The judgment is hence nothing but an explicit guarantee for B that by his personal retribution, $r\dfrac{B}{A_c}$, he does not run the risk of $r\dfrac{\Delta}{B}$. The judgment gives him a free hand to deal with his antagonists. Certain prehistoric legal institutions lead one to conclude that the enforcement monopoly of Δ did not always originate as prerogative, but, on the contrary, that it arose from retributive assistance given to B in case he was weaker than A_c. . . .

4. A further distinctive characteristic of the specifically legal order is the *reaction allotment*. Spontaneous reactions are of an indeterminate kind. At the moral level we do find a secondary norm[2] which states that a norm violation shall be punished by Ω, but it remains uncertain in what form and with what severity the r should occur. In practice it will vary from case to case with respect to the same offense. Nor, by the way, are there any fixed standards for the reaction in the extralegal systems of order in modern society. The same offense against the public or group morality will be dispatched in one case with a disapproving shake of the head and in another case will result in social boycott or other painful consequences. This is in

[2]   Geiger calls "secondary" those norms which call for a sanctioning reaction in case of the violation of primary norms.—Ed.

part due to the fact that in the various cases the $r\dfrac{\Omega}{A_c}$ is not carried out by the same MM_Σ and that the individual MM_Σ react in different ways and with different degrees of severity.

Such variability for the $r\dfrac{\Omega}{A_c}$ must be interpreted as a concomitant manifestation of spontaneous reactions. Within given limits a certain value scale may be evolved even in primitive societies, whereby a given relationship between offense and reaction appears "equitable" while more extensive punishment is considered excessive. However, a number of ethnographical observations indicate that the more primitive the level of the society, the greater the tendency to maximize the reaction. The reaction seems here to be directed less against the specific type of offense as against the violation of the social order in the Σ per se, that is, regardless of which norms are involved. By disregarding the prevailing order in the Σ, A_c automatically places himself outside of the Σ and forfeits the security of its order. In any case, as far as the personal reaction of the victim is concerned, at the primitive level he does not seem to have been inhibited by any established limits. The gradations of spontaneous reactions, which apparently come into being during the course of further development, depend purely upon emotional evalutions and moods, and that fact alone provides for extreme variations.

The reactions imposed in organized proceedings by instance Δ, on the other hand, have been measured and graded by reflective evaluation. The model of adequacy (equivalence) comes to guide the legal administration of instance Δ, whereby each offense has a "corresponding" reaction which is specifically adapted to it according to kind and degree. We do not mean that r, in an objective sense, is adequate for the c with which it is associated. There is no such thing as objective equivalence between "crime and punishment." What we mean is that the secondary norms determine which reactions are considered adequate for the various kinds of norm violations. The decision concerning what reaction is commensurate with a given violation cannot, of course, be subjected to any objective criticism. . . .

5. As a general rule we find that in the realm of the legal order the norm violator also enjoys norms guaranteeing his "rights." Instance Δ "owes it" to him to observe the formal norms of procedure. The Π gives him the assurance that he will not be subjected to any legal disadvantages beyond those reactions monopolized by Δ, and the reaction imposed by Δ is specified in terms of kind and degree according to the offense involved. . . .

The Objects of the Legal Order

The legal order is never the only type of social order prevailing within a differentiated society. Mores and conventions also occupy important positions, a manifestation which we call *pluralism of the social ordering systems.* . . .

Here again we are presented with a genetic question: How does this differentiation of the ordering systems come to pass? If we accept the hypothesis that a larger social organization under a central authority, and hence a legal order, originates endogenously within an already existing but previously decentralized society of the same substance, then we must assume the following. At some given point in time there exists a society governed exclusively by mores. As the society crystallizes about a central authority, a legalization or "jurification" of certain parts—but only of parts!—of the social order existing in Σ occurs, while other social relationships continue to be regulated by the spontaneous functioning of morality. Some social relationships are thereby elevated into the legal sphere while others are not.

If, on the other hand, we choose as our starting point the hypothesis of an exogenous origin of the central authority, then the legal order appears from the very beginning to be associated with a new social entity—not only with regard to its formal structure, but also according to the human aggregate involved. A larger society governed by a central authority is created when, through conquest or by bloodless subjugation, two or more previously independent social units are welded together under the supremacy of one of them. In this case the relationships between rulers and ruled and the functions of the newly created larger unit establish an entirely new category of social relationships. This category constitutes a natural object for the legal order, which then gradually extends its jurisdiction from this area into the internal relationships of both of the given population strata and there absorbs or succeeds the previous, spontaneously maintained orders.

In the case of either hypothesis the question is raised: According to what principles are those relationships selected which are to be legally regulated? Is it possible to conceptualize the general principle governing the choice of certain relationships for legal regulation, while dispensing with legal regulation for other relationships? As in the case of our previous enquiry into questions of selection (cf. pp. 60–67), here too our answer must be "no."

In spite of the fact that all modern legal systems are concerned with essentially the same kind of social relationships—security of life, property, reputation, the family, etc.—and that they even regulate these relationships, by and large, in much the same way, this by no means indicates that these are the "natural" objects and forms of solution of the legal order. The relative similarity of legal systems only corresponds to the general similarity between social structures and ways of life. A glance at the legal orders of totalitarian states shows that the choice of objects as well as the choice of solutions in the legal order can be considerably altered as soon as a sufficiently fundamental dislocation of the social structure has occurred.

It may appear obvious that we should seek a formal answer to the problem of selection in the fact that the central authority, by the guarantees of monopolized and regulated sanctions, will attempt to enforce those norms which appear to be indispensable to the existence and functioning of the society in its given structural form, specifically where directly functioning interdependence and spontaneous reaction do not sufficiently ensure the maintenance of these norms following a decline in the instinctive, emotional solidarity among the members of the legal community. These ideas, in various forms and modifications, recur in a number of philosophical theories of law, including, strangely enough, Lundstedt's theory of social utility, whose metaphysical basis and empirical fallaciousness I have elsewhere demonstrated in detail.[3] Reduced to its basic conception, this kind of explanatory attempt only says that the central authority includes those relationships in the legal order whose regulation along certain lines is regarded as indispensable to the interest of the legal community (and enforceable within a given power constellation). But the only indication that the regulation of a certain relationship is held to be indispensable for the existence of the legal community is the fact that it has been included in the legal order. It is hence nothing but an empty tautology, a circumlocutory pseudo-explanation.

One will therefore have to be satisfied with the observation that legal orders of temporally and spatially different legal communities regulate various bodies of social relationships along different lines and that these historical variations are apparently traceable to a multitude of presently unexplained factors. One of the tasks of a comparative sociology of law is to investigate correlations between certain social structures and the characteristics of those social relationships which are regulated by their respective legal orders, as well as the form of this regulation. Care must be taken, however, to avoid such platitudes as "in a theocratic society the religious cult is legally sanctioned," or "private property is a cardinal legal institution of capitalistic society,"—for these are also nothing but tautologies in disguise. . . .

[3] *Debat med Uppsala on Moral og Ret* (Lund, 1946), pp. 108–128.

4

UNORTHODOX REMARKS ON THE QUESTION OF THE SOURCES OF THE LAW

Custom—Custom and Statute in Archaic Law

THE JUDICIAL instance Δ is requisite to the legal order, the legislative instance Θ^1 is not. A legal order which is based exclusively upon norms of habitual origin and in which the institution of statutory maxims is unknown is theoretically conceivable and historical examples can even be cited.

1. According to the hypothesis of endogenous origin of the legal community, it is quite apparent that the earliest stage of the law, having just emerged from a purely moral order, is familiar only with habitual norms. The central authority, Π, which has been consolidated within Σ and about which the Σ has crystallized into a *legal* community, is first confronted with a morality emerging from habit, maintained by the mechanism of spontaneous reaction, and adequate for the present needs of social life. The nature of these norms may remain substantially the same. It is possible that nothing happens except that, for example, a cooperative, "democratic" popular court, as an *ad hoc* instance Δ for a given case, establishes to what extent the conduct of A_c has broken previously observed moral rules and decides on the sanction commensurate with the wrong.

---

[1] This symbol, introduced in a section here omitted, stands for any person, group, or institution functioning as norm-sender or norm-giver (*Normstifter*).—Ed.

The sanctioned norms are still those which were previously maintained by the spontaneous reaction of the Ω. Instance Δ, therefore, decides first and foremost in accordance with "customary law." . . .

The appearance and maintenance of Δ in the life of Σ, as well as its procedures for the administration of sanctions, are of course obvious objects for new norms, which will first come into being when the legal community has been consolidated. But in their substance these norms are also the products of habit. It is difficult to imagine that an *endogenous* central authority, acting as Θ, will explicitly install the instance Δ and then lay down the rules for the exercise of its functions. It must, on the contrary, be assumed that the transfer of the reaction function to an instance Δ is a gradual development and that procedural norms and rules of sanctioning emerge directly from its actual operation. These new legal norms differ from those carried over from prelegal times in that they did not change over from the moral to the legal category, but were, from the very beginning, legal norms in the strict sense.

The habitual origin of additional legal norms may then take the following form: new habits of behavior and moral rules arise spontaneously in the daily life of Σ, for example, when the course of development alters certain external conditions and creates new typical situations, for which corresponding new behavior models come into general practice. If occasion then arises for instance Δ to reinforce these new behavior models through the imposition of sanctions, we know that they have been incorporated into the legal sphere and that new customary law has come into being. On the other hand, a previously nontypical situation, for which no behavior model has come into general practice, may come before Δ to be adjudicated. Thereupon Δ passes its judgment on the principle of "equity" and the decision becomes precedent. We will discuss the creation of legal norms by instance Δ in greater detail below.

Legislation in a hypothetically endogenous legal community would occur either cooperatively and democratically through the resolutions of a popular council, or monocratically by the directives of a dominant chieftain, or theocratically in the alleged revelations of a godhead, mediated by a politically powerful priesthood.

2. If, however, one accepts the (in my opinion more probable) hypothesis of an *exogenous* impetus for the origin of a central authority and legal community, we may expect changes in specific details but otherwise little variation in the general picture as far as the relationship between law and custom is concerned. Here one has to imagine that a warlike tribe subdues, with or without bloodshed, one or more settled tribes, usually agricultural, so that out of the formerly separate tribal elements a single political unit is welded together. The ensuing process by which the "state" and the law come into being may take many diverse forms, the possibilities of which are to some extent known to ethnology and prehistory, but which will not be described here. A schematic outline is sufficient for our purposes.

The first phase is characterized by a purely coercive relationship between rulers and ruled. It may be presumed that the masters as well as the subjects bring their own respective prelegal orders with them into the new political unit, but that neither party had a legal order in the technical sense beforehand. What occurs when either the conqueror or both parties had made the change from the prelegal to the legal condition before the unification will not be considered here, as we are dealing exclusively with the first origins of the law. The conquerors as well as the subjugated must be thought of here as prelegally organized tribes at the moment of their unification. A legal order then develops gradually, step-by-step together with the social merger, as the two ethnically distinct tribes occupying the same territory become a single, politically united people.

Within the two groups the mores which each brought with them into the new larger unit may continue to exist, to the extent that they have not been abrogated by the change in the sociopolitical situation—which is more likely to be the case with the conquered group. But the relationship between rulers and ruled will first be one of sheer coercion rather than law. (If the larger unit comes into being because a settled tribe is threatened by an aggressive warrior tribe and voluntarily seeks and pays tribute to another warrior tribe for its protection, then the phase of purely coercive domination will be passed over and a condition of regular exploitation will be established at once.)

The legal relationship subsequently comes into being when the arbitrary acts of government on the part of the rulers settle into a steady routine, control and exploitation crystallize into habits so that a certain tranquil stability develops in the relationship between the two elements—the first step toward fusion. Hence in this case, too, there is at first no call for legislation. Instance Δ finds the norms which it shall maintain by sanctions partly in the past acts of government and partly in the mores of the prelegal phase, to the extent that they are still applicable and viable under the altered circumstances. Although we must think of instance Δ as having been installed by an official act of Π, its formal functions under such primitive conditions can hardly be specified to such a degree that one could speak of orally proclaimed legal norms.

The oldest manifestations of the legal type were presumably not proclamative normative maxims for the conduct of the populace, but rather the directives of the central authority to its various organs, specifically executive orders as well as general instructions for the exercise of the functions of Δ. Government and legal administration were, for instance, still entrusted conjointly to the same agents at the time of the Frankish kings. In the Δ-function of these organs the directives were put into effect as the royal court commissioner (*comes*) endeavored to institute royal law in place of tribal law. These directives resemble the type of law proclaimed orally or in writing in that they not only assign certain tasks to a person for his area of responsibility, but also give specific instructions as to how and in what forms these tasks are to be carried out. This constitutes the characteristic *prospectiveness* of the law: the directive regulates future events and conduct "until further notice." It also involves, however, a certain submission on the part of Π to its own law; once issued, such directives continue to function automatically and become binding even for cases in which the Π would have preferred a different *ad hoc* handling of the matter. In order to cancel such a directive it must be expressly revoked, and the necessity of such a positive act alone exercises a certain amount of restraint. Moreover the organs of government, the officials, are already engaged in the execution of the directives and have in the meantime developed their own techniques of implementation. This apparatus thus acts as a retarding force against any arbitrary alteration of the principles.

The sources of legal norms therefore appear to emerge in the following historical sequence: first the custom, followed immediately by instance Δ and considerably later by instance Θ—and much, much later, by legal science. . . .

Metamorphoses of the Customary Legal Norm

. . . When a subsistent norm of habitual origin is given the form of a declarative normative maxim, it has no great significance for the existence of the norm. Basically nothing has changed. The normative maxim merely states that the subsistent norm really exists; thus the maxim as such is entirely irrelevant for the social order of the Σ. Its significance lies only in the fact that it is a reflection of the subsistent norm. It has now become an abstract idea; it is released from the particulars of a given case and can be communicated and transmitted. This, however, has certain consequences.

Habits come into being by a gradual process, habits can cease to exist in the same way, and habits can change in an imperceptibly gradual process. Habit is a manifestation of adjustment to the milieu. As the milieu changes, the adjustment process is repeated. Whenever a collective habit (i.e., a custom), on being transformed to a moral norm, assumes the character of a subsistent norm so that the association of an s with a g becomes obligatory, the resulting model $s \rightarrow g$ is nevertheless none too rigid. With changes in the social milieu the actual situations considered to be of type *s* will undergo certain, barely perceptible alterations, and unconscious modifications of the type *g* will accompany them. As long as the model *s* → *g* is more concretely perceived than mentally abstracted, the moral norm will retain a high degree of flexibility. That does not necessarily mean that it is actually in constant independent fluctuation. On the contrary, it is usually quite stable, since the total social milieu at the stage of development of the exclusively moral order, because of its relatively static structure, seldom provides occasion for readaptation within the ordering system. In the swiftly changing contemporary milieu, on the other hand, mores are short-lived.

This changes with the verbal formulation of the behavior model into an abstract idea. The physical perception does not register the gradual transformation, since the perceptual image itself participates in these transformations through the series of repeated situations. But once the model with its obligation-stigma has been captured in words, regardless of how casuistic or concrete the formula, it is—in a more or less metaphorical sense—truly "captured." It is conceptually fixed and thus has a certain constancy of meaning. Through its concretization in the form of a declarative normative maxim, the moral norm loses some of its flexibility. A particular verbal formula is devised for it and in this form it is handed down to subsequent generations as obligatory, although the life that it is supposed to regulate develops along its own lines. In this way a tension is generated between the variability of living conditions and the stability of the institution (here, the moral norm), a tension that must be constantly and repeatedly overcome. Hence only in an abbreviating procedure is it admissible to write the behavior model always in the same manner as *s* → *g*, whether it appears in the formula $(s \rightarrow g)_{v\frac{AA}{\div}}$ or $w[(s \rightarrow g)_{v\frac{AA}{\div}}]$. As soon as it is prefixed by a *w*, *s* → *g* takes on a new aspect. It ceases to be the iridescent image of the habitual, nonverbalized norm and becomes the conceptually fixed, abstract scheme of the normative maxim.

The habitual behavior standard, on the way to becoming a

legal norm, undergoes the same stabilization process—if not already in the prelegal stage, then at the latest with its formulation as law. This formulation is, moreover, especially emphatic. We will first consider the case of the judicatory option on the habitual standard. Viewed schematically, instance Δ always decides in accordance with the habitual standard as it exists at the moment of judgment. It does not therefore interfere with the future development of the standard. One can actually observe how the judiciary in its decisions to a certain extent follows the fluctuations of social life. The application of the habitual standard by instance Δ is meant retrospectively: "Thus it is deemed lawful in the present case because people have always acted according to this standard in the past." The deciding of cases in accordance with habitual standards is, however, always accompanied by a declarative formulation of the standard. The *êosagari*[2] "found" law in the moral heritage of the tribe and propagated it in their recommendations. They gave emphasis to the moral norm by expressing it as a precedent, thus making it serviceable as a general standard for future decisions. The modern judge must, in his decisions, somehow formulate the habitual standard on which he is basing his judgment, that is, he must express it in a declarative maxim. By virtue of instance Δ's authoritarian position as holder of the sanctioning monopoly in the Σ, such a normative maxim carries special weight. Even though a particular decision of instance Δ, in accordance with the habitual standard, is not intended to put a stop to the process of gradual change, the precedent will inhibit further spontaneous development of the standard. A norm has been formulated in concise terms and has become the basis for a verdict. Although it has itself been derived from the life process, in this concise form it acts upon the process as a stabilizing force. . . .

Although the habitual standard actually loses flexibility

[2]   Under Teutonic law, an institution of legal advisors. Basing their recommendations on intimate knowledge of customary practice, the *êosagari* did not pass judgment on cases but merely provided the deciding instances with a legal (precedential) foundation for their verdicts.—Ed.

when it is set down in a declarative maxim, as a matter of principle this flexibility is preserved. This is different in the case of a legislative option on a habitual standard. In the first place its substance is not formulated *ad hoc* and with respect to a particular case—as in the reasoning of instance Δ, but as a highly abstract and general principle for the handling of a certain category of cases. In this way it may possibly acquire greater conceptual breadth, but in its conceptually abstract form it will also become inviolable as the programmatic command of the Σ, enunciated by instance Θ. The crucial difference is that the modality of its function is now no longer retrospective; the future is no longer left open. When set forth as a statutory law in a proclamative maxim, it assumes the prospective modality of a standing rule: "Thus it was decided today and thus shall it be done—until further notice—in the future." Instance Θ removes a habitual standard in its momentary condition from the flux of social life, formulates it in concepts, sets it down in clear, succinct terms, and promulgates it as a general principle for the future. Thus the substance of the habitual standard is frozen and intentionally made static. The modality of its normative function from now on is that of law and no longer that of morality. . . .

Norms and Norm Systems

When we above spoke of ordering systems and of norm systems we meant to designate the totality of order-phenomena manifested within a given Σ, the sum of the existing norms. On the other hand we must not necessarily assume that these norms, with respect to their substance, constitute a coherent whole. If that were the case in the exclusively moral (habitual) order of a Σ, then we would have a most curious situation. Every primitive ordering system emerges independent of all rational control as a miscellaneous collection of individual behavior models with an entirely casuistic nature. If this is the case, one can hardly expect the individual norms, regulating different types of situations, to be mutually coordinated as if based on some guiding pragmatic principle. The myth of autogenous rationality in social life (cf. pp. 57 ff.) may give the impression that this kind of thing exists, but it remains merely a myth.

It is something else again when, retrospectively, by means of a penetrating, detailed analysis of an existing norm system, certain basic features of a consistent affinity can be discovered —at the risk, to be sure, of interpreting more into the facts than one derives from them. Such an affinity, such a "spirit of the laws," can only be understood psychologically—that those persons living together in the order-bearing Σ and participating in the invention and propagation of the behavior models obligatory in various situations, are all of a similar mental character, and also that a once created system of behavior patterns and institutions, by virtue of its own momentum, governs the conception and form of its own new features. The internal coherence, the unity of purpose which may be effected in this way is, however, in any case more of an aesthetic than of a rational nature and does not exclude a logical conflict of norms.

Archaic legal orders are likewise of a casuistic, unpremeditated nature. That much is obvious as long as they are based on the institutional implementation of habitual standards. A first attempt at a rational coordination of norms may then occur when contradictions and lacunae in the norm system become more conspicuous in the formally delegated administration of order by special Δ instances than under the rule of spontaneous order. Hence those persons acting as instance Δ, by judicial modification of the habitual standards, will work toward a certain coordination of norms for contiguous spheres of social activity. This norm-generating activity is also casuistic. Hence the mutual coordination of norms will be effected more in the form of a revision of existing norms than by a master principle governing the composition of the entire norm system. Even the highly sophisticated legal system of Rome's Golden Age—thanks to its basic institution of the granting of praetorial *actios*—bears the trace of the casuistic and the unsystematic.

A further step toward total coordination of the norm system follows with the (private or official) codification of customary law and judicial practice. The collection and subsequent ordering of legal principles and precedents make comparative observations unavoidable, and these comparisons lead by and by to editing, polishing, and coordinating.

The conception of a unitary legal system, derived "deductively" from guiding legal premises, is, however, a late product of intellectual contemplation of "the law" as a closed system. It is, in a word, the product of a legal theory presuming to be a self-sufficient discipline. (A parallel is the morality of principles, the creation of formal ethics.) No such legal system is to be found anywhere in sociopolitical reality. The grandiose experiment of the *Code Napoléon*, undertaken under the influence of the Enlightenment, was attempted only in various major branches of the legal order and its more recent developments are again deviating from the idea of a closed system. This is no doubt related to the fact that the legal orders of modern states must regulate an ever increasing quantity of social relationships, as a result of the shift from political restraint of the state in the liberal era to its increased political intervention in all fields of social and human activity. A norm system derived from a few basic legal ideas and coordinated in all particulars presupposes a high degree of continuity in the social life it is to regulate. Such continuity can only be assumed in the realm of very general, fundamental human and social relationships. As soon as legislation begins to concern itself with regulating the minutiae of social life, it must demonstrate great agility, that is, it must be able to modify certain norm complexes in accordance with new needs. The legislative machine is continuously in operation and its unwieldiness makes the task of creating norms by means of ordinances difficult enough already. It is impossible to thoroughly revise the norm system in each such case, or even to anticipate the possible imbalances (norm collisions) between old and new norms.

The strict systematic unity of our legislation has already been disrupted by the fact that laws from various historical periods, with substantially different social structures, exist today side by side. Our private and criminal law, in their basic elements, originated in the period of bourgeois ascendency; at the same time we have welfare legislation produced by the intellectual and moral climate of the immediate (and certainly no longer bourgeois) present. Jurisprudence strives, on the basis of its comprehensive technical knowledge of contemporary norms, to influence the forces of legislation in the interest of maintaining a modicum of internal unity. And the Δ-instances are confronted daily with the task of smoothing out, by means of mediating constructions, inconsistencies in the relationships between various norm complexes. . . .

5

THE OBLIGATORY CHARACTER
OF LEGAL NORMS

Real and Ideal Law

THE SUBSTANCE of "valid" law here appears to be the behavior models which can be actually observed within an organized social aggregate Σ under a central political authority Π, as well as those norms which actually influence the course of events in that social aggregate—in other words, the actual legal condition in Σ. An appraisal of this condition is pointless and impossible. Certain modes of behavior are the normal pattern of events in Σ. Π employs the coercive means at its disposal in order to enforce these modes of behavior. Hence this is the real legal condition in Σ. A friend of mine—a legal scholar—once countered my remarks on this topic with the statement: "I refuse to acknowledge as valid law that external order which the government manages to put into effect on the basis of its coercive powers." This utterance was greeted with applause by colleagues of his who were present. He would probably emphatically deny being an adherent of natural law; nevertheless, on the basis of this statement, he is one.

According to this point of view, whether the ordered pattern of events in Σ actually enforced by Π with the help of its organs Θ and Δ is "law" or not should depend upon whether or not the substance of this order corresponds to standards or criteria existing independent of it. We are here no longer dealing with law as reality, but as an ideal. Such standards can only be derived from the "essence of the law," interpreted as a conceptual reality—and that is a postulate of natural law. Such preconceptions are the products of fantasy and have nothing to do with science. "Ideal law" is something outside the realm of empirical knowledge. . . .

What should the scientific study of law have as its object if not the actually existent legal order? There is no reason why one should not give vent to his disapproval of certain characteristics of this order, or even its basic principles, by calling them "illegal." Only one should not forget that illegal does not mean nonlegal, but rather badly legal, i.e., a moral or political—in any case a scientifically irrelevant—appraisal. Even bad or perverted law is "law". . . .

Hence the "validity" or the obligatory nature of a legal norm can only mean, in the scientific sense, that within a given legal community this norm (to a hypothetically measurable extent) is enforced. . . .

Obligation and the Calculation of Obligation

. . . The obligation of the legal norm is in principle a quantitatively measurable alternative, a statement of probability regarding the course of future events. As far as the past is concerned, it is possible to give a mathematically founded, statistical description. Even if the concrete problem of determining the numerical quantities involved constitutes a methodological barrier, it does not alter the fact that measurement is theoretically feasible. The number of prosecutions for negligent destruction of property in which instance Δ allowed damages and the verdict was carried out can be accurately established by means of legal statistics. It cannot be ascertained, however, how many cases there were in which negligent destruction of property actually occurred, nor in how many cases the negligent party voluntarily (out of court) made compensation. Both classes of cases are, however, definite—albeit unknown—numerical quantities as far as the past is concerned. If one had access to a motion picture showing all members of the legal community at all times, then it would be possible to establish the specific numerical values of these unknown quantities. For the past, that is, a somehow delimited previous period of time (for instance, the last ten years up to the present moment), one may therefore set up the equation:

$$v = s \xrightarrow[x]{\pi} \left[\begin{array}{l} \rightarrow g \\ \rightarrow \bar{g} \rightarrow r \end{array} \right.$$

where π means "probability" and x represents the hypothetical value for the degree of probability.

Such a statement of "legal history" is of little value, however, to the lawyer who must deal with the question of obligation in the context of an actual legal situation. With respect to the past, the above formula says two things, namely (1) that in $x/100$ of all s-cases either g or ($\bar{g} \rightarrow r$) actually occurred and (2) that in every single one of these cases there was a $x/100$ chance that g or ($\bar{g} \rightarrow r$) would occur. These statements cannot, however, be applied without qualification to the future, that is, to events which have not yet run their course. . . . The legal situation varies with time and what in the present case is obligatory always remains uncertain. Being practical, one will in many cases simply say: "For twenty years now an overwhelming and constant proportion of all s-cases have led either to g or to ($\bar{g} \rightarrow r$), so it is not likely to be significantly otherwise today or tomorrow." Hypothetically, however, any new case may mean the first step toward a change in the legal situation, the inception of a new norm or the extinction of an old one. . . .

Each case in which the question must be asked, "What law is here valid?"—the actual question of validity—is always the first link in a chain extending into the future and as such is subject to the general uncertainty regarding the future. In this sense it is *res integra*. The question of "validity" or of obligation can therefore only be answered in terms of a *calculation of expectation*. . . .

The Mechanism of Obligation

When a norm is obligatory it means that it is probable that behavior will either be in conformity to it or that a reaction will follow its violation. The motor which keeps this mechanism running is social interdependence. The social interdependence existing between the members of a Σ acts directly upon the individual as the vital impetus for his actions: he either behaves unreflectively in consonance with the norm, whose behavior model has become second nature to him, or he is consciously motivated to abide by the norm as a dictate of the community. Otherwise the reaction of the environment Ω will painfully remind him, if he steps out of line, "that he is not alone in the world" and that his freedom of action must be kept within bounds if he wishes to enjoy the privileges of society.

Exactly the same thing applies, in principle, for the legal order, with the qualification that the reaction function here has a greater significance. At this point we will take up our discussion from page 71. The legal community is extremely large in terms of numbers, intrinsically heterogeneous, and highly differentiated in structure. Social interdependence, as a vital relationship, therefore assumes a more diffuse character, it functions with reduced clarity, the individual's propensity for uninhibited behavior is increased, and his voluntary and almost natural conformity is no longer necessarily the general rule. This is balanced and compensated by the fact that social interdependence is institutionally concentrated in a central authority Π and that social control is administered by a special instance Δ. The fact that the reaction is organized as a special social function, that an extensive apparatus for the infliction of sanctions has been created—this fact alone gives the reaction a special significance. But why, on the other hand, should a society weigh itself down with this extensive apparatus if one could generally expect that the norms would be obeyed voluntarily, and if not, that a spontaneous reaction of Ω would be sure to follow? The very existence of the sanctioning apparatus (the organs of adjudication and enforcement) is proof that the maintenance of the legal structure stands and falls with the sanctioning of norms.

That certainly does not mean that the citizen only obeys the norms out of fear of sanctions and that "deterrence" is the first principle of legal efficacy, especially since we are dealing here not only with criminal law but with law in general, and since "sanction" does not only mean punishment but also injunction as well as many other things. As in any other kind of ordering system, conformity to the norms usually takes place in the legal community without coercion and without the actor ever considering the threat of a reaction. He acts legally because he is accustomed to the behavior models of the legal order and because many of these models simultaneously coincide with widespread moral attitudes. Moreover, conformity to a behavior model (even though it may be subject to criticism) appears to be a lesser evil, the alternative being a threat to behavioral coordination, the *sine qua non* of social existence. Finally, the mere fact that the community or its leaders demand this or that induces a blind or conscious respect for their dictates; the prestige of the instances Π, Θ, and Δ is in fact a strong motivation for obedience. If therefore the sanction does not always constitute a motive for individual action, it would nevertheless be a great mistake to assume that it has nothing to do with voluntary obedience. It has been occasionally noted how the threat of sanctions—especially the sanctions of criminal law—first makes it clear that the social authorities are serious about their demands. The threat of sanctions does not so much act as a deterrent as it serves to underline the demands of society and to stress their importance. Another mechanism however, as far as I can see, remains generally ignored. Those who comply "by volition" and without coercion could no longer be obedient if the norm were not enforced by sanction and threat of sanction against the delinquent and those inclined toward delinquency. I cannot respect the property rights of others as long as the protection of my own property is not guaranteed, or else my existence would be endangered. The principle of reciprocity, the coordination of behavior, is the cornerstone of the legal community. Even if the sanction does not therefore motivate the compliance of the individual, it is nevertheless the indispensable prerequisite for a social milieu in which voluntary compliance is possible.

A common criticism of the so-called coercion theory—the idea that the law is a coercive order imposed from above—points out the impossibility of maintaining by sanctions a norm whose substance is generally rejected. Accordingly, voluntary $(s \rightarrow g)$ behavior "by volition" would have to occur in a certain (overwhelming) proportion of all cases of s in order for the sequence $s \rightarrow \bar{g} \rightarrow r$ to prevail in the remaining cases. Hence it is concluded that it is not the sanctioning function of instance Δ, but the legal consciousness and morality of the citizens which actually impart validity to the norm. But this argument does not contradict the theory advanced here. In the first place we have located the sources of validity not in the sanctioning function but in social interdependence, of which the sanctioning function is but one of the results. Secondly, we have just pointed out that the sanctioning function and readiness to sanction of the instance Δ is important also for voluntary conformity to the norms. Thirdly, the feasibility of establishing unpopular norms appears to be greatly underestimated as result of a poorly understood collective psychology. The dictatorships have taught us better—or should we say, worse. But this question is mentioned here only in passing.

As a result of the institutionalization of the legal order, instance Δ—as holder of the sanction monopoly—occupies the key position in the mechanism effecting the realization of the law. In the final analysis instance Δ decides whether or not a norm has validity. By putting the norms enacted by instance Θ into effect, instance Δ first establishes their substantial validity. By declaring habitual standards to be customary law, it confirms as legal those norms which were previously not thus obligatory. By deciding according to judicial discretion, according to the nature of the matter, and according to considerations of equity where appropriate norms are lacking, it creates valid law. By (possibly) refusing to apply normative maxims proclaimed by Θ, it divests these maxims of their obligatory character. The sanctioning habits of instance Δ thus determine, more than any other single factor, the behavior of the populace....

. . . If there is a legal norm which states that a certain behavior model is obligatory for certain persons, then there will also be a legal norm which states that it is obligatory for instance Δ, in case of breach of this norm, to react against the offender with the infliction of (civil or criminal) sanctions. . . . If, however, Δ neglects to impose sanctions when $s \rightarrow \bar{g}$ has been committed (or imposes sanctions other than in the prescribed manner; or imposes sanctions, even though $s \rightarrow \bar{g}$ has not been committed), it has violated the sanctioning norm. . . . Thus one can see the kind of circumstances connected with the "validity" of substantially determined norms which are to be put into practice by instance Δ. The limits of their validity are set by the readiness of instance Δ to impose sanctions in their behalf. . . .

Norms and Factual Circumstances

. . . According to the classical conception, instance Δ is under obligation to certain definite rules, especially the directives of instance Θ, the so-called laws. Adjudication, according to these rules, means that certain facts are investigated and those norms applied which correspond to the nature of the case. The circumstances of the act are subsumed under the norm. This image corresponds to the naïve, rationalistic idea that concepts duplicate the reality they seek to describe.

No jurist still believes today that adjudication is limited to this simple logical process in which the judge plays the role of an automaton: the facts are inserted at the top, the button is pushed and the finished judgment is dispensed at the bottom. This miracle is supposedly explained by the fact that the highly sensitive machine—called "the judge"—contains in his interior a sorting apparatus calibrated with the contents of the law. Every modern jurist knows that judicial activity is partially constructive. Otherwise it would be impossible to speak of the practice of the courts as a source of law. Nonetheless the old prejudice clings to life and jurists find it difficult to throw it overboard. There are apparently only few practicing jurists who, on closer examination, recognize that there is no such thing as a logical process of subsumation of facts under norms, and that the construction of new law by the judge is not the exception—when the lawbooks let him down—but the general rule.[1]

Above everything else, we must here emphasize that this idea of the subsumation of facts under norms cannot refer to what we have called the norm in the actual sense, namely, the subsistent norm: the eidetic image, provided with v-stigma, of a typical mode of behavior. Since in this context a logical process is meant, only a normative maxim can be involved, whether proclamative or declarative—or to be more exact: the conceptual substance which is expressed in normative maxims. The basic problem therefore concerns the relationship between the conceptual scheme of facts, $s \rightarrow g$, as set down in the normative maxim, and the concrete facts $s' \rightarrow g'$ or $s'' \rightarrow g''$, etc., ad infinitum. The factual scheme supposedly circumscribes its own scope of meaning in such a way as to cover certain concrete facts. The facts of social life appear as concrete variants of the abstract scheme of facts contained in the norm. Figure 1 is an attempt to represent this relationship graphically. Every point corresponds to a concrete fact, whereas the circle symbolizes the presumable scope of meaning fixed by the factual scheme of the norm. It is supposedly then the task of the judge, on the one hand, to investigate, determine and analyze the facts which have been presented for judgment according to their nature (that is, without objective error), and on the other hand to establish the scope of meaning of the factual scheme given in the norm. On the basis of these two operations he must then decide whether or not the norm is valid for the case,—whether $s' \rightarrow g'$ lies inside or outside the field of reality indicated by the factual scheme of the norm. If affirmed, then judgment is to be made according to the norm or, in other words, a sanction is

[1]   Knud Illum, *Lov og Ret* (Copenhagen, 1945), pp. 120 ff., places great importance on this. But although we agree here on the basic issue, Illum draws essentially different conclusions.

inflicted.[2] In short, the judge supposedly identifies the concrete deed $s' \rightarrow g'$ as a case of $s \rightarrow g$ or of $s \rightarrow \bar{g}$.

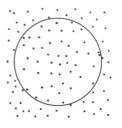

Figure 1

The conceptual scheme of facts and behavior, as it is verbally formulated in the normative maxim, has in reality however no objectively limited or limitable scope of meaning whatever. There is no definite set of concrete facts for which, by virtue of their nature, the normative maxim is inherently "valid." The substance of the normative maxim is conceived and understood as a mere point without extension. It is nothing other than a *conceptual point of reference* for the judge, and as such cannot encompass a field of concrete cases, but only determines the perspective from which they are seen. Consequently the judicial interpretation of a normative maxim does not state its given scope of meaning (rightly or wrongly), but rather imparts a scope of meaning to the norm. . . .

Are the Lawyers Aware of That?—Critique of the Juridical Question of Validity

. . . The language of the law, by appealing to allegedly objective standards, conceals and dissimulates as much as pos-

[2] The operation must, of course, be carried out for every single element involved in the given circumstances: Does s' fall under the norm type "s"? Is the actor A' an "A" within the meaning of the norm? If there is a plaintiff B', is he a "B" within the meaning of the norm? Does g' satisfy the conditions of "g" as foreseen by the norm, or is it $\bar{g}$ in terms of the norm?

sible the creative activity of the judge. For his part, the judge would prefer to discover, rather than invent, the law called for in a given case.

Beyond all doubt we are confronted here with a classic example of occupational ideology and it is tempting to analyze its structure and to trace its psychological origins. Two principal motives are suggested.

1. Professional fascination with the idea of order per se, involving the conception of fundamental unity and consistency of events. This may be the source of the ideal image of the sub-sumation of all conceivable particulars of an act under general and objective standards, that is, the idea of absolute coordination of events and of perfect certainty in the law.

2. Hypothetically however it could also be due to an *acade-mization* of the professional mentality. I will attempt to de-scribe this process as conceived. The professional judiciary has had a practical, scientific education and occupies an official position in the body politic. The former circumstance may con-tribute to a certain inclination toward professional and *techno-logical* theoretization of their functions as a deciding instance. A corollary thereof is the instinctive prejudice against any func-tions which lie outside the normal technical routine. One at-tempts therefore to hypostatize an objective ἐξωτῆϛγῆϛ from which all specific problems may be projected onto a level where the learned technical procedures may be applied.

The official position in the body politic may, in its own way, have the same effects, inasmuch as it is unfavorable for the development of free (that is, not circumscribed by exact limits of responsibility) initiative. The mentality of the civil service may be one of the reasons why the professional judge prefers to feign application of an objective rule and to assert the existence of an instance controlling his responsibility, instead of admitting that he is in fact creating law on his own free initiative. We may take it as a confirmation of the implied assumptions that the aversion to making such an admission is apparently more pro-nounced on the part of the academic, lower middle-class judges of (for instance) Germany or France than among the less numerous, academically less encumbered, gentried English jurists.

It is in any case a fact that juridical terminology feigns the existence of legal standards to which one may appeal in a given case, even when there are no appropriate statutes or established precedents. In fact, however, instance Δ actually creates law even where it appears to be only applying already valid legal maxims. . . .

The Function of the Normative Maxim

. . . The expression, "without delimited scope of meaning in regard to concrete facts," naturally does not mean that the substance of a normative maxim can be interpreted at will and correspondingly applied. Even with respect to relatively elastic concepts, one can imagine examples of opposite extremes, for instance when one must ask: If this act is not a betrayal of military secrets to a foreign power, then what other acts would correspond to this conceptual scheme? And on the other hand: If we choose to regard it as a betrayal of military secrets, then what is nonmilitary and what is nonsecret?

The conceptual scheme of the normative maxim has no fixed scope of meaning in relation to concrete acts, but is instead a point of reference for such circumstances. This relationship implies a certain tolerance, however, and this tolerance is determined by nothing but the conventions of the language. Referring again to the above graphic illustration we may express the essence of the present discussion as follows. The conceptual scheme of the normative maxim potentially has a maximum and a minimum radius of reference. Somewhere in the zone delimited by these two radii is located the fluid boundary of the scope of validity of the norm, such as it is legally administered. The circle described by the minimum radius of reference then represents the nucleus of the field of validity, i.e., the aggregate of classical cases corresponding to the letter of the normative maxim (Fig. 2).

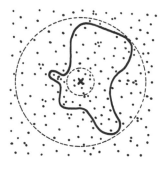

Figure 2

The normative maxim as such is of course by no means obligatory, i.e., the proclamative maxim and the conceptual substance expressed therein have no effect whatever on the processes of social life. There is always the theoretical possibility that instance Δ will not bother about the norm. In that case there will be no equivalent subsistent norm and no trace of obligation. It is exactly the same as if it had never been enacted and never appeared in a lawbook. *If* however instance Δ wishes to appeal to the normative maxim for purposes of a decision, then its interpretation and application are limited by the conventions of the language which determine—albeit vaguely—the minimal and maximal radii of reference of the conceptual scheme expressed in the normative maxim. In this restricted sense one can attribute substantive validity to the normative maxim. On the other hand, that is the most that can be meant when it is said that a given statute is "valid" for certain factual circumstances. . . .

Nevertheless the general practice is to impute "validity" to proclamative norms, i.e., to the statutes. . . . When a statute is enacted, it is true that it remains nothing but words as long as instance Δ does not give reality to the *v*-stigma by applying the maxim in court. But instance Δ could ignore the maxim. If all the judges in the land, or a majority of them, follow suit, then there will be no equivalent subsistent norm for the statute. But under normal circumstances there is only a slight probability that this will happen, even if the individual judges have no personal desire to apply the norm. The psychological influences of professional morality and honor may well determine the motives for action in the case of each individual. Seen as a social phenomenon, however, the transformation of a proclamative norm into a subsistent norm has more tangible causes. . . . Decisive for the transformation of the conceptual substance of a proclamative norm into a subsistent norm is not the imposition or omission of sanctions by any particular judge, but rather by instance Δ as a whole, i.e., the entire judiciary. If the judiciary were to reject en bloc the normative maxim enacted by Θ, then it would simply collapse. The political authority Π can coerce an individual judge, but a judiciary with established convictions can be coerced as a whole only by means so drastic that their employment would be tantamount to a coup d'état. It need not come to such general rejection, however, even if internal resistance to a law is widespread among the individual judges. Personal and group attitudes can contradict each other. The individual judge who feels tempted—for example because of reservations concerning the consequences of interpretation— to ignore a statutory norm, must take into account that "the other Δ's," and especially the higher instances, will not stand by him, but will reverse his decision—even though he suspects that they secretly share his reservations against the norm. He risks not being able to effect in legal practice his objection to the norm enacted by Θ. . . .

The obligatory character of the proclamative norm is therefore based on the willingness of instance Δ to apply sanctions in the spirit of the maxim, and on the willingness of instance Δ as an institution to enforce the application of the maxim by the individual judges. The legal obligation of a judge toward the normative maxims enacted by Θ is not based on considerations of legitimacy but on the improbability of being able to implement a juridical act which is at odds with the substance of the normative maxim against the opposition of the entire judiciary. . . .

The Calculation of Obligation

. . . It is of no immediate interest for legal life what was legally binding yesterday. In practice it is only important to know what is *now*—today or tomorrow—obligatory. *A* wants to know the risks which are connected with the potential conduct g' in a given situation s'; *B* wants to know what kind of g' to expect from *A* in a given situation s'. *A* wishes to be able to rely on promised guarantees of immunity from legal disadvantages within his legal sphere; *B* wants to be able to expect with certainty that *A*—or else instance Δ—will behave in a given way.

These guarantees are entirely relative, and are to be found in what we have occasionally referred to above as the "calculation of obligation." In spite of its relativity, the degree of certainty is by no means insignificant. Where are the reference points for such a calculation of obligation to be found?

The written law, i.e., the entirety of all proclamative normative maxims, represents one system of conceptual reference for concrete facts. The manner in which the obligatory content of the subsistent norms, administered by appealing to these maxims, is determined, can be observed in the practice of the courts. Here, however, the question of validity in the perspective of legal history also becomes (indirectly) significant for legal practice. The great majority of important legal prescriptions are so well established that in pursuance thereof a fairly consistent body of precedent has been accumulated. Moreover, the greater part of the relationships in real life fall into the center area of the field of facts which constitutes the scope of meaning of a norm. One knows, in other words, the general meaning and scope which is given to the legal paragraphs by the interpretation of the courts. Hence the calculation is, in practice, absolutely certain. The element of uncertainty which is theoretically always present is infinitesimally small. If jurisdiction has remained fairly stable over a period of twenty years, then there is no reason to expect a radical change today or tomorrow.

If, however, a process of change is taking place, and if the facts of the case lie at the periphery of the scope of meaning of a norm, it is possible that they will be affected by a gradual change. But in this case as well, reference points for a calculation are provided by the past adjudication. By tracing the development of previous decisions, the trend of the legal interpretation can be established without difficulty: Extension? Restriction? Shifting of emphasis? Experience shows that one can rely on a certain constancy in legal judgment, even if it only be with respect to the continuity of its transformation. The geometrical position of the currently valid law is to be found somewhere on the extension of the curve of previous adjudication, depending on the amount of time elapsed since the last decision on a case.

That applies in the case of the *desuetudo* as well, for which the English legal system provides a prime example in its sanctioning of suicide. Today a coroner's jury hardly ever forgets to add the clause "while of unsound mind" in its verdict on a suicide case. The effect is tantamount to nullifying the spirit of the law, while showing all due respect for its letter. The present situation is the final result of a long process, in the course of which the rules pertaining to an immunity from sanction on grounds of mental incompetence have become increasingly lenient. The scope and intent of the law regarding suicide remain basically unchanged. The judiciary, however, has reduced its practical validity to nil. One could now strike these laws from the books without really changing anything in the English legal system. Anglo-Saxon traditionalism prefers to retain the forms and alter the facts. Similar instances can be cited by the dozens.

Thus far we have assumed the existence of a fairly frequent adjudication, a continuous chain of decisions in which a certain tendency could be discerned. There are situations, however, where this condition is not given. As examples I will mention: (1) The passage of a new law, where a body of judicial precedent does not yet exist. (2) A norm for which there is no continuous adjudication because for a long period of time there has been no issue to which it could have been applied. (3) Changes in the actual social structure (technological innovations, economic transformations, etc.) leading to the development of new living conditions, as yet unknown in their specific nature, and for which it is not yet certain whether or not instance Δ considers any existing norms to be applicable. . . .

1. Let us now consider the first of these cases, a new law which has not yet been put to the judicatory test. In this case one will first calculate that presumably *some* subsistent norm is coming into being in connection with the enactment. It is known by past experience that instance Δ generally uses the normative maxims proclaimed by instance Θ as reference points for the judging of specific cases and that Δ more or less conforms to terminological convention with regard to the words used in the maxim. . . .

In certain cases it is not difficult to foresee that a newly passed law is going to be a fiasco. If, for example, at a time when new automobiles are not available and a renewed supply can only be expected at much higher prices, a law fixing the maximum price for a used car at its original, new-car price can be expected with certainty to have a very low intensity of obligation. The A-persons have no desire to sell at the legal price. The supply, which was already insufficient to meet the demand, becomes even more meager. Those B-persons buying for an excessive price feel themselves by no means victimized; on the contrary, they are happy to be able to buy at that price. Instance Δ therefore, for lack of private complaints, is only able to apply the law when the police on its own initiative ferrets out instances of violation, whereby the B as well as the A persons will employ all possible means to obstruct them. The ineffectiveness on the $\bar{g}$-branch then undermines the remaining efficacy on the g-branch. . . .

Assuming however that as a rule a newly proclaimed statute results in the development of a subsistent norm, it is nevertheless at first uncertain what kind of an obligatory content it will acquire through the action of instance Δ. In this case as well, the calculation of obligation has certain reference points:

a) Even during the preparation and parliamentary discussion of the proposed law, it becomes a topic of debate in legal associations and in professional journals, as well as in those segments of the population which are directly affected by the law. Certain points of view, tendencies, and interpretations can already be discerned at this stage.

b) If the law has finally gone into effect, then—even before the first concrete case has been brought before instance Δ for judgment—the public will begin to feel its way out onto the *g*-branch. A law has been passed. Hence something has been altered in the legal situation. The bulk of the population will first prefer, "just in case," to plan for a very wide instead of a too narrow interpretation of the presumed obligation. Those individuals who are less concerned about the possible consequences, and who generally make it a practice to take fullest advantage of their freedom of action, may calculate in the opposite direction. In the case of a special law, for example, one pertaining to real estate transactions, joint-stock companies, the practice of a specific occupation, etc., those persons who are about to make a decision and who are even possibly affected by the new law will seek the advice of a lawyer. Hence the manner in which the public practice becomes established on the *g*-branch pursuant to the new law *prior* to any decision on the part of instance Δ is determined (1) by common sense and terminological convention with respect to the words of the legislator, and (2) by familiarity with the general legal situation of the society, which manifests certain guiding principles. It is thus expected that instance Δ will apply the new law in a manner consistent with these principles. . . .

c) The preceding discussion regarding the consequences of the law for the legal situation applies to the formation of a provisional calculation of obligation. The public receives its orientation in part directly from commentaries in the daily press or in special publications, and in part it has the indirect benefit of legal discussions via the advisory activity of the lawyers or the legal counsels of professional associations.

In this way the public practice first feels its way out onto the *g*-branch, whereby the cautious evaluation of the freedom of action confronts and is confronted by the bold exploitation of what are taken to be the outer limits. In its decision on the first such case to come before it, instance Δ then has this fact of actual practice to consider and will more or less make allowances for it—consciously or unconsciously. The resulting adjudication is likewise at first uncertain about the exact delimitation of the obligation. By correcting the popular interpretation of the norm, and by defining and clarifying its own by virtue of its administration of the law, it becomes—thanks to the guiding authority of the higher instances—more sure of itself and gradually finds its equilibrium. . . .

2. Some additional aspects must be considered when we analyze the second of the above-mentioned examples: a norm for which there is no continuous practice because for a long period of time no concrete cases have been adjudicated which the norm could have been applied to. How should the calculation be made when such a case finally does occur?

We will first take a hypothetical example. The criminal code includes special provisions for time of war. Thirty years have passed since the enactment of the law, during which the country has not been involved in a war. There is no doubt that instance Δ will apply the relevant paragraphs of the code in the event of a war, albeit that at first the determinants of the obligation will be uncertain.

Here is a contrary example. The *Loi Le Chapelier* of 1791 and the *Code Napoléon* of 1810 forbid the union of laborers, especially for the purpose of strikes or wage wars. Even at the time of the Bourbon restoration these prohibitions were evaded by disguised labor unions, but not until the *Loi Waldeck-Rousseau* of 1884 were they formally repealed. Moreover, as early as 1868 there existed a kind of gentlemen's agreement to the effect that no action would be taken against violations. Around 1880, therefore, there must have been complete certainty in the calculation of obligation. The instance Δ was no longer prepared to inflict sanctions in accordance with sections 414 through 416 of the *Code Pénal*. The sixteen year silence of the courts on the question was not because no cases occurred in which these regulations could be applied, but rather because they were not brought before instance Δ for the simple reason that it was recognized that the norms corresponding to the legal prescriptions were hopelessly obsolete and therefore void. The law was still on the books, but a contradictory subsistent norm had come into being. Application of the legal prescription would have been irreconcilable with the social and economic situation existing around 1880 and with the corresponding public opinion. . . .

In the first case the law was not applied for lack of an occasion. In cases of the second kind, however, nonapplication is a symptom for the extinction of the norm. The calculation of obligation knows to distinguish the latter circumstance as significantly different from the first. . . .

3. Finally, the third of the above-mentioned cases pertains to technical or organizational innovations which lead to the advent of a previously unknown type of siuation, for which no appropriate norm has yet come into being. Neither the law nor legal interpretation can here offer any immediate reference points for a halfway certain calculation of obligation.

Daily practice has the first word. Some kind of adaptation to the new situation will be attempted. In this endeavor the persons involved—the actors and those affected by the actions of others—will of course to some extent have contradictory ideas about the most desirable order of things. Here, too, a preliminary theoretical discussion may warrant certain conjectures regarding the probable attitude of instance Δ. The invention of the radio or the airplane, etc., gives occasion—even before the introduction of broadcasting or scheduled air service —for the juridical discussion of the new legal questions thus raised. The first signs of the emergence of a new kind of business organization lead to discussions among corporation lawyers, from which the layman may pick up a certain preliminary practical orientation. The first controversy which cannot be settled amicably then forces instance Δ to take an official stand. One alternative is to apply an already existent legal prescription, extensively interpreted. A second possibility is to relate the case by analogy to another type of situation and to apply the relevant prescription. Thirdly and finally, instance Δ can construct law autonomously, whereby it may—in conformity with legal practice—make a shamefaced appeal to "the nature of the case." Whichever way instance Δ chooses, it will essentially be guided by the desire to find a legal solution which fits as neatly as possible into the letter and spirit of the precepts governing the whole existing legal system. . . .

Another fact deserving comment is that the calculation of obligation on the part of the individual acting in a legally relevant manner has its counterpart in the *calculation of success* on the part of the judge. He functions as instance Δ, but he is not "the instance Δ." It would be too simple a formula to say: The judge renders his decisions in concrete cases in accordance with his professional knowledge and convictions. Were all judges in all cases to act in this way without compromise, we could expect the body of legal precedent to be far less consistent than it actually is. Just as the layman regulates his conduct according to a calculation of which possibilities of action are safely left open to him by the existing norms, the individual judge bases his decisions, among other things, on a calculation of what prospects of success his verdict will have within the juridical system. No judge likes to see his decisions reversed and corrected by a higher instance. Therein lies an essential retarding factor in the adjustment of the obligatory content of established norms to changes in the social order: the first new decision must always reckon with a particularly intensive review by the appellate courts. Hence the tendency, whenever problematic decisions are involved, to take cover behind the prestige of the legal profession, inasmuch as this prestige presumably also carries some weight with the higher instance. And therefore, finally but most important, the tremendous— not always wholesome—respect for the precedent established by the higher and highest instance.

In short: what is administered as binding law in a modern legal community is the final result of mutual adjustment and concurrence—partly through precalculation, partly through subsequent corrections—between a multitude of factors whose structured interaction constitutes the "legal life." It is not the individual ΔΔ's who create law with their decisions. The legal norms which are binding at a given time in the history of a legal community are rather determined by the collective system and its total structure. The calculation of obligation of the average citizen, and the calculation of success or tenability of the Δ-persons, have—apart from the various reference points mentioned in passing—a certain basic foundation: the relative consistency of legal decisions and the predictability of changes in this area. This also provides that degree of legal security which is necessary for civil life.

6

LAW AND MORALITY

The Genesis of Law and Morality: Externalization and Internalization[1]

HERE WE WILL once again take as our starting point the communal order of a primitive society. This was dealt with above as the first genetic preliminary to the legal order. The fact that the habitually established standards of this communal order are maintained by the spontaneous reactions of Ω against deviant behavior therefore occupied a central position in our discussion. It has also been occasionally implied that at the same time a superstructure of magico-religious beliefs evolves to consolidate these behavior models. One may indeed search in vain in primitive and even in archaic communities for customs, morals, or other standards which are not associated with certain religious ideas, usually of the taboo type. . . .

In the primitive communal order therefore a moment of external coercion and a moment of internal reverence exist side by side, mutually entwined in complete unity. . . . By transferring the control mechanism preserving the order from "the community itself" Ω to a functionally specialized instance Δ, the internal participation of the individual in the order wanes. It now appears as something external to himself, an organizationally objectified social system which approaches him with certain demands from the outside. . . .

That by no means implies that the previous moment of internal participation is suddenly abolished as far as the legal

---

[1]   In the original text the subtitle is: *Genetischer Zusammenhang zwischen Recht und Moral.*—Ed.

order is concerned. The substance of the norms as well as the central authority which maintains them are at first objects of religious reverence. What I wish to say is only this: The process of progressive *secularization* of one part of the social order, namely, the law, begins with the institutionalization of the control of the order in instance Δ. Thus begins that externalization, that transition from participation to restriction, from divine *fas* to plain *jus*—developments which are, in retrospect, unmistakable.

This integration of the elements of external coercion has the corollary of setting free the element of internal participation, which likewise operated in the communal order as an independent force. This too subsequently undergoes an integration process, the phases of which we will consider below and out of which the system of morality is evolved. It is my intention to show how through a process of polarization, beginning with the communal condition, law and morality develop as two distinct systems of action, each based upon different principles. . . .

Spiritualization

The original moral attitude is an emotional affirmation or negation, confirmed by the social environment, toward certain modes of behavior. I call this the *primary evaluation*. It involves nothing but a more or less conscious feeling of approval or disapproval.

But by objectifying this emotional relationship in such a way as to reinterpret it as a quality of "good" (or "evil") intrinsic to the mode of behavior, "good" comes into existence as a value-idea (*Wertidee*) and standard. In other words, it is not the case that one can establish deductively, by derivation from an abstract idea of "good," which modes of behavior are good and which are evil. We here find a development analogous to that described for the legal order (p. 88 ff.). To begin with, no such uniform system exists, but only a confused heap of "accidental" behavior models, generated by social life and collectively maintained, which are given the designation "good." If it is possible to find a common, consistent characteristic uniting them all, then certainly only in the sense of a similarity of style, to be explained on the grounds of a collective psychology. The application of the designation "good" (or "evil") to a number of modes of behavior (and their opposites) leads by induction, with the emergence of abstract thinking, from actions and action-patterns which are designated as good to a general concept of "good." This concept, the value-idea of "good," can now become an object of speculation. A theoretization takes place. "Good" is affirmed, on the grounds of conceptual realism, to be an existent entity and an attempt is made to establish its essence and substance. Accordingly the good actions deductively appear to be good to the extent that they partake of the value-idea of "good." I call this the *value judgment* in the true sense. It is the act of relating something empirically given to a preconceived value-idea and its evaluation in terms of that idea. . . .

This process, the spiritualization of morality, is the counterpart of the institutionalization of the law. Spiritualization brings with it, however, a transfer of moral authority from the outside to the inside; it leads, in other words, to the so-called autonomous conscience morality.

In the communal order the motivations of social pressure and of reverence are combined. If we regard them together as an early form of morality as well as of law (*primae mores et primum jus*), then we may say: The authority of this order, seen as law, was not only external (social pressure on the part of Ω) but also internal (reverence). The authority of the same order, seen as morality, was not only internal, based on reverence, but also external, based on social pressure. With the polar development of law and morality as two distinct, independent systems, the external authority—represented by the state —became specifically legal and in the course of time progressively increased its priority in regard to law. The internal authority, conscientious reverence for the "good," became specifically moral and attained priority in that sphere, outweighing external considerations. But not all at once and not completely, even today. In the folk morality corresponding to the stage of development of mores, the community does not only present the individual with the substance of the moral norms, but he must learn and practice what is "good." The control of moral conduct also depends partly on the conscience of the individual, and partly on the ostracism of the environment. And that is still the case today wherever a moral value community exists.

The internalization of the authority judging one's actions results in a consequent transition from a morality of deeds to a morality of convictions. In the eyes of a third party the most important consideration is the physical act and its effects, although a more differentiated interpretation, modifying a judgment based on actions alone, may to a certain extent make allowances for the intentions of the actor, as these are revealed by certain symptoms. In the case of self-judgment (conscience searching), will and intention become the most important considerations. Allowances made for the intentions and opinions of the actor in the moral judgment of a third party are the direct consequences thereof. But that is not all. To the extent that my own conscience, and not the social environment or even the state, is the arbiter of my conduct, morality extends beyond the realm of the social order. I am responsible to others for those actions whose consequences affect others. I may be responsible to myself for actions which affect only myself and for ideas, desires, and intentions which are not put into action. Only in the eyes of the authority of the individual conscience can there be such a thing as a sin against myself or a secret sin.

Morality is thereby partially dissociated in its substance from the concept of social interdependence. It is not only a social morality for the ordering of life in relation to others, but also an individual morality, a guideline for that solitary existence in which the human being stands alone before his value-idea (i.e., his god).

In the foregoing we have spoken of the authority of the conscience as moral arbiter, meaning that the instance of moral control is transferred to the individual. That however does not preclude the conscience from receiving from external sources those moral norms whose implementation it naturally controls. On the other hand we have not yet considered that highest degree of internalization which culminates in the idea of the moral autonomy of the individual. The personal conscience is not only moral judge, but also its own moral legislator. We are here presented with an analogy to the development of the law: in the same way that instance Δ originally administers habitual norms and instance Θ does not enact norms until a later stage of development has been attained, in the realm of morality the conscience is first a judging authority before it becomes a norm-making authority within the *morality of the autonomous conscience....*

This highest internalization of morality corresponds to the increasing self-reliance and emancipation of the individual to be found in the social history of Western civilization. In this way morality as a social order must logically cancel itself.[2] Everyone is his own moral legislator, but at the same time the moral norms which he proposes and conforms to should regulate his conduct in society and his relationship to others. This contradiction can be reconciled only if all autonomous moral speculation leads to approximately the same conclusions. There is, however, no guarantee whatever that this will be the case. . . . Hence we can theoretically recognize our mutual rights to subjective moral principles, but in reality and in practice the application of our own moral principles to others is a violation of *their* moral integrity.

Morality is no longer useful as a social regulator. The divergence of individual moralities must, on the contrary, lead to the eventual disintegration of society. If, in spite of this, the result is not complete anarchy, it will not be on account of moral forces, but, on the contrary, because of *the diminishing importance of morals in an increasingly institutionalized society. . . .*[3]

Law and Morality

We have proceeded here from the assumption that a primary social order undergoes, on the one hand, an externali-

---

[2]   The following is taken from my *Debat med Uppsala*, p. 72 f.
[3]   In the original German text this and the preceding paragraph belong to the section entitled *Drei Formen der Moral.*—Ed.

zation and institutionalization process whereby the law emerges as an explicit ordering system, while at the same time a parallel process of internalization and spiritualization occurs, the result of which is called morality. Consequently then, law and morality must be regarded as conceptual opposites which in the course of linear development draw farther and farther apart. Morality is founded on internal obligation, law on external. Morality is what I feel obligated to do; law is what the state obligates me to do. The idea of the growing gap between morality and law can be supported by a number of observations from legal history and legal psychology, which need not be discussed in detail here. I will simply mention in passing archaic-sacral law and rational, profane law; the growing multitude of moral rules, which although widely accepted, are no longer legally sanctioned; and on the other hand the great number of legal rules whose substance is regarded with moral indifference. I will also mention the critique directed at the substance of modern legal orders based upon various contradictory moral standpoints.

The conceptual difference between morality and law does not prevent a certain overlapping of their respective spheres; on the contrary, the nature of this difference directly implies such an overlap.

1. Even in a society whose moral thinking is perfectly homogeneous as a result of tradition or dogma there will be (generally accepted) moral norms which remain completely outside the legal order, be it that their sanctioning is basically impossible or that the substance of the moral imperatives themselves are of no interest to the legal community as such. On the other hand there will be legal norms whose substance is of a purely technical or conventional nature and hence morally indifferent (procedural rules of order, traffic laws, terms, and dates, etc.). Between the two extremes there will be a great body of norms which are legally sanctioned as well as morally recognized. In a society with heterogeneous, discrepant moral thinking the situation will be more complicated. As far as the collective morality is concerned, the legal order may possibly be under the strong traditional influence of the moral doctrines

of a prevailing ideology. It will, moreover, in large measure bear the stamp of the general moral ideas of the dominant social class. Increasing concessions to intellectual and religious minority groups as well as to a strong social opposition will be the general rule. Thus the positively charged moral field of the legal order will be severely limited, inasmuch as concessions can only be made by means of a reduction process. The legal order ceases to support with sanctions those moral demands which a growing minority no longer recognizes. . . .

To the extent that the demands of law and morality coincide there is a cumulation of incentive for compliance; to the extent that they are contradictory there is a conflict of norms.

2. A certain moral conception may contain the precept that it is a moral duty to obey a legal norm qua legal norm, regardless of its specific substance. This attitude (legalism) places a formal moral obligation especially on those norms which are by virtue of their specific substance morally indifferent. In addition it is conceivable that even legal norms of a morally questionable nature may be invested with a moral obligation, to the extent that—on a hypothetical scale of moral demands arranged according to their importance and urgency—the fulfillment of a legal norm is considered more important than compliance with the norm of personal conscience. In any case this formal moralization of legal prescriptions assumes that the legal order itself or the legal community with which it is identified—the state—must be considered as moral values in their own right.

3. From the point of view of the legal community the most important thing is that under all circumstances behavior be in accord with the legal norms. Whether or not the individual in a particular case acts in a legally correct manner because of an internal or external duty—or completely without regard for any conception of duty, simply because of habit or interest, etc.— is irrelevant. It is likewise irrelevant whether he violated a legal norm because his conscience forced him to, or whether this violation was contrary to his personal morals, or whether he violated his personal morals by complying with the legal norm. . . .

If there are minor variations in the moral conceptions within the legal community, the legal order can accommodate them by reducing its moral substance to the common core of the various moral conceptions involved and being in other respects morally indifferent or tolerant.

Thus it is possible to maintain the internal as well as the external obligations toward legal norms. In this case there are only the following kinds of obligations: (a) legal-moral, (b) purely legal but morally indifferent, and (c) purely moral but legally indifferent.

Contemporary Western society, because of the obvious internal antagonisms resulting from its differentiated structure, does not possess the here necessary prerequisites of moral structure. To the extent that only some special moral sentiments are involved, allowing the individual to put the moral subjectivism of conscientious autonomy into practice as far as he himself is concerned, one could easily overlook their ethical deviancy. This is impossible, however, with respect to deep-seated moral schisms existing between various groups within the population. It is a vain and self-deceptive venture to try to whitewash these schisms by calling attention to consensus on major issues, specifically those resulting from a common heritage of ancient classical and Christian moral traditions. Here we are not dealing with mere variations but with inexorable contradictions, with discrepancies not at the periphery but at the core. As far as the concept of private property is concerned, one should have recognized that a long time ago. Similarly the discussion in recent years between the resistance movements and flexible noncooperation in the occupied countries reveals profound discrepancies in the moral valuation of human life. Other points of controversy may be cited by the dozens. The degree of real consensus on basic moral issues still to be found in a legal community recognizing the principles of free conscience and thought is in any case inadequate as a moral foundation for a contemporary legal order.

Under these circumstances there are three possibilities:

1. The moral character of the legal order will continue to be maintained, as is presently the case—thanks to the zealous, if

philosophically and sociologically ill-advised efforts of our legal theorists. The result is that every day scores of citizens are constantly subjected to norm conflicts of a moral nature. . . .

2. The legal order can—by a change of attitude on the part of the political, legislative and judicial organs, as well as by a sober reevaluation of popular political, social, and legal philosophy—give up its claim to internal obligation. That certainly does not alter the fact that individual citizens and whole (nondominant) groups of citizens will be confronted with norm conflicts between the demands of the law and those of their personal or collective moral values. The difference is that it no longer involves a conflict between two different *internalized* conceptions of duty. . . .

3. The third possibility, however, is the consequence of value nihilism, i.e., that the general conception of "internal" obligation, derived from imperative value-ideas, be gradually destroyed, meaning that value morality itself disappears as a form of life. It is precisely the maintenance of legal morality in a morally discordant society, compromising all value conceptions, which can contribute more to this development among the general public than popularization of the philosophy of value nihilism. Words such as justice, honor, public spirit, etc., have been overworked to such an extent that today there is amazingly little moral weight behind the rhetorical gravity with which they are used. The (often phony) pathos associated with them is sometimes irritating, sometimes ludicrous—to the extent that it is not simply overlooked as an oratorical convention.

In a society where value nihilism had become the rule, undisguised social interdependence would once again become the ordering principle, morality—by its internalization and spiritualization—having led itself ad absurdum as a social order. Incongruencies between the modes of behavior demanded would still exist, inasmuch as one social group would make different demands than the others. Hence cases might occur in which it would be difficult for a person to move safely in different circles. But the incongruence here is of a strictly real nature; it is not a question of moral values but a practical problem of maneuvering within a given social milieu.

At all events, in an antagonistically differentiated society with contradictory individual and group moral values, the obligatory nature of the legal order can no longer be based on moral categories. The *v*-stigma of a legal norm must hence be objective, i.e., the expression of a real fact. The *v*-stigma of a norm based on moral values is subjective and imaginary. The moral norm is obligatory for those who worship the imperious value concept looming behind it—and only for them. The obligation is rooted in the imagination of those believing in the value. If you violate a legal norm, something happens *to* you; if you violate a moral norm, something happens *in* you. Therein lies the difference between external and internal duty or obligation. The former is fact, the latter is imagination. That every belief in a value is, before the bar of epistemology, nothing but blind faith may be a debatable point. That a legal order cannot regulate the external coexistence of a conglomeration of citizens with divergent values on the basis of internal obligation, however, should be evident even to those who wish at all costs to maintain a positive philosophy of values.

II. Ideology and Truth

Introduction

GEIGER'S THEORY of ideology is so closely connected with his methodological position that the former does not become fully understandable without a knowledge of the latter. For this reason Geiger devoted one full chapter of *Ideologie und Wahrheit* (chapter 3 in the original) to the methodological foundation of his conception of ideology, and this must therefore be the starting point for this brief introduction to the following translation, even if it sometimes means repeating what has been said in the opening chapter of this book.

In keeping with the analytical theory of science, Geiger held that the object of science is cognitive reality (*Erkenntniswirklichkeit*). This he defines as the sum total of spatially and temporally located phenomena which are directly or indirectly accessible to sense perception. Cognitive reality is objective reality as it exists external to and independent of the perceiving subject, an assumption which Geiger introduces as axiomatic. Although human experience of this reality is selective and mediated by our senses and the fundamental categories of perception, cognitive reality nevertheless permits a particular type of statements to be made about it. Geiger calls them theoretical statements. They can be empirically verified or falsified by the use of proper techniques and research designs, because they are based on an analysis of observations according to the rules of logic.

From the concept of cognitive or theoretical reality Geiger distinguishes pragmatic or existential reality, which is essentially reality-as-subjectively-experienced. With regard to cognitive reality, theoretical statements can be either true or false, i.e., in agreement or disagreement with *objective* reality. With regard to existential reality, on the other hand, this criterion of truth is not applicable; statements about it can only be said to be either adequate or inadequate to the existential situation of a given speaker.

Tracing the history of the concept of ideology, Geiger points out two important variants which are connected with these two conceptions of reality. The first is ideology as a *false* judgment, the making of which may be motivated by interest. The second is ideology as a judgment which is or is not in accordance with the life situation of the speaker: "right" or "wrong" ideology. This second view of ideology Geiger finds especially in Marxist theory (e.g., "false consciousness") and also in Mannheim's notion of "total ideology". He urges that a clear distinction be made between the two standards involved, the frequent use of the term "false" in both cases having obscured the difference.

For his own treatment of ideology Geiger chooses the first approach. His rationalism and positivistic convictions must have made him feel extremely uncomfortable with the notion of existential reality, which he rejects as point of reference for scientific analysis. If science aims at making statements about objective reality, the term ideology as meaning a false judgment should be restricted to refer to such statements which can be proved to be either true or false, i.e., theoretical statements.

However, Geiger realizes that the applicability of the criterion of truth presupposes that it is possible, as a matter of principle, to make statements which are in agreement with reality, or whose agreement or disagreement with objective reality can be established. If all thinking were in fact inescapably determined by the existential situation, i.e., if Mannheim's assumption of total ideology were correct, it would be impossible to distinguish between true and false judgments and hence the concept of ideology as false judgment would become meaningless. This is briefly pointed out in chapter 3 below. Elsewhere Geiger goes into the matter more extensively. He rejects Mannheim's distinction between particular and total ideology, not only because, as stated in the translation below, what is involved is in Geiger's opinion merely a matter of degree as far as the second concept has an acceptable meaning, but also for a number of other reasons. In the present context, his criticism of the concept of total ideology is most relevant. In Geiger's view this notion can serve and has served to justify ideological thinking by declaring it to be inevitable—a social consequence of Mannheim's theory he considers to be extremely harmful, which gives him a powerful motive to refuse it.

Geiger does not deny the existence of "styles of thinking" as implied in the notion of total ideology, but he argues that to the extent that real factors (*Realfaktoren*) influence thinking, they do so at the level of the concrete individual and not at the collective level. Secondly, he argues, "style of thinking" should be understood as a concept of cultural sociology rather than of epistemology. His argument against the epistemological conception which he attributes to Mannheim is that although social structure, social position, and cultural heritage may influence an individual's thinking (in ways to be explained psychologically), this influence is not in the nature of a strict determination. He finds supporting evidence for this in the fact that there have been persons who did think "contrary" to their social position and even to the spirit of their time, and in the related fact that individuals in the same life situation often think quite differently. But such empirical evidence is only of secondary importance. Geiger's main argument is that as a matter of principle, observation of the canons of scientific method affords the chance to think objectively.

It may be recalled that Mannheim himself tried to point out a way of offsetting the bias or perspectivity of thinking which is due to the existential determination of cognition. Geiger rejects this solution, which exists in the strategy of synthesizing partial perspectives. If the existential determination of cognition holds universally, as the concept of total ideology implies, the best that can be achieved by following Mannheim's strategy is to clarify the exact boundaries of our blind spots without being able to eliminate them. The crucial question is therefore whether it is actually possible to escape from the existential determination of cognition, and this Geiger affirms by pointing to the objectivity of scientific method.

As Geiger well recognizes, this objectivity is predicated upon the claim that the rules of logic, laws of thinking, and fundamental categories have universal validity rather than being culturally conditioned and historically relative. Should the latter be true there would be no possibility to refute the assumption of total ideology. To fend off such an attack, Geiger devotes a short chapter in *Ideologie und Wahrheit* (chapter 8 of the original, not translated here) to a discussion of this problem, but his treatment of the subject is rather unsatisfactory compared to the level of sophistication achieved by contemporary philosophy and theory of science. Geiger's main points are that although there may be some change in such basic categories of thinking as matter and movement, time and space, and causality, this does not seem to be linked to changes in social structure, but rather reflects an advance in knowledge. As regards the possible cultural relativity of (Aristotelean) logic, Geiger remains unconvinced by those critical arguments which have come to his attention and concludes that our logic seems to correspond to the structure of objective reality and cannot hence be said to be existentially determined.

While Geiger maintains that correct thinking leads to full truth, he also recognizes that this is a process of gradual and very slow approximation, constantly hindered and jeopardized by the intrusion of interests and emotions which make for a neglect of the canons of scientific objectivity. He therefore demands that conscious efforts be made to raise the level of intellectual morality and theoretical imagination. By intellectual morality he means the deliberate effort to raise one's own interests, emotional relationships, value premises, etc., to the level of full consciousness in order to eliminate them from thinking, whereas theoretical imagination refers to gaining distance from one's own social situation and cultural context. Together this constitutes the attitude of detachment which he advocates, and which he believes to be furthered significantly by the experience of social differentation, by differences in culture and mentality, multiple group-membership, and specialization.

Though Geiger does not quote Weber, it is obvious that his precepts correspond closely to the postulate of value freedom. However, just as Weber never denied the importance of values for the choice of problems, Geiger similarly points out that questions are and indeed must be stimulated by nontheoretical impulses, and that this in itself does not influence the validity of the statements or theory designed to answer the questions. The charge of ideology can only be made where nontheoretical elements are carried over into theory.

Geiger's preliminary definition of "ideological" as deviating from reality (in a sense yet to be specified) leads him to adopt a very narrow concept of ideology: only of cognition can it be said that it is true or false, i.e., agrees with or deviates from reality. Geiger therefore applies the concept of ideology neither to consciousness, or even to thinking and cognition as activities, nor does he apply it to art, law, or religion (with the exception of religious doctrine or dogmatic theology). These restrictions he himself emphasizes; indeed, in the text below he mentions several times the decision to limit himself to the analysis of statements which claim to be cognitive. This, however, is still a rather large category, including not only theoretical statements in the strict sense but also pseudo-theoretical statements such as value judgments, metaphysical statements, and statements of religious doctrine. Geiger also applies the term ideological to concepts which lack precise empirical referents, their content being evaluative or the generalization of some emotional experience; examples would be "virtue," where the substance of the concept is a value, or "freedom," which has a high emotional charge and lacks specific empirical referents unless defined in a certain way, e.g., as freedom from, or to, something specific.

At this point a possible source of confusion must be noted. The first more general definition of ideology which Geiger offers below (p. 143) does not apply to all the different types of statements just mentioned. The definition seems especially tailored to value judgments, and while it also covers other types of pseudo-theoretical statements, it certainly does not apply to (false) theoretical statements. Yet it becomes clear from the subsequent discussion that Geiger's concept of ideology does in fact also include false theoretical statements, i.e. statements which express a testable, empirical proposition. Such a statement is not ideological if and because it is false, but is called ideological only if nontheoretical impulses, such as interests or an emotional relationship to the object, are either the cause of the observational and logical error(s) committed in making the false statement, or if they motivate continued belief in the truth of the false statement after contradictory evidence has become available. Thus Geiger states in one place that while pre-Galilean, geocentric cosmology was always a false theory, it became ideological only when still believed in after Galileo.

The statement about advertising which Geiger analyzes below as an example of ideology makes clear that one of the errors which can be motivated by nontheoretical impulses is the failure to specify explicitly certain limiting conditions which circumscribe the scope of validity of a theoretical statement. This bears emphasis because overgeneralization, i.e., the formulation in universal terms of a proposition which holds only under specific conditions, is indeed a frequently committed mistake but may not immediately come to mind when speaking of the errors which make theoretical statements false.

Finally it may be pointed out that Geiger's analysis of the statement about intellectual freedom has a problematical and possibly misleading implication. He shows that this statement may be rephrased in terms of an empirical proposition, but argues that it will still remain ideological unless the underlying value premises are explicitly declared. In Geiger's example the value premises consist in the assumption that the dependent variables (or effects) involved in the empirical proposition refer to something which is desirable. Such assumptions, however, i.e., a positive or negative evaluation of the dependent variables in causal relationships, are often if not generally made where nontheoretical impulses guide the choice of a question. This, as Geiger stated elsewhere, does not in itself make the answer ideological; it does not at any rate make the proposition empirically false. Hence one might conclude that in a case like this it is not the theoretical statement which is ideological, but that an ideological element enters only if the evaluation ("*Y* is desirable") is subsequently carried over to the causal factor ("*X* which causes *Y* is good"), or if unconditional action directives are derived from the causal relationship irrespective of the fact that the effect in question is not necessarily desired by everybody.

In another passage of *Ideologie und Wahrheit* which is not included in the translation, Geiger apparently recognizes these implications more clearly. There he analyzes two examples which show that certain statements which imply valuations may yet be epistemologically admissible and nonideological. Thus if it is said that alcohol is harmful (has bad effects) or that paper is useful, certain objective standards are implied which, if specified and formulated in operational terms, make testable theoretical statements of these judgments. The standards with reference to which the effects of a phenomenon are assessed rest upon value premises, but as long as the latter are recognized as such (which also implies that they are subject to debate), even evaluational terms in an empirical proposition are admissible. This, incidentally, implicitly recognizes the basic postulate upon which functional analysis rests, namely that "(eu)functional" and "disfunctional" are judgments which can only be made with reference to a clearly specified goal-state which must be seen as postulated rather than objectively given in any absolute sense.

Renate Mayntz

1

THE VALUE JUDGMENT

AS AN IDEOLOGICAL

STATEMENT

EPISTEMOLOGICALLY admissible[1] statements about a real thing either (1) establish that X is such and such or that Y is this and that, or (2) they can be put into the form of such an "is-proposition" without distorting their meaning. We call such propositions *theoretical statements*. We distinguish them from such statements as "I wish I could afford a car" (desire), or "Thou shalt not lie" (imperative), or "Ah, cruel fate!" (emotional outburst), or "Leave my dog alone!" (command), and other kinds of verbal expression.

A theoretical statement, *i.e.*, an is-proposition, joins two words with the verb "is," not by using it as an auxiliary verb, but by designating A as identical with or as equal to B; or in the sense that A falls into the wider category of B; or that B

Translated from *Ideologie und Wahrheit* (Stuttgart and Vienna: Humboldt Verlag, 1953), pp.53–68, 92–104, 164–186, and printed here by permission of Luchterhand Verlag as the present holder of copyright of this volume.

[1]   Geiger uses here the word *erkenntniszulässig;* subsequently he also uses the synonyms *erkenntnislegitim* or *erkenntniskritisch zulässig* (and the corresponding negative forms). These term have been translated as "epistemologically admissible (legitimate, etc.)." What is meant is that a statement does (or does not) meet the criteria of positive, empirical science, i.e., that it is (or is not) a theoretical proposition from the point of view of positivistic epistemology.—Ed.

is one of the distinguishing characteristics of *A*. Such statements are the result of the logical interpretation of observations and their content may be tested by the same means, i.e., verified or disproved.

Certain propositions have the same grammatical form, "*A* is *B*," but do not satisfy these requirements. The *value judgments*, for instance, are such propositions, and we shall now examine these more closely in regard to their content, structure, and origin. . . .

Here is an example of a value judgment: "Hyacinths are fragrant"[2] ("smell good"). What is here stated is: (1) there are plants called hyacinths with certain characteristics which distinguish them from other plants; (2) the blossoms of this plant have the quality of being "fragrant." The first statement is correct; the second is debatable. If it is true, as will be shown, that there is no such quality as "fragrant" or "fragrance," then we may conclude that the given value judgment must be one kind of ideological statement, i.e., a certain quality is attributed to a real phenomenon which does not belong to its real and empirically testable properties. Specifically in our example it is claimed that the object "hyacinth," which is given in spatial-temporal reality, possesses the quality of "smelling good," which does not exist in spatial-temporal reality.

We could take the easy way out and simply say: There are people who detest the smell of hyacinths and even get headaches from it. They do not share the positive value judgment. How can we decide who is right? The flower appeals to one person's sense of smell and is repulsive to someone else's—but it is obviously impossible that it *is* fragrant and at the same time the opposite. That may appear to be idle hairsplitting, inasmuch as everyone knows that "you can't argue about taste." And if that were all there was to it, a serious discussion of the matter would certainly be superfluous. But, firstly, it will be shown that other, highly controversial value judgments are just as pointless as those of taste. The latter have been selected

2   The corresponding German adjective *wohlriechend* is more clearly evaluative, its literal translation being "pleasant smelling."—Ed.

to open this discussion only because they can be dealt with without arousing deeper emotions or psychological resistance. Secondly, it is not enough just to concur that tastes differ. It is of far greater cognitive-psychological importance to understand how it happens that preferences of taste are, nevertheless, expressed in generalizing, objective statements. In other words: How do value judgments of sense and taste (and every other kind of value judgment) originate, and in what structural form are they expressed?

What happens when a value judgment is made is this: person *A* confronts a real object *O*. While observing object *O*, *A* establishes a number of objective traits which, taken together, indicate what the language by general agreement calls a hyacinth. The sentence, "This thing is a blue hyacinth," is the theoretical statement corresponding to the visual examination of the object. It is of no importance here whether or not most people are sufficiently acquainted with the appearance of a hyacinth to be able to express their first impression in the above words. If there is another plant very similar in appearance to the hyacinth, the first impression may be deceptive; the premature identification of an object as a hyacinth will then be proven false when more specific characteristics are considered.

Simultaneously with the perception of the object and its proper assignment to the category, something else occurs which is completely nontheoretical. *A* has the sensation of a pleasant (or offensive) odor. He sniffs and says "Ah!" or he wrinkles up his nose and says "Phooey!" Those are not statements about the object "hyacinth," but reactions to the sensual impression which it makes. So far so good. But it so happens that every time *A* has an object before him which he recognizes by its objective characteristics to be a hyacinth, he has the same olfactory sensation. This concomitant relationship is so invariable that *A* inadvertently transfers his perception of odor from the level of sensation to the level of cognition. Green, oblong leaves, a stiff stem, a cluster of blossoms, a certain form and color, etc., *and* a pleasant (or unpleasant) olfactory sensation appear invariably together. Instead of saying, "The hyacinth has these objective characteristics—in addition to which I find its smell pleasing," *A* says, ". . . and it is fragrant." *B* says, because of the same kind of invariable concomitance between the objective characteristics of the flower perceived and an unpleasant olfactory sensation: "The hyacinth is . . . and has an unpleasant odor." It is impossible for both *A* and *B* to be right; but it is not that one is right and the other wrong. Taken literally, they are both talking nonsense.

Let us now express that a bit more scientifically. The perception of the senses and of taste is something peculiar to the individual, something subjective. This subjective relationship of the individual to the object is objectified in the value judgment. It is reinterpreted into something materially given, i.e., attributed to the object as one of its qualities, and hence made subject to expression in the form of a theoretical statement ("*X* is *Y*"). This procedure is epistemologically inadmissible; the statement is not legitimate.

Does that mean that it is not legitimate to render judgments about things and other phenomena? Certainly not. It only means that value judgments are epistemologically illegitimate. This distinction will now be illustrated by a series of examples.

1. Let us assume that you, the reader (like myself), delight in smoking a cigarette on an empty stomach upon awakening and gravely miss it when you cannot do so. This fact is a *primary valuation* on your part and it would be pointless to call it illegitimate. It is simply your immediate feeling ("feeling" used here in a very broad sense) which you can't do anything about. The moralist or the physician may explain that it is reprehensible or harmful to *yield* to the temptation. Both may try to make you overcome this impulse, which is rooted in a valuation of sense and taste, by appealing to other valuations, such as considerations of health. But your primary valuation remains unchanged; only the impulse is suppressed. Moreover it is obvious that without primary valuations, life would come to a standstill. Every act presupposes a conscious or unconscious choice between alternative courses of action, and this choice involves the comparing or weighing of primary valu-

ations. Up to this point no theoretical statements are involved, but only mental processes.

2. Early in the morning, still lying in bed, you light up a cigarette, inhale deeply, and fall back on the pillow with a satisfied "Ahhh!" You haven't "stated" anything, but you *have* given voice to your primary valuation of the morning cigarette. And why shouldn't you? Such utterances, known to grammarians as interjections, may be designated here as *expectoration* of the primary valuation: one gives vent to his gratification (or displeasure) with an exclamation.

3. Referring to your daily habits you say, "My greatest pleasure in life is my morning cigarette." That is an "is-statement," and as such completely legitimate. Maybe you are telling the truth. Perhaps—in fact probably—you are slightly exaggerating. Coming from some people it could even be an outright lie; a young person, for instance, might merely have the childish ambition to appear "wicked." All that is beside the point here. The content of the statement concerns phenomena in spatial-temporal reality, namely, the speaker, the object-category "cigarette," and the speaker's recurrent sense of pleasure. Here we have a statement of *reflective evaluation*. It expresses the nature of the subjective relationship between the speaker and the object after the speaker has given himself an account of this relationship. A real theoretical statement is being made—not about the thing, but about the speaker: "I am a lover of the morning cigarette."

4. Only now do we come to the value judgment, which is expressed thus: "There is nothing better than a morning cigarette on an empty stomach." This statement is not legitimate. In this general and objective formulation, the pleasurable sensation of the speaker is transformed into an inherent, given quality of the object. But the cigarette has no such quality as "good." Different people experience different sensations. What you *can* say, for instance, is: The object has that or that objective quality, which arouses this or that sensation in me. Returning to the hyacinth: It gives off a strongly aromatic, almost intoxicating smell, which *I* find pleasing (or displeasing).

Hence the value judgment objectifies a subjective relationship of the speaker to a thing, and makes this pseudo-objectivity an element in a sentence taking the form of a theoretical statement about the thing. This is not legitimate. Again, someone might object: "You're whipping dead horses. We already know all that. And what difference does it make whether I say, 'I like it,' or, 'It is delicious'? Everyone knows what I mean and that I can only speak for myself."

But it is exactly this last point which is not so certain. Have you never heard a mother tell her children, when they won't eat a certain food, how "delicious it tastes"? Or *A* tell *B* that he was crazy if he didn't like oysters and that he "didn't know what was good"? But let's leave the subject of value judgments of sense and taste, about whose pointlessness, at least in principle, we all agree, even though in practice the idea of their objective validity still exerts an unconscious influence.

What is true of value judgments of sense and taste likewise holds for other value judgments. But as soon as we begin to consider artistic-aesthetic value judgments, toleration (there is nothing there to be tolerated) suddenly becomes more dubious. If I am moved to call the Madonna Sixtina "trash," the "educated people" descend upon me and explain how "wonderfully beautiful" the painting is and that I have "very bad taste" or that I "don't understand anything about art." I want to know why. I prefer any El Greco at all to the Sixtina, which I simply can't stand. And when someone objects that he finds the emaciated, deformed limbs repulsive, and explains to me that Rubens's voluptuous wenches are far more pleasing to the eye—then I leave him to his own opinion.

Why, however, are aesthetic value judgments taken so much more seriously than those of sense and taste? I believe I can provide an answer. It is of no considerable importance to the social environment (in our societies anyway) whether I prefer caviar or veal, whether I would rather have red wine or beer, or whether I place roses or carnations on my table. But it is another matter with art, music, or literature. In every historically given culture there exists a certain similarity of aesthetic valuations, partially as a direct result of the propagation of value judgments. Certain modes of aesthetic valuation are standardized by a fashion-setting elite, which gives its approval to a certain style in the handling of a theme or to a preference in the choice of a theme. This approval guides the process of selection in the cultural market and leads to the creation of aesthetic habits in the general public. For those who do not know a great deal about art themselves, the authority of the experts and of the "cultured" people plays a major role. Nor is the influence of snobbishness to be underestimated where aesthetic valuations are involved. By expressing a certain taste, you identify yourself with the "best connoisseurs," and the expectation of social prestige to be gained in this manner may well give rise to aesthetic hypocrisy. In addition, familiarity with works of the predominant fashion causes a certain unresponsiveness to new or deviant forms. It is always small groups of experts who are not dependent on orthodoxy for their social standing that break the bonds of tradition.

After a certain kind of valuation has been generally accepted, the claim to objective validity of the corresponding value judgment finds support in the fact of general consensus. If most other people judge an object the same way A does, then A draws the conclusion that the value must be inherent in the object itself. Collective agreement may give the appearance of objective validity, but it is by no means the cause of it. Other eras and other societies—today even other groups within the same society—have different aesthetic values.

Nor is the value judgment "beautiful" (or "ugly") anything but an interpretation of the pleasure or displeasure found in a work of art as one of its intrinsic qualities. I am speaking now not of scholarly analysis, which usually applies other, far more objectively defined standards of aesthetic judgment.

Coming finally to the matter of moral value judgments, we find that by contradicting them or criticizing their validity we arouse outright animosity, for moral value judgments are associated with the strongest of social interests. That is why we began the present analysis with a discussion of unemotional, strictly perceptual value judgments. The moral conduct of *A*—and the primary valuations which motivated it—are of vital importance to those around him. Interpersonal relationships are governed by social institutions. The social pressure exerted on an individual to enforce conformity to certain behavioral patterns gives the distinct impression that certain acts are per se good or evil. The favorable or unfavorable reaction of public opinion or group authority, as well as training from earliest childhood, contributes to this impression.

It is well known, however, that practically every kind of behavior forbidden in one society has at some time been permitted—or even prescribed—in another. That applies to everything from lying to feuding and from incest to cannibalism. Nor is it possible to prove with logical arguments that one morality is right and the other wrong. Hence a particular act can hardly be inherently good or evil, but it is only evaluated in one way here and otherwise somewhere else. At the present time even various levels of the same society evaluate certain modes of behavior differently, even to the point of contradicting each other. In short: a society does not prohibit one mode of behavior because it is bad or put a premium on another because it is good; rather the members of a society ascribe the value characteristic "evil" to what is prohibited and "good" to that which is socially advocated.

This also constitutes the basis of the moral value judgment. Act *X* is socially disapproved of. Instead of saying, "We disapprove of the killing of fellow human beings" (reflective announcement of valuation), we say, "Murder is reprehensible." Notice that the term "murder" is already a suggestive valuation and not merely the objective description of an act. "Murder" is the designation for all socially objectionable cases of killing human beings. The executioner, on the other hand, is "doing his duty" and the soldier "is a hero" when he kills. And to remove the moral stigma from the taking of one's own life, the expression "voluntary death" is substituted for "suicide."[3] Ob-

---

[3] The German *Selbstmord* means literally "self murder."—Trans.

viously opinions differ widely as to when and under what circumstances the taking of human life is reprehensible, when acceptable, and when praiseworthy.

By designating a certain kind of act as good or bad, one either thinks that "good" and "bad" are qualities inherent in the act and characterizing its real nature, or that there is such a thing as a value of goodness (and a negative value of evil) which the act partakes of or embodies. But neither of these interpretations can be substantiated in empirical reality, and all attempts of philosophy to found a universal and objectively valid system of morality have failed miserably for this very reason.

Let us now summarize our findings. Every kind of value judgment is based on the fact that personal or collective primary valuations (i.e., affective relationships of individuals to an object) are interpreted as qualities of the object itself, that is, they are objectified. Things *are* not beautiful or ugly, acts *are* not good or evil, etc., but people and groups find pleasure or displeasure in them, approve of them or disapprove of them. Note that when we say here that it is not true that the taking of human life is reprehensible, we are not saying that the taking of human life is permissible or praiseworthy. Such a reversal of a value judgment is just as much of a (contrary) value judgment and hence is epistemologically just as illegitimate.

Although these conclusions have been reached in a somewhat different way, everything presented in this chapter thus far is essentially in agreement with the teachings of the Swedish school of A. Hägerström and his successors, known as the Uppsala philosophy. From this point on, however, I emphatically part company with this group.

After the Uppsala philosophers had discovered the origin of the value judgments, they reasoned thus: a theoretical statement is a statement about a *something*. A value judgment is an utterance about a *nothing*, since the word "value" corresponds to nothing given in spatial-temporal reality. A value judgment is hence nothing but an expression of the feeling (approval, pleasure, etc.) which underlies it. It doesn't say a bit more than if the person making the judgment had exclaimed "Ah!" or "Phooey!" The value judgment is therefore a theoretically meaningless statement. It does not contain a theoretical opinion. Astonishingly, this serves as a justification to Hägerström and his school when they themselves make value judgments with a vengeance. "Why shouldn't we," they ask, "as long as we know that nothing we say has the least bit of meaning?"

But it is not true that the value judgment is without theoretical meaning, for its genesis is by no means decisive for its structure and its intended meaning. The basis of a value judgment is of course nothing but the sensual or emotional relationship of the judge to the object being judged. In the imagination of the judge, however, this relationship is transferred into an inherent quality of the object. The fact is that he detests lies, but he *says* that the lie is bad. Occasionally this can be quite clearly demonstrated in the case of moral value judgments. Someone declares: "I detest lying." When asked for his reasons he replies: "Because deceitfulness is a bad character trait," or, "Because lies are reprehensible." What is actually happening here? Genetic analysis of the value judgment has shown that calling a lie "bad" or "reprehensible" is nothing but the objectification of personal distaste or social rejection. First of all, therefore, the feeling of disapproval is objectified, whereupon this apparent objectification is cited as a rational ground for the disapproval.

When someone says, "The life of others is sacred," or "Cruelty to animals is despicable," he really means it. Or, to use the language I have imposed upon myself thus far by limiting my critique to *statements*: statements must be judged on the basis of their structure. They may have their genesis in the sphere of the emotions and as such be without theoretical meaning. But in expressing his personal relationship to an object in a value judgment, the speaker employs the form of an is-statement. And in this form the value judgment, posing as a theoretical statement, makes a claim to objective validity. "Anyone who says the contrary—or even anything different— is wrong" is the attitude implicit in the value judgment. It pretends to be a valid theoretical statement. As such, however, it is not legitimate, since the thing it applies to does not exist in empirical reality. Objectification of valuations into a value-idea is illusory. The value judgment is an is-statement about something which is only alleged to exist. It is not legitimate because its structure is not consonant with its content.

This is the nature of ideology. It lies in the objectification of the nonobjective, in theorizing the nontheoretical. It is pseudo-theory, perhaps better designated as *para-theory*. Hence it is not false in the usual sense. Logically speaking, it is neither true nor false. Since there is actually nothing whatever "real" at issue, but only the illusion of reality, we are not dealing with anything that can be corrected or refuted by logically coordinated observations. The critique begins at a prior stage: the statement is declared epistemologically illegitimate or para-theoretical and therefore incompatible with cognition.

.

THE SOURCES OF IDEOLOGY

WE HAVE described and analyzed the value judgment as an example of an ideological statement. It was called ideological not because it expresses a valuation, but because it cloaks a valuation in the form of a theoretical statement of fact and thus imparts to it a claim to objective validity. These ideas can now be expressed in more general terms in order to formulate a definition of the ideological statement.

A statement may be called ideological if, by virtue of its grammatical form and its expressed meaning, it appears to be a theoretical statement of fact while at the same time containing nontheoretical elements, i.e., elements which do not pertain to objective, empirical reality. . . .

The above definition attributes the ideological character of statements to their infiltration by nontheoretical elements, which then become not only objectified, but also (apparently) theorized. How this occurs has already been illustrated by the example of the value judgment. The human being may approach an object or a sum of objects—all the way up to a universe containing all perceived, presumed, and possible objects —in two different ways.

First, as *observer*. That means that he occupies a position vis-à-vis the objects he is considering and regards them as exterior to and independent of himself. They hence belong to the external world and as such are subjects for theoretical state-

___

The first five paragraphs of this chapter are taken from chapter 5 of the original text, entitled *Para-theoretische Aussagen;* the remainder are selections from chapter 6 of the original text, entitled *Ursprungsschichten der Ideologie.*

ments. His sole relationship to them is that he observes them. This is also known as the disinterested or detached attitude.

The other and opposite position is that of a *participant*, one who has a living relationship to things and sees them in connection with himself or himself in connection with them. One can call this a *vital relationship* in the widest sense. The statements which can be legitimately made from this position are by no means statements about the object itself, but rather about the speaker in respect to the object, or about the meaning of the object for the speaker. This is the vitally interested or attached attitude. To the extent that statements do not reveal that they only pertain (reflectively) to the *vital relationship of a participant to* an object, but are so phrased as to appear as *factual statements of an observer about* an object—to this extent are they ideological. They theorize—or, as we usually say, rationalize—a vital relationship.

. . . The ideological distortions in our statements result from the fact that vital relationships of the speaker to the object involved enter into his statements and give them a pseudo-theoretical character. The main question for the analysis of ideology is then: Where are the sources of ideology to be found? Every statement can be conceived as the final link in a chain and is predicated on a body of premises from which it is —correctly or incorrectly—derived. Even in the most pedantic of scholarly works, only some of these premises are explicitly mentioned and developed. The question, therefore, is at what point in the chain of premises do we find vital relationships entering the material context? By asking this question we by no means deviate from our stated intention to concentrate on the statement itself, focusing instead on the cognitive process preceding it. The expression "at what point" does not refer, psychologically, to what goes on in the mind of the speaker—hereafter called "the ideologist"—before he makes his statement, but is directed logically and epistemologically at the structure (the content) of the statement itself. Occasionally—in fact quite often—the door appears to be opened to ideological distortions by the very fact that the ideologist does not think through the whole chain of premises leading to the statement, but begins at some later point and takes all antecedent premises "for granted," or else leaves out some part of the chain ("short circuit").

When a statement is suspected of being ideological, therefore, the problem is to find that point in the flow of its premises where a muddy stream of uncontrolled sentiments empties into the clear water of the theory. Sometimes one does not have to look very far. Occasionally, however, the source of the distortion may lie a good way back. Thus one may speak of more and less *remote ideologies*. The more remote, the more difficult it is in general to expose the ideological distortion and to locate its point of incursion. It would be a tempting and presumably also a worthwhile task to investigate ideological statements or those suspected thereof with respect to the source of the ideology and to the distorting mechanism. The expected result would be a classification of ideologies. Such a systematic, comprehensive investigation has never been attempted, nor can it be performed here. It requires the collection and analysis of many hundreds, perhaps thousands, of possibly ideological statements. The epistemologist would be better equipped for this task than the sociologist. Nevertheless the attempt will be made here to illustrate with examples at least certain typical points of ideological incursion. . . .

The most obvious of ideologies are those which can be traced to direct material interests of the speaker. For that reason they were for a long time the only ones which people were aware of. When later more complicated and less conspicuous cases of ideological distortion were discovered, it seemed reasonable to describe and explain them in terms of interest theory. Strained attempts were often made to find a connection with material interests where the unbiased observer was not capable of seeing such a relationship.

The recognition of ideology based on interest (in the narrowest sense) has repeatedly found expression even in everyday speech. This is illustrated by the popular phrase, "He thinks with his stomach," or in such sayings as, "The desire is

the father of the idea," and "Whose bread I eat, his tune I sing."
The connection between the content of a statement and a material interest of the ideologist in the object of the statement is
here direct, without any intermediate links. It may be called a
surface ideology. . . .

At this point we may mention an objection to Mannheim's
basic distinction between particular and total ideology. Ideology based on interest he calls particular, whereas the total
ideology is supposedly based on an existential determination
of cognition. It is impossible, however, to make a clear distinction between the two, inasmuch as it does not involve a difference of kind but of degree. The particular ideology is a surface
ideology. In the case of the total ideology, however, the point
of incursion of the vital relationship on which it is based is very
remote. It is *depth ideology.* Between the most superficial and
the most deep, however, there are innumerable intermediate
possibilities. The differences in degree quite adequately explain
the fact that, according to Mannheim, the particular ideology
can be corrected without presumably affecting any other cognitive activities of the ideologist, whereas the total ideology
permeates the entire mind like a fermentation process. Here,
according to Mannheim, critique cannot be restricted to the
statement(s), but rather must investigate the foundations of
the cognitive process itself. It is obvious: the more the ideological element of a statement lies on the surface, the less is the
danger—schematically speaking—that it will encroach on other
systems of statements. The deeper the source of the ideology,
the more extensive will be the region of single statements which
is endangered.

There are, however, other statements whose ideological nature lies as close to the surface but which have nothing to do
with any "material interest." One may consider, for instance,
the rationalization of personal likes and dislikes. The Bavarian
dialect has an appropriate saying: "Likin' makes beautiful."
We have here a striking instance of the transformation of a
primary valuation ("liking") into a value judgment ("is beautiful"). It is even possible that an apparently objective reason

will be given as explanation by referring to certain valued characteristics of the object concerned. A lover discovers virtues possessed by the object of his affections, i.e., characteristics which are either visible only to his loving eye, or which, if really present, dominate his image of the loved one. Love is known to be blind.[1] . . .

The concept of "interest" is rapidly fading into the background of scientific discussion because of the inadequacies of its definition. Especially in regard to the theory of ideology, it has given way more and more to the concept of "engagement of the will," which although far more comprehensive is more clearly delimited. . . .

Henrik Ibsen's much quoted "life lie" belongs in this category; it is any conception, belief in which—regardless of how unfounded or even contradictory—helps make human existence more endurable and gives man the courage to go on living. Every metaphysical theory about "the meaning of life" is such a lie. It is entirely mystifying how human existence can be attributed with any meaning which transcends it. Ibsen appears to have been convinced that man has an urgent need for such a lie, and the fact that most people believe in one would seem to prove him right. Such lies are indispensable, however, only to those who are too tender-minded to bear the idea of a self-contained and self-sufficient existence. The ascetic stoic or cynic has no need to deceive himself.

Here follows another case of engagement of the will, a case involving an ideology of equally great importance for both sociology and politics. In the fervid discussions of recent years on the democratic system and way of life, the guarantee of so-called freedom of thought has been emphasized as especially important, the lack of which being one of the main arguments against the totalitarian "people's democracy." It is sometimes contended that this intellectual freedom to hold personal convictions and to express them publicly is a "social benefit" at

[1]   As rudely expressed in a Danish folk rhyme: "Kåerligheden har sin egen vilje—den falder på en lort som pa en lilie." (Love has a will of its own—it falls on filth as easily as on a lily.)

least as valuable as a high material standard of living and economic security. It can hardly be said, however, that the intellectuals who give voice to such comparative value judgments are interested in maintaining the economic inequality prevalent in capitalistic society. Their own economic situation under latter-day capitalism is by no means enviable; at any rate it is not so desirable that they should defend it with ideologies. On the contrary, we could sooner expect engagement of the will to be manifested on the other side.

Most of us intellectuals, however, place so much value on full freedom of creation and expression that we would not be inclined to sacrifice it for our economic advantages. That is our own matter and has nothing to do with ideology. It is presumably wrong, however, to impute to the bulk of the population—consisting of the working as well as the middle classes— the same relative evaluation. For those parts of the population who get their intellectual matter second or third hand—and that is the overwhelming majority—material goods are far more important. Most of them have never experienced "freedom of thought" in the full sense of the term. Their reservoir of concepts and ideas has always been imposed upon them from some higher authority; hence it is not too important which authority it is or which ideas are propagated to the masses. During the transition from a society based on the free competition of ideas to centrally coordinated totalitarianism, the living adult generation would object to, or at least resent the denial of free choice between competing authorities. Nor is that something totalitarian rulers have ever been in doubt about. Following generations, on the other hand, growing up in a culturally unequivocal and monolithic environment, would in the absence of contradictory ideas have no feeling of constraint; hence they would, in the psychological sense, be truly free. A continuous, constant pressure would only be felt by those who had made thinking their major purpose in life and the substance of their existence. Hence, when the social hedonist advocates the happiness of the greatest number, it is at least debatable whether economic advancement and security does not mean more than an intellectual freedom which for the majority cannot be more than nominal. . . .

From the democratic point of view it would be very easy to say that the well-being of a handful of intellectuals is not decisive. And when such intellectuals refer to a "human" need for intellectual freedom as an argument for liberal democracy, they are obviously projecting their own personality type in order to support their demands by claiming that they have a majority character.

To avoid misunderstandings I must add that it is entirely another matter when intellectuals argue, for instance, as follows: We know that the man in the street cares much less about freedom of thought than do we who require it for our professions. But if, nevertheless, we desire this freedom not only for ourselves but in the name of the entire democratic society, and if we declare it to be indispensable even though we are the only ones who have the opportunity of making full use of it, we do so for the following reasons: (1) Without complete freedom for intellectual creativity and communication, cultural life would stagnate as soon as presently inherent possibilities have been exhausted. Political shackles on intellectual production prevent the "dynamic" structural change of the existing cultural system. (2) In the long run the political equality and civil freedom of the population at large is indirectly contingent on the presence of a freely creative intelligentsia which is not subjected to any pressures from above. . . .

Such a "functional argumentation" for the necessity of intellectual freedom would in any case not be ideological in the same sense as the generalization based on psychological projection mentioned above. The former would even be theoretically tenable, provided that we accept two premises: (1) A dynamic, progressive culture and (2) political equality and civil freedom of the masses are desirable. Only if these two premises are explicitly acknowledged as choices of volition can the "functional argumentation" cited above be considered valid, and of course only within the boundaries set by these premises. "If a dynamic cultural life and democracy are desirable, intellectual freedom must be guaranteed." In the event that these value premises are tacitly overlooked or even passed off as objective fact, an ideological element enters the functional argumentation for the social necessity of intellectual freedom.

The hypothetical argumentation for the necessity of intellectual freedom as outlined above suggests another type of ideology which, for lack of a better term, we shall call *occupational ideology.* . . . In exactly the same way, the farmer may point out that the city dwellers would die of starvation if he didn't plant wheat and raise cattle; the existence of the entire nation supposedly depends, therefore, upon the agricultural community. He forgets thereby, or underestimates, his own functional dependence on urban society, on the industry which supplies him with the tools of his trade and the consumer goods for his daily needs, on the government which maintains order in the social system in which he lives and works, on the science which stands behind the entire technology of production, including agriculture. In short: he forgets the fable about the stomach and the limbs. Or the clergyman argues for the indispensability of his profession by pointing to the inborn need of man for religion and to the necessity of providing a religious foundation for moral behavior. He neglects to mention that the clergy does its best to engender a need for religion in many and to keep it alive, it being dubious whether in the absence of such efforts the need for religion would not long since have vanished; and moreover that moral and immoral behavior can be found without major differences among believers and nonbelievers.

Such an occupational ideology has various roots, the most superficial of which is interest in the occupational existence. One lives by following an occupation. If an occupational function is regarded as superfluous by the remainder of society, the members of that occupation lose their basis of existence. The higher the function is held in the public esteem, the more favorable will be the income prospects of the corresponding occupational group. Advertising for the occupational function never hurts.

There are also, however, less manifest sources of ideology.

In a society in which the division of labor is highly specialized, it is exceedingly difficult to gain insight into the interdependencies of the whole system. By the daily practice of our own function we become familiar with it in all particulars, with the result that we have not only a distinct idea of the difficulties it presents, but also of the scope of its social effects. Our idea of other occupational functions is generally quite foggy, if we even have one at all. The farther they lie from our own field of activity, the less clear are our own notions about them. It is no wonder, therefore, that when we try to imagine the entirety of functional patterns in the society, the contribution of our own occupational group assumes the most concrete aspect.

There is, however, also a third factor involved. Most occupations today require a certain training; many even demand an extremely high degree of specialized education. In the course of such a curriculum one not only attains a certain level of knowledge and skill, but also develops a specific way of thinking. The engineer, the doctor, the lawyer, the educator, each has a philosophy of life common to his profession, a particular point of view from which he regards his enviroment. The same thing holds, naturally, for the artisan and the businessman, for the farmer and the office worker, for the day laborer and the desk clerk. . . .

3

THE ANALYSIS OF IDEOLOGICAL STATEMENTS AND THE ROLE OF INTROSPECTION

IF THE concept of ideology is applied to statements, and only to statements, then it may only be applied to cognition. Music or fine arts do not produce statements; and poetry or literary description, while making use of language, do not use it as a medium for statements, but rather to communicate the tone, rhythm, coloration, and nuances of experience.

We need not deceive ourselves, however, about the difficulties connected with this restriction to statements, this ascetic renunciation of introspection. We must remember that designating a statement as ideological does not simply mean to say: "The statement is false." There are innumerable statements which can be proven false without therefore being ideological. A statement is false in the ideological sense only if it is para-theoretical, i.e., if it has been corrupted by the infiltration of a vital engagement. But how can we claim that this is in fact the case without introspection, i.e., without recourse to the mental process by which the statement was produced? If we cannot, then only two possibilities remain. One would be an introspective analysis of ideology. The other would be a renunciation

---

This chapter comprises pp. 164–72 of chapter 9 in the original text, entitled *"Ideologie"—Ein Makel der Erkenntnis.*

of the concept of ideology, inasmuch as this would be completely without meaning in a nonintrospective context. In this case one would be limited to demonstrating that certain statements are false, without being able to distinguish the specifically ideological nature of the error.

1. The most simple case is that of the value judgment. Here it is possible, on the basis of a concrete proposition isolated from its context, to say with certainty that it is ideological, the para-theoretical expression of a personal engagement. Indeed, the proposition contains nothing but a specious theoretization of the engagement, a positively or negatively emotional attitude toward the object of the statement. The ideological character of the value judgment is directly visible in the substantive structure of the proposition itself. The only question then remaining is: Is the value judgment, coming from the lips of the speaker, his own ideology, in the sense that he has reinterpreted his primary valuation of the object of the statement into an ostensibly factual statement? Or is he only repeating a value judgment which has been suggested to him by his education and environment? In this latter case the engagement of the speaker with the value judgment itself—as a dogmatic conviction—would be primary, and his corresponding emotional point of view toward the evaluated object secondary, a conditioned reaction.

In any case the value judgment cannot be anything but an ideology. It is the pure and classic example of the para-theoretical statement, and recognizable as such by its structure.

The same applies to all statements having transcendental metaphysical content, in short: all statements which either (a) refer to an unreal object or (b) refer to a real object but make assertions about it which cannot apply to real objects (e.g., attributing to it empirically nontestable characteristics).

2. As soon as a statement claims to be a factual statement about a real object, however, it may be demonstrated by conventional testing methods (observation and logical critique) whether the statement is substantially true or false. In the latter case, however, it is impossible to specify with certainty whether

or not the mistake has ideological grounds. Not every wrong statement reveals directly and, so to speak, on the face of it whether its author simply blundered in his thinking or whether he was tripped up by a vital engagement—whether he *erred* or was *blinded*. Such statements, therefore, may be *suspected* of being ideological, but a final *accusation* cannot be made without introspection.

Wherever the ideological critique of scientific propositions occurs, however, it never involves isolated statements, but only entire systems, e.g., a book or a treatise. The individual statement appears in a larger context; it is a derivation. I do not have to make introspective assumptions about how the author came to make such a statement: he tells me himself, since his train of thought is communicated to me in the series of statements. What cannot be determined on the basis of the statement alone can be established by an analysis of the context. By checking step by step the ideas put forth, it is possible to find the point at which an error has been made. The proof that the statement is ideological here means the same thing as locating the source of the ideology in the derivation of the statement. Somewhere along the chain we may find, for instance, a metaphysical premise, or a hidden value judgment, or an appeal to an obsolete conceptual model, which is no longer consistent with current knowledge and only used because it is an old habit, etc. What was formerly only the suspicion of ideology now becomes a definite accusation.

3. In a third case—sociologically the most important—the accusation of ideology made against a particular statement is based on entirely different grounds. The following proposition may be taken as an example: "Advertising for name brands serves the consumer by insuring a high standard of quality for the product and, by increasing sales volume, reducing its price." At a certain stage of economic development this proposition was, at least partially, true. Today it is false—but I will here spare the reader going into the reasons why. For our present purposes it is not important whether the assertion is really false or whether we only assume it to be so for the sake of our ex-

ample. If someone makes this statement, and if I can prove that it is false, the question still remains completely open whether or not it is ideological. The speaker may have investigated and analyzed the economic relationships involved to the best of his ability, coming to the stated conclusion. That it is false may be the consequence of a simple observational or logical error. If however the speaker is the manufacturer of a brand-name product or the owner of an advertising agency—i.e., if he is dependent on advertising for his living—then we may suspect him of ideological partiality. It is as yet merely a suspicion, and only the consumer—who is also under suspicion of ideology—will state: That *is* the ideology of the speaker; because he has an interest in advertising he is attempting to justify himself and to make it more palatable for us. The unprejudiced observer will leave it at *suspicion* of ideology and let it go at that. He cannot make any introspective statements about what went on in the mind of the speaker before or while he was making the statement in question.

If someone who does not have a vital engagement with advertising can reach the same false conclusion, then why can it not also be a simple case of erroneous judgment when coming from a person who has an interest in advertising? The mere fact that there is a congruence between the substance of a statement and the interests of the speaker is never sufficient grounds for the contention that the statement is ideological. Even entirely accurate statements may be consonant with and support the interests of the speaker.

That is generally true of all statements which have any bearing on the speaker's interests, his social or economic situation, or any other determinants of his existence. If someone makes a statement—accurate or inaccurate—which "corresponds" to his life situation, we should not jump to the conclusion that it was dictated by the speaker's engaged attitude toward the object.

Before we attempt to solve this dilemma, we must make some remarks on the subject of introspection. While reading points 1 and 2 above the reader may already have had doubts about whether the concept of ideology as presented here is not also of an introspective nature. Is it possible without recourse to introspection to assert, for instance, that in the value judgment the emotional relationship of the person doing the judging becomes theorized or objectified? Is it possible to speak at all of emotions and engagement? Strictly speaking, no. But if we were to go to this extreme of orthodoxy, it would be impossible for social science to make any statements at all about human values and other highly important subject areas. The practical question appears to be not, "Is introspection admissible?" but rather, "To what extent is introspection admissible, if we wish to stay within the bounds of reasonable judgment?" . . .

I know by direct experience that I have emotions and I am quite aware of my vital engagement with certain objects. I proceed from the assumption, moreover, in all of my actions, behavior, and being in general that I am not the only living human being in the universe. Implicit therein is the—albeit introspective—certainty that the bodies I have identified as human beings in the material world about me also have a consciousness of their own. That other egos are there, that they too have emotions, that they, like myself, are vitally engaged with things or events—these are immediate certainties upon which my entire existence is predicated. It would be quixotic to eliminate these practical certainties from our theory simply because they are introspective. By observing and testing myself, however, I discover one other thing, namely, that my emotions and vital engagements have occasionally played tricks on me, clouded my judgment, and betrayed me into making objectively questionable statements.

a) I therefore have the immediate certainty that every statement is the final product of a cognitive process. About the process itself in any given instance, however, I know nothing. If this process is explicitly described (point 2 above), then I am dealing with a chain of statements and not with an individual statement. In the case of an isolated statement, every attempt to reconstruct the underlying train of thought is based on an introspective interpretation, with no recourse whatever to any objective points of reference.

b) In general and in principle, however, I also know by direct experience that what has been defined as ideological distortion (i.e., the influence of vital engagements on cognition) is a real possibility. Without inadmissible introspection I am therefore justified in taking any and every statement under scrutiny with a view toward this possibility. We saw under point 1 above in which cases an individual statement, on the basis of a content analysis, could be designated with certainty as ideological. Under all other circumstances it would be in *particular* and *casuistically* inadmissible to say: This particular statement coming from this person is ideological. Since it cannot be objectively proven what went on in the mind of the speaker before and while he was making the statement, any assertion made about it can be nothing more than an introspective presumption.

On this understanding we may now return to the question, whether or not and in what sense individual statements which are not pure ideology (e.g., value judgments or transcendental, metaphysical tenets) can be called ideological. Let us again take the example given above, the statement about the effects of name-brand advertising. In view of what we have just said, it would obviously be inadmissible to say: The statement as such is an ideology, regardless of who makes it. The statement *can* be the result of simple ignorance of the given facts or an erroneous conclusion. It would likewise be unfounded to say: "This person is the owner of an advertising agency. Advertising is his business. Therefore he defends it. Coming from him the statement is ideological." He could just as easily as anyone else be the victim of a disinterested error. Any doubts, therefore, must be interpreted in his favor. No one has sufficient objective grounds to be able to say: "He says that *because* he sells advertising."

What can be asserted however, if supported by the evidence, is this: "The statement that name-brand advertising improves the quality of the product and lowers the price is an ideology of the sellers of advertising and of those whose products are marketed with high-pressure advertising methods." Not "It is an ideology of this particular person," but "It is an ideology of the category of persons to which he belongs." In the same way we may speak of a laborer's or government worker's ideology, of an ideology of farmers or intellectuals, of a national ideology or the ideology of an era. How does that happen?

A preliminary observation reveals that there is a frequent repetition of a statement X or of similar such statements, or of statements containing X or contained by X. The distribution of the statement is investigated and it is found that it is especially common among a certain kind of persons. Within a certain objectively defined category of people the statement is encountered regularly, or at least quite frequently, while having few advocates outside of this circle. By means of a statistical test a correlation is established between the statement and an objectively delimited category of persons. It is, in other words, legitimate to say that the statement is typical of persons in the given category.

Now let us assume that empirical evidence proves the statement to be false. The statistical correlation between the false statement (opinion) and this specific category of persons demands an explanation. We can see that in such cases we are dealing with frequently repeated, so-called standard statements. When referring here to a speaker, therefore, we do not mean that everyone making this statement arrived at his conclusion by means of an independent process of thought. The statement will have been originally formulated by a particular individual on the basis of his own deliberations, or else by several individuals who came to similar conclusions independently of one another. The frequent repetition of a statement is an indication that it has found agreement and been accepted by others. The question, precisely formulated, is therefore not, "How does it happen that the people in category N all 'think that way,' " but rather "How does it happen that an especially large number of people in category N agree with the error X and profess it as their own opinion?" The explanation is to be found by (a) an

analysis of the content of the statement and the logical consequences of the errors contained in it, and (b) an analysis of the
life situation of the category of individuals in which the erroneous statement has such a large following, i.e., for which it is
statistically typical. The life situation of this class of people
reveals a common trait, a determinant which is consonant with
the faulty component in the statement. The fact that advertising
has a vital significance for businessmen, especially for a given
group of businessmen, and that these people are vitally engaged
with advertising, is a fact which can be derived from the nature
of their life situation. That this engagement on the part of an
individual must be responsible for a derailment in his thinking
cannot be proved. But only one rational explanation can be
found for the fact that the majority of people in this specific
category are especially liable to believe this particular erroneous statement, namely, the content of the statement appeals to
a vital engagement on the part of these individuals.

The various representatives of this category can only be
suspected of ideology—a suspicion which can never be confirmed with certainty. The category as a whole, however, may
be *accused* of ideology. Ideologies of this kind—i.e., most political, social, and economic standard statements, as well as
most other fashionable opinions—are to be treated as mass
phenomena, and the analysis of ideology should not refer to
the individual cognitive process, but should restrict itself to
making comparisons between the content of statements and
the life situation of their adherents.

4

THEORETICAL AND PRAGMATIC CRITIQUE OF IDEOLOGY

THE CONCEPT of ideology implies a criticism. When using this concept, one must necessarily be aware of nonideological thoughts and statements which correspond to reality —if not as practical alternatives, then at least as a theoretically possible ideal. Otherwise one could simply refer to "thought" and "idea" and "statement" and ignore the concept of ideology entirely, inasmuch as it would not imply any more than already indicated by these terms.

If however an ideology is a thought, idea, or judgment which deviates from reality—i.e., is in some way false or untrue—then the function of a critique is to investigate this deviation. That is in fact the objective of a *theoretical critique of ideology*: it criticizes ideology in cognition or in the form of theoretical statements. . . .

One will immediately ask why this task calls for an independent discipline, or in any case a special branch of sociology. What do we have logic and epistemology for? The question is thoroughly justified, and many a zealous advocate of the theoretical critique of ideology could have saved himself a great deal of trouble—and much confusion—if he had attempted to clarify this point before plunging into profound analyses.

Logic can expose fallacies in two different ways.

1. In the case of a concrete statement whose object is accessible to direct (sensory) observation, an error can occur

because the observation was false on which the statement is based. The person thinking and speaking made an observation and drew from it a conclusion. The conclusion may be entirely correct as far as formal logic is concerned, but in substance it is nevertheless false because the observation was in error. The speaker believed that he saw something which "in reality was not there" or was other than he thought it to be. In such cases logic is not involved. The source of the error lies in the technique of perception and observation.

On the other hand, the speaker may have made a correct observation, but then made an error in the logical interpretation of what he perceived. He has "drawn the wrong conclusion." . . .

Logical critique is here presented with no technical difficulties whatever. One always has access to the factual data which constitute the object of the statement, and it is possible by repeating the observation and checking the steps of logical proof to show whether an error has been made in the observation or in the logical inference.

2. Metaphysical, transcendental statements are liable to logical critique only to the extent that they contain an "internal flaw." In this case there is no possibility of confirming or refuting the substance of the statement by checking observations, since there is nothing there to be observed. In substance such a statement does not refer to any perceptible reality, but to something lying beyond ("transcending") the realm of experience. The individual statement can be dealt with logically only by showing that by the rules of formal logic it contradicts other statements within the same system. . . .

Epistemological critique goes deeper than formal logic. An argument or statement is declared to be legitimate or inadmissible according to standards set by the possibilities and limits of cognition in general. It it possible, for instance, to demonstrate that the object of a statement lies outside the realm of possible cognition. Or, that the problem to which the statement claims to be an answer is spurious, i.e., merely imaginary. Or, that the fundamental concepts used are faulty. Or, finally, that the conclusions are correct according to the rules of formal logic, but cannot be supported by the premises from which they are derived. Epistemologically one can, for instance, criticize the basic axiom of some transcendental metaphysic, and thus the entire system built upon it.

For all of these methods of critique, no controls are called for which were not available to traditional, orthodox philosophy. Indeed, if no other critical problem were involved than to establish whether a statement is true or false, or whether it is epistemologically admissible, then we would have no need for a critique of ideology.

This latter kind of critique, however, attacks the *genesis of the error*. It does not ask, "Is this proposition right or wrong?" but rather, "How did it happen that this thinker made this kind of error in observation or deduction?" "Why was it that this thinker violated the limits and conditions of cognition at this point and in this way?" . . .

The critic of ideology does not establish whether a statement deviates from reality; to do this we would not need him. His specific function is to relate the established deviation to some factor found elsewhere than at the theoretical level. One could say that the logician and the epistemologist judge whether statements are true or false, whereas the critic of ideology looks for the laws which govern the making of the false statements.

But at this point we must call attention to an important aspect which deserves more consideration than it has previously received: these nontheoretical points of reference are not necessarily social factors. Ideologies may also be rooted in character, and perhaps in biological factors as well. . . .

So much for the theoretical critique of ideology. Four major points should now be clear:

1. The concept of ideology postulates that there is such a thing as nonideological, unbiased statements.

2. If one considers such statements to be humanly possible —either in general or with respect to certain objects—then ideological statements are, judged by the criterion of truth, illegitimate. In terms of cognition such statements are worth-

less, or at least inferior. They do not meet the standards called for in the search for truth.

3. If one regards completely nonideological statements as humanly impossible—either in general or with respect to certain objects—then the question still remains whether there are not various degrees to which the cognitive ideal of being nonideological may be approximated, and whether revealing the sources of ideology does not help to promote such an approximation.

4. Theoretical critique of ideology itself is by no means a correction of the statements, but only serves to point out the external sources of their fallacies.

But there is also such a thing as *pragmatic* critique of ideology. That a statement incongruent with reality is, from a theoretical standpoint, inferior because it deviates from the truth—this is a judgment which is valid only on its own premise. This premise is that truth, in the sense of "congruence with reality," is the goal. As *theory* the ideological statement is disqualified.

If, however, someone contends: "Truth, objectivity, congruence with reality is not decisive for the value of a statement. What is really important is the influence which the statement has on (social or historical) events." Then what? Indeed, this view has been propounded by not a few prophets of darkness: Marx, Pareto, Nietzsche, Sorel, the Nazis, the historian von Harnack, and many others. On the other side are those who believe that mankind can only be served by the progress of objective thinking. In this category belong Bertrand Russell, Harold D. Lasswell[1]—not to mention many others—and in which I emphatically include myself.

In this deep antagonism between "cognitive truth at all costs" and "appreciation of untruths which serve life"—in this antagonism lie the most extreme positions of a pragmatic

---

[1]   "Without science, democracy is blind and weak. With science, democracy will not be blind, and may be strong." (*The Analysis of Political Behaviour* [London, 1947], p. 12.)

critique of ideology. Here the statement is not judged on the basis of its truth value, but of its practical expediency. Or, the measure of truth is its function for man.

Theoretical critique of ideology as described above is a scientific endeavor. It analyzes real data, namely, the relationships between erroneous statements and external factors. Pragmatic critique of ideology, on the other hand, has nothing to do with science—or very little. It results in the making of value judgments. It is impossible to have a theoretical dispute—and eventually be convinced by logical arguments—about whether "Truth" or "Life" (whatever "Life" may mean) is more valuable and more important and which must be given priority. Therefore if I declare my own standpoint in this matter to be, "The truth of a statement is for me decisive. A statement deviating from the truth (i.e., verifiable agreement with reality) goes against my grain, even when I have to admit that it may be somehow 'useful' "—then I do not intend it as a statement which claims to be theoretically correct. Rather, I give scientific standards the preference when it comes to rendering judgments about statements. My opponents do the opposite. Both parties choose as they do not as scientists, not by appealing to the authority of theory, but as individuals and on a nonscientific basis.

But even those who pragmatically give preference to ideological thinking are forced to admit that ideological thought or judgment *as theory* is inadequate. They must limit themselves to saying: "As theory the statement may be inadequate, but inadequate theory has a function in social life which I approve of." That, for instance, is essentially the standpoint of Pareto; Marx, on the other hand, or Nietzsche, the Nazis, and Bolshevists go much farther. They contend not only that untruth has a social mission, but deny that efforts at objectivity can be justified—even as theory. Here "the mind stands still," and that in the most literal sense.

To repeat: pragmatic critique of ideology, whether it be the positive or the negative evaluation of ideological statements from a nontheoretical (activistic) point of view, is not a matter of science. There is, however, a version of such critique which is—or at any rate, could be—scientific. It restricts itself to studying and describing the influence which certain ideologies have on social action and the course of history. It can also go further and analyze the influence of ideological thought on social and historical life in general. As in the case of the theoretical critique of ideology, though with a different perspective, an attempt is made to establish the correlations, covariants, and constant relationships between ideologies and tangible phenomena of the external world. There can be no scientific objection whatever to such a pragmatic critique of ideology as long as it remains within the limits of establishing such relationships and refrains from making evaluations of such influences as it may discover. One may, for instance, find that certain ideologies are more conducive than others to aggressive behavior. Or one may find that ideologies in general, regardless of their specific nature, help to intensify those social conflicts which have an objective basis. It cannot be said that scientific authority, however, whether aggression is detrimental, or whether the intensification of social conflicts is advantageous for the historical process.

For the sake of literary integrity, therefore, I have explicitly characterized the exposition of my own sociopolitical evaluation of ideologies as a nonscientific book,[2] as the manifestation of a particular evaluative point of view and preference. It remains to be seen whether this will spare me the accusation of combatting ideology with scientific arguments. Readers who are not able to distinguish between theory and politics because, as confirmed ideologists, they insist on lumping the two together, will presumably accuse me of inconsistency. And the faithful rationalists will perhaps take over my evaluations and transform them into "scientific arguments" against ideologies (of others). I feel myself to be misunderstood by both parties and I do not want to be put into the same category with either of them.

[2]   *Demokratie ohne Dogma*, (Munich, 1963), the book from which the remainder of this volume has been taken for translation.—Ed.

III. Pathos and Rationality
in Mass Society

1

THE MASS SOCIETY OF
THE PRESENT

"Mass society" is the phrase with which the social form of the twentieth century has been branded. It is intended to express more than merely the quantitative magnitude, the enormous populations today incorporated under a nation-state. "Mass" at the same time has a qualitative connotation: it implies a supposed lack of structure in contemporary society, the absence of an organized arrangement of the gigantic units encompassing millions of anonymous individuals. In this sense of the term, Röpke[1] laments the lack of an "organic vertical structure" of the society. Thus conceived, the concept of mass society is the common denominator for all those defects attributed—with or without justification—to our society: the homelessness and isolation of the individual within his social environment, the leveling process and uniformity, "Americanization," bureaucratization, excessive specialization, the decline of cultural standards, the subversion of values, and the end of the metaphysical orientation toward life. . . .

Atomization—this disquieting term applies primarily to the disappearance of the corporative vertical structure of society. Large-scale modern society is no longer so organized that its constituent individuals belong to cohesive primary

Translated from *Demokratie ohne Dogma* (Munich: Szczesny Verlag, 1963), pp. 35–74, 115–134, 150–175, 176–208, 211–238, and printed here by permission of the publisher.

[1]   Wilhelm Röpke, *Die Gesellschaftskrisis der Gegenwart* (Erlenbach/Zurich, 1942), pp. 89, 109.

groups, which are then arranged in pyramidlike units of a higher order. The individual now belongs directly and in his own behalf to the larger and more comprehensive structures—especially the nation and the social class. The society as a whole is composed "atomistically" of so innumerably many persons that the individual loses his importance as a person. The atomization of society thus corresponds to the *anonymity* of the individual, and both together constitute what is conceived to be "mass society": an agglomeration of countless, nameless persons. This kind of structure is supposedly to blame for the deracination of people in contemporary society and for their leveling and uniformity. We will have to examine to what extent this is true, and if true, to what extent it constitutes an evil. . . .

"Atomized mass society" is a one-sided and distorted expression for the contemporary form of society. In order to confirm this and to get at the heart of the matter we must first describe certain basic types of interpersonal existence. Such types can be grouped according to several different aspects and various characteristics. Here however we need only one pair of types, which we will illustrate with the following examples.

A family or circle of friends consists of a very *small number* of persons feeling close and intimate with one another. Every member stands in immediate *personal* contact with every other member. There are subtle differences in the personal relationships between particular pairs of relatives or friends. The friendship or the familial relationship can be described as types, the latter having as special subtypes the marital, paternal, maternal, and sibling relationships. Regardless of these distinctions, however, every relationship between two given persons has its own individual character. Within the same circle of friends, the friendship between A and B will have a different personal tone than that between A and C or between B and C. Between father and children there exists a relationship which can be generally described as the paternal type, but the relationship of a father to one child is never exactly the same as his relationship with the second or third child. The standard type of paternity varies with the individual. The same is true with each pair of siblings. The family embraces its members as nearest of kin and the friendship circle unites its members as companions—regardless of the hundred other social ties held by the members of these groups. Nevertheless every member enters these groups with all of his individual peculiarities. Thus the relationship between each two members of a specific group assumes a particular character, determined by the special way in which both parties, on the basis of their individual personalities, react to each other. Tension and discord between two members of a family spoils the atmosphere in the home for the others. Possibly two siblings regard each other coolly and without understanding. This creates a dissonance in the family and disrupts the naturally warm and intimate atmosphere of family life.

At the other end of the continuum we find a social unit of a completely different nature. The working class—or any other class for that matter—numbers in the hundreds of thousands, millions, a countless multitude. The reason they appear as a social unit is because of a similarity of external circumstances, which in turn creates a similar view of life and common socioeconomic interests. As individuals, the members of a class remain anonymous to one another. Each regards the others as "people who are in the same situation as myself," i.e., as representatives of a type. And in the eyes of the others he is likewise a nameless unit among his countless equals. It is important for him, and it contributes to the way in which he perceives his own experiences, that numberless others are in the same situation. But only with a tiny proportion of these others does he ever come into personal contact. As flesh-and-blood human beings, as unique personalities, each with his own cares and joys, virtues and faults, they are of no interest to him; they are only meaningful for him in their capacity of proletarians. It may appear that a social class is a poorly chosen example, inasmuch as it is not even clearly delimited. Who belongs to the working class? That is a matter of definition. It may be that a number of those who are commonly included in this class do not consider themselves as such, and vice versa. But among the kind of social units to be described here can also be found some whose boundaries are fluid, a feature associated with other characteristics, which we shall now point out.

The Protestant church in Lower Saxony has several million members, a considerable proportion of the total population. No one expects the members of so numerous a social unit to personally embrace each other with mutual love and affection. What unites them is not a personal relationship between individuals but a religious faith, although even this is questionable in view of the great body of indifferent members. In any case, here too the members maintain a mutually anonymous relationship and are not personally involved with one another. The individual does not feel himself to be associated with every other member, but with the religious community as such, and his connections with the other members are indirect, i.e., mediated by the social unit. In this sense the church is not an association of persons, but an impersonal structure which is superimposed on the individuals concerned; it is a set of tenets, means of grace, and symbols, administered by clerical officers—pastors, deans, superintendents, and bishops.

An indirect relationship of a similar kind exists in all larger associations organized for the pursuit of a special interest or in the service of a "cause." Such social units are held together not by bonds of affection, but by those of order. Of course feelings and affective emotions may also be involved, but they are not directed toward the fellow members but rather toward "the common cause." The other members are for me only participants in the cause we have in common. The structure of such social units requires no personal affection between its members, who, for their part, expect none from each other. Lack of interest in the other members, as persons will be the rule, and personal dislike between two members need not harm the common cause, just as long as everyone remains loyal.

What makes a direct, sympathetic relationship here impossible from the start is the so-called mass structure of the social unit—above all, of course, the great number of associated individuals, which alone makes it impossible to perceive the unit as a whole. The relationship among its members is anonymous for the same reason, since no single member is able to conceive of all the thousands or millions of his fellow members as individuals. He comes in direct contact with only an insignificant minority of this multitude. All the others are for him nothing but people who, like himself and with himself, comprise the body of a large social unit, such as the nation. In this manner—and not by means of direct contact between its members—is the character of a large social unit determined. Everyone realizes that he is surrounded by "a multitude of others" with whom he has no personal contact, for the simple reason that he is physically incapable of knowing all individually. The relations between a single member and the rest are only indirect, i.e., they are determined by and limited to membership in the large unit as a whole.

Where a great number of persons are associated in a social unit, each regards the others not as individuals but as molecules, as numbered but unnamed members of the same species. The expression "mass structure" thus conveys—*lucus a non lucendo*—the idea of the absence of structure. Each lumps all of the others together, well knowing that he too is only one among many for the rest. The relationship between the members is subjected to a categorization and leveling process. One does not think of Miller, Schulz, Hofmann, and the thousand others, but thinks rather of "us Bavarians," "us Catholics," etc. The others are for me not individuals, each different from every other, but people playing the same role, and only by virtue of this role do they enter into my life.

What we have here is a *depersonalized* social relationship. One realizes that he is not bound together *with* other persons, but is engaged, the same as they are, *in* something, namely, in the objective of the social unit. This depersonalization of social relations, belonging in its more pronounced forms to a recent stage of social development, is connected with what has been called the differentiation of the various spheres of life or reality, and which has been principally approached as a problem of cultural development.

How natural it seems when we speak of economics, art,

technology, religion, science, politics, etc., as separate fields of human endeavor. It is not as if these were regarded as mutually exclusive, hermetically sealed compartments, but nevertheless as if the entire culture appeared to be functionally separated into these various branches or areas. . . .

. . . The division of the culture into different areas has its counterpart in the functional or occupational specialization of creative cultural activity. One person's purpose in life is science, others devote themselves to artistic creation, while still others are concerned with the production of economically useful commodities; still others live and work in the world of politics. But only in the creation of culture elements, in the *productive* culture process, does a division of labor between persons reflect the division of the culture into various fields of activity. Cultural life also has its *receptive* side, and here all have a share in each and every aspect of the culture. In the productive culture process the various sectors of the culture are kept functionally separate, whereas in the configuration of the cultural milieu of the society as a whole, as well as in daily life, they are combined.

They converge, meet—but even then they do not completely unite. The partitioning of the life-spheres within the culture is projected into the consciousness of the individual. He has a more or less clear idea that in the course of daily life he is constantly moving back and forth between separate spheres—from the providing of economic commodities to the sensation of aesthetic pleasure, from religious reflection to political conflict. In each of these instances he assumes the internal attitude and external posture appropriate to the circumstances. He feels and acts alternately as *homo oeconomicus* or *politicus*, *religiosus* or *intellectualis* and is well aware of this change in his mode of conduct and experience in these various roles. The professional politician presumably subscribes to a special morality of power, the executive to a special morality of business—both of which differ from (and in some points directly contradict) the *usual* standards of moral behavior. But even one and the same person occasionally acts according to mutually incompatible moral standards; in his political behavior he is guided by other norms than in the pursuit of his occupation, and still different norms apply to his relations with friends. He is fully aware that in each of these cases he is acting in accordance with different, perhaps contradictory norms. His conscience does not condemn the actions based on one moral attitude, seen from the standpoint of the other, as "immoral"; it is more likely that he will explain the discrepancy to himself and to others by pointing out that the various life-spheres and their corresponding behavior patterns are governed by different moral rules.

This alternation of roles, the conscious idea of moving back and forth between separate spheres of life and their respective situations, is underscored by the structure of the society itself; to the extent that the different human pursuits and intentions are the object of collective action, they are carried out in differing social milieus. Religious faiths, economic interests, political movements, etc., have all led to the formation of specific groups within modern society. The society is differentiated, in a certain sense specialized, in accordance with the organization of the cultural sectors.

While moving back and forth between the various cultural sectors, the individual also changes from one social unit, i.e., from one circle of associates, to another. Each of his various interests and ideas (religious, aesthetic, political, economic, etc.), together with its corresponding mental attitude and mode of behavior, is thus identified with a specific group milieu. Each life-sphere, each field of interest, has a given place in the group structure of the society.

At this point the present line of thought converges with the previous one: membership in a group distinguished by a specific type of endeavor is defined and bounded by a particular intention. The purpose embodied in a given group becomes the common denominator of the group members; it defines the basis—and the limit—of their solidarity. All other aspects of the personality of the individual members remain outside of this group relationship. What was here described could be called the *objective-detached social relationship*. The relations between members of functionally specified groups do not depend on the individual personalities of those involved; they are associated merely as participants in the same cause. . . .

The specialization of group formation far exceeds, however, the differentiation according to larger cultural sectors. Thousands of narrowly circumscribed specific goals and special purposes are the basis of association in thousands of groups. The more narrowly defined, the more precise the aim and intention of a group, the more impersonal and objective will be the relationships among its members. That is especially true in the case of goals relating to calculable, material interests. A real estate owners' association, for instance, exists for the purpose of representing the interests of its members in matters relating to credit and tax policy. Such a purpose cannot generate an affective personal relationship between various individual real estate owners; their relations are cool and rational, and in extreme cases, of a purely business nature.

Groups with *ideal* objectives appear at first glance to be of a completely different character. The struggle for world peace or for the idea of democracy is conducted in a different spirit than that against inconvenient tariffs or for higher wages. For that very reason the professional organizers of economic interest groups endeavor to find idealistic slogans in which to clothe their aims. Directed towards nonmembers, this camouflaging of egotistical motives is usually not very successful; the opponents generally see through the mask and publicly expose the hypocrisy. As a rule, however, such an idealistic superstructure is a source of strength for the group itself; in the cause of a noble idea people feel morally justified in acting collectively with an unscrupulousness which many of them would shun if it were only a question of consciously egotistical objectives. By representing the object of a struggle as a holy cause, the use of the most brutal means in its behalf can be justified.

The fervor and fanatical zeal of those dedicated to a common idealistic (or idealized) goal should not, however, let us overlook the fact that the relationships between the various members are just as impersonal and detached as in groups with overtly pragmatic aims. In both cases the binding tie is "the common cause" and not a feeling of personal affinity. Of course communist A maintains a friendly relationship with his like-minded comrade B—as long as B remains faithful to the sacred political creed. But if B dissents, this is also the end of A's friendship with him. A was never emotionally involved with B as a person, but with "the cause of socialism," and only for the sake of this cause does he have a derived and wholesale attachment to its supporters.

The functionally specialized social unit is hence in its final form not so much a group of persons, but an impersonal *system of ends, means, and functions*, an objective apparatus which the individual serves—or makes use of for his own purposes.

Between the extremes here described—the personal-intimate and the objective-detached social relationships—are to be found intermediate forms and variations. The essential fact remains, however, that interpersonal relationships, *ceteris paribus*, become more impersonal and estranged the greater the numerical size of the social unit and the more clearly specialized it is with respect to its given goal. At one end of this continuum specific persons are actually living together, at the other end there is only an abstractly organized collection of nameless individuals.

The latter type corresponds to the frequently invoked mass society of the present, whereas the former is closely connected with the organic *Gemeinschaft* extolled and longed-for by the romantic critics of contemporary society. Certainly both structural types characterize certain historical stages of development, but not in the sense that the one type is found only in the past and the other only in the present. It is indeed the case, however, that abstract and formal organization first occurs in a relatively far advanced civilization, whereas the other type of social organization is prevalent at an earlier phase. In the following we will designate the personal-intimate type (called "face-to-face group" by the Americans) as primary groups, and the objective-detached type as secondary groups.[2]

[2]   Geiger, speaking more abstractly, uses the terms "groups of the primary order" and "associative units of the secondary order."—Ed.

Primary groups correspond to direct, vital needs, whereas secondary groups satisfy complex social needs and require an entirely different psychological type. Among primitive peoples the senses and the emotions are more developed than are the intellect and conceptual thought. Their mental life is essentially limited to what is directly perceptible. Their field of social action is therefore confined to groups which are perceived by the senses as finite units comprised of such and such a number of people. But not too many people, otherwise the boundaries become indefinite and the perceptibility is lost. Secondary groups, on the other hand, require a certain capacity for abstraction. They are too large numerically, as well as too specialized in their objectives, to be grasped as units by direct sensual perception, and their structure bears the stamp of well-reasoned organization. Not only the internal structure of these groups, but, perhaps even more so, the entire social system of which they are components makes certain demands on the mode of conceptual thought of their members. The primary group embraces the individual. He is a part of it; it is the firmly banked channel in which his life runs its course. Secondary groups, however, are designed for and limited to a specific purpose. The individual belongs to a number of such groups and moves with an easy rhythm back and forth between them. In primary groups life can be mastered with *substantial* conceptions, whereas life in secondary groups is based on *functional* concepts. . . .

. . . Large groups organized on a rational, impersonal basis appeared on the historical scene long before our time. They did not come into being overnight and out of nothing, but developed step by step, becoming more prevalent with the advance of civilization. This fact should be pointed out to the romantic critic of so-called modern mass society. Even while the social form of the primary group is still predominant, the abstract social units of the secondary order begin to emerge as superstructures. But the converse of this proposition is also true: primary groups are not absent in the social system of an era characterized by secondary groups.

That is something so obvious that one is almost ashamed to have to put it into words. This is unavoidable, however, in view of the more recent social and cultural criticism, with its thoughtless, crude comparison between medieval organic *Gemeinschaft* and contemporary "atomized mass society," which gives the impression as if the mass structure has simply supplanted those former relationships of personal intimacy. But we still have family and neighbors, friends and acquaintances, colleagues and clubmates. It is an irresponsible exaggeration to assert that the social life of the present is "atomized" and that the corporative, hierarchical structure of the Middle Ages gave way to that mixture of chaos and stupid uniformity called "mass society."

The concept of mass society takes into account only one aspect of the change in the social structure which has occurred in modern society. What has really happened can be more accurately described as the *separation of the public and private spheres of life*—a basic form of the above-mentioned separation into sectors of purpose. The course of this development may be briefly described.

The glorifiers of the Middle Ages have no idea to what an extent the society of that day held the individual in its clutches. If one could sentence these dreamers to two weeks of life in a medieval society they would return thoroughly cured. In order to be oneself, one had to be a Trappist or a hermit. There must have been a great dearth of what we today call private life. There was no clear boundary between public and private spheres of activity. The primary groups in which one lived with his relatives and friends had a number of public functions as well, whereas the larger organizations which existed primarily for public purposes made deep inroads on personal life. . . .

Since that time the private and public spheres have become differentiated from each other to the extent that a specific social milieu now corresponds to each. The expression "atomized mass society" hence gives a wrong idea of contemporary life. Only in the sphere of public life has an atomization taken place, in the sense that the individual has become a mere number in a large series, a molecule in a mountain.

In economic life he is a tiny cog, forced to revolve in time with the whole huge machinery. Labor in factory and office is so thoroughly organized that activity at the lower levels is reduced to eternal repetition of a single standardized routine. Even in relatively "independent" positions in economic life, the individual's freedom of action is more formal than real. The intrinsic laws governing the system thrust him with invisible hand in the predetermined direction. . . .

In political life the individual is a free citizen enjoying equal rights, but in mass democracy he cannot get a hearing for his personal views, nor can he assert his own political will. The sole opportunity for the expression of political volition is provided by joining one of the opinion and interest blocs known as parties. The individual is merely one drop in the ocean. Even the possibility of influencing the course of events by means of his vote, as one among hundreds of thousands, is today more negative than positive. . . .

Thus in political as well as in economic life, apart from a few privileged exceptions, the individual as a person carries no weight, but only as one of the great multitude of nameless individuals. In this respect—and only in this respect—can we speak of anonymous mass society. At another level of social life, however, a movement in the opposite direction has occurred. If public life has become more public, that is, more impersonal and masslike, private life has also become more intimate and private. The same development which brought about the much abused mass existence has at the same time made possible a depth of personal, inner life previously unknown. It is this solitary form of life—being by oneself—which has gained the most by the dissolution of patriarchal and corporative ties. Moreover, certain primary groups have thus been "privatized," in that they have been relieved of their secondary, public functions. . . .

Mass existence and atomization are confined to the public sphere of life and are compensated by a corresponding individualization of private life. Mass organization here, personal singularity and intimate association there. It is not mass existence as such, but the polarization of forms of life, the *dualism of social spheres*, which is the distinguishing characteristic of contemporary life.

More than a hundred years ago, Honoré de Balzac lamented in his novel, *Le Curé de Tours:* "In our time the governments are making the error of trying to adapt man to society instead of shaping society to fit the needs of man." Today the "homelessness" of man in society is a popular theme. It often occurs in the form of a slogan which, once uttered, is repeated in chorus because it is consonant with certain moods and because it offers an easy excuse to those who are not equal to the demands of their existence and who thus feel themselves confirmed in their self-pity. With the help of the plaintive word "homeless" they try to shove the responsibility for their own failure off onto the external circumstances. No one stops to consider what this homelessness actually consists of. If the word is to have any precise meaning, it must express one of two ideas, or perhaps elements of both: (1) a kind of social atrophy or "undernourishment" (W. Röpke), or (2) an uncertainty in social orientation. The first question is then whether or not these shortcomings actually exist; if so, the second question is whether they may be traced to structural deficiencies in the society, or whether they are the result of other factors. . . .

The isolation and cold impersonality which go with the functional specificity of social contacts is a specter which the romantic social critics invoke with particular enthusiasm. There are a number of possible rejoinders to this. In the first place, in one entire segment of society, the intimate primary groups, the need for human warmth finds satisfaction. Secondly, the casual, incidental social contacts in the anonymous mass milieu hardly play such a large part in our lives as the critics would like to have us believe. Such relationships are mainly limited to the urban environment, whereas a large part of the population still lives in villages and towns. No one has yet taken the trouble, by the way, to establish how much truth there is in the phrase about the increasingly mass character of life. The limited but systematic observations I have made myself indicate that even in the urban milieu, personal relationships clearly predominate.[3] And finally, one may call attention to the fact that the anonymous mass milieu is not infrequently preferred—generally in order to avoid a confrontation with oneself. . . .

The catchword phrase about the homelessness of the individual in the society can, as we said, also refer to an uncertainty in orientation. The citizen has, in other words, no definite idea about his place in society; he is not entirely sure where he belongs and has no clear idea of the network of relationships in which he finds himself. Hence he is without roots. Supposedly this is, on the one hand, a consequence of the social structure per se, namely the abstract nature of our huge organizations and the complicated interrelationships between the various elements of the social mechanism as a whole. Karl Mannheim, for instance, is of the opinion that modern man is beset by primitive fears because he cannot grasp the functioning of industrial society.[4] I very much doubt whether men in earlier times, with their even less trained intellectual faculties, were better able to comprehend the relationships of their society, even though they were simpler. I even doubt whether this theoretical, technical understanding and insight into the working of society is of such great importance.

On the other hand, some seek the origin of rootlessness and uncertainty of orientation in the looseness of the individual's relationship to the various social bodies to which he belongs. Certain associations having profound and far-reaching effects on his life cannot be concretely perceived by him because of their tremendous proportions. That applies to the state and the nation, economic relationships, the church, etc. Here again we find the model of the "atomized mass". The individual feels himself to be a mere atom in a vast aggregate and sees himself irresistibly carried along by a stream whose direction he does

[3]   Geiger reports in detail the results of this systematic self-observation in a chapter of the original text which is here omitted.—Ed.

[4]   Karl Mannheim, *Man and Society in an Age of Reconstruction* (London, 1940; reprint Routledge & Kegan Paul, 1960), p. 59.

not know. Within such gigantic systems the coherence of individuals can be accomplished only by formal organization. That however means the existence of a perfected apparatus, consisting of official organs, material facilities, and schematic rules for their administration. The creation of such apparatus has contributed much to making a clear sense perception of the society impossible. Especially the state assumes the form of an abstract, impersonal apparatus in popular conception. The individual is subject to the pressure and coercion emanating from it without having any "living relationship" to it, and thus feels forced into a passive role. . . .

And finally, we have the highly complex differentiation of social functions, i.e., the functional specification of groups described above. While moving from the economic to the religious to the political and then to the recreational sphere, the individual is changing in the same alternating rhythm from one group to another. Each of these obliges him to fill only one functionally specific role, and each unites him with a differently constituted body of associates. In each group he plays at given intervals, so to speak, a guest role; he belongs with body and soul to none. In short: his collective existence does not take place within a firm and stable framework, but consists of a chain of situationally determined events and occurrences. This episodic configuration of social life may create confusion in a simpler mind.

However, the main source of uncertainty is probably the fact that the individual is not provided with a fixed set of social ties. He is for the most part able to move about freely within the society. It is his own affair which political party he wishes to support, and no one forces him to subscribe to any particular one. He can even choose between trade unions with divergent lines of policy, e.g., socialist, Christian, etc. Should he join a religious congregation? Which one? Should he break his ties with the one his parents made him join? Hundreds of associations, movements, and leagues cast out their lures, trying to catch followers. The individual becomes an object of competition between the groups, a competition which is conducted by all sides by means of blatant propaganda. He is torn to and fro by suggestions disguised with pseudo-arguments, or by objective arguments about matters which he has only the vaguest notion of. Not only for commercial advertising, but even more so for the propaganda of ideas do Betrand Russell's trenchant words apply: "Are we to be forced for all eternity to put up with the dictatorship which scoundrels with their seductive arts practice on fools?"[5]

But "homelessness" in the sense of orientation uncertainty is not necessarily a consequence of social degeneration. It is more likely a result of shortcomings in the deveolpment of the human intellect. A population better trained in *conceptual* thinking could not be so easily bewildered by the abstract nature of social interrelationships, by the complex structure of society, and by their own flexible and loose relationships to a number of social groups. A bit of exercise in the independent, *critical* application of healthy reason would put the average citizen in a position to choose and to take a stand, instead of being, as he is today, psychologically pushed and shoved by multivoiced, untruthful propaganda.

[5]   Geiger gives no source for this quotation, nor has it been possible to locate it; it was therefore retranslated from the German.—Ed.

2

SOCIETAS HOMINIS
SAPIENTIS

THANKS TO thousands of years of intellectual effort,
mankind has been able to subdue the forces of nature and to
create an incomparable arsenal of tools and techniques for the
mastery of its environment. This fine technical apparatus would
be able to insure us an infinitely rich life, spiritually as well as
materially, if it were not for the deficiencies, tensions, and conflicts in interpersonal relations which prevent mankind from
making full use of the existing opportunities. Occasionally,
these resources are even diverted to the purpose of mutual
annihilation. What we gain by the advance of technology we
lose by the folly of our social behavior. What Penelope weaves
by day she unravels at night.

Man makes bad use of his talents. As he is today, he is not
equal to the external apparatus which he himself has created
for the enhancement and enrichment of his existence. Mankind
is apparently not yet competent to manage its own civilization.
Why does the whole machinery of human existence function so
poorly, in spite of a highly developed technology for the mastery
of that existence? A disparity between the level of the objective
culture and the subjective development of man has been accurately identified as the true source of the permanent social
crisis.[1] Beyond this point, however, there is no consensus in

---

[1]   E. Spranger, *Die Kulturzyklentheorie. Sitzungsbericht der
Preussischen Akademie der Wissenschaft* (1926), p. 17; and many others
after him.

the evaluation of the problem of existence in our time. It all depends on the specific nature of this discrepancy, and how it may be accordingly rectified. There are, as far as I can see, three different possible answers:

1. Cultural pessimism regards the entire rational and *technical civilization* of the present as an abortive development bearing the evil seed of Satanism. Our external cultural apparatus itself is supposedly overdeveloped and hence bad. The rejoinder is that technical means as such are neither good nor bad, but indifferent. It all depends on what they are used for. . . .

2. Others see the source of the calamity in the *structure of society*. The "atomized mass society" supposedly hinders the individual in the full development of his spiritual capabilities. The fatal discrepancy exists between the structure of society on the one hand and the psychic nature of man on the other. Man supposedly feels unfulfilled and discontented in his social environment; he withers and pines away because society in its present form suppresses his deepest spiritual needs. All live human fellowship is said to freeze in a world of cold institutions and machines. Hence people no longer live and work with and for one another, but apart from and against each other, while the institutions senselessly proliferate. . . .

3. An answer can also be sought in the opposite direction. It is possible to take issue with many serious flaws in the makeup of modern society—but its mass structure does not belong to this category of ailments. The incongruity between the social structure and the psychic nature of man has its origins not in the degeneration of society, but in the fact that man is retarded *in his personal development*. The objective civilization has rushed ahead and left the subjective one behind. In comparison with the achievements of their objective culture and civilization, people are social imbeciles. The problem is to advance the level of personal development of the individual to that commensurate with the structure and apparatus of his society.

Where this idea occurs—and it is really not very new— it is generally directed at human moral standards. Our knowledge and know-how, and the power which they give us over things and events, demand the highest level of morality. Otherwise this power will be used not for constructive purposes but for annihilation. The fatal discrepancy is therefore seen to obtain between the intellectual and the moral level of man's development. With respect to mass society in particular the following argument can then be found: mass society is an established fact and an inevitable stage of development. Social life however is a matter of morality. As the radius of our social relationships increases, we must accordingly learn to embrace ever larger, less directly perceptible masses of fellow men with our moral sentiments and to open our hearts to the brotherhood of the human race. Our capacity for moral conceptions is too narrow and inadequate. It encompasses those nearest to us, but is incapable of fostering a living sense of responsibility for those outside our everyday circle of acquaintances.

At a later point I will explain in detail why I do not place all too much importance on morality in the usual sense. For now I will only advance the thesis: *The technical apparatus of civilization as well as the structure of society demand, quite to the contrary, a shift of emphasis in favor of the intellectual powers, a systematic intellectualization of the individual and his training in emotional asceticism.* What is here meant, it should be noted, is not only advancement of the intellect and sharpening of the faculties of the mind. Of course this too. Mainly, however, a modification more than an augmentation: a readjustment of the form of life. What is involved is the encouragement of a more intellectual, less emotional attitude toward social life. The *homo intellectualis* must be led to victory over the *homo sentimentalis*.

Concurrent with this development, an *individualization* is also called for, a shifting of emphasis toward the solitary form of life. In modern society there is not so much a lack of "togetherness," but rather, in a certain sense, too much of it. The average person is not sufficiently capable of defending his inner independence against those social bodies which he is dependent on for his external existence. With all due reservations I wish to make a plea for the *emancipation of man from the community*, i.e., for his liberation from certain forms of emotional collectivism. It is not necessary to point out that an individualization in this sense goes hand in hand with intellectualization and is unthinkable without it. . . .

Why, however, should man be adapted to the structure of society? Why not vice versa? . . . There is only one compelling reason to accept people as they are and to modify the society accordingly: the immutability of human nature. The familiar phrase that "it is simply human nature" is, however, a cliché and frequent repetition will not make it any more true. The mentality of the European apparently underwent certain changes between the time of Aurignacian man and that of Thomas Mann and Niels Bohr, and there is no particular reason to believe that the average man of today is the last word in evolution. Karl Mannheim also regards a transformation of man as not completely out of the question,[2] and in this connection it makes no great difference that he is referring to a change in the moral character rather than in the intellectual one which I am speaking of.

. . . I contend—and will later demonstrate—that the average contemporary habit of mind is anything but the general standard of human nature. It is not the "nature of man" but a cultural product—unfortunately an inadequate one. If there is one thing which is fundamental to human nature, it is man's nearly infinite adaptability and modifiability. I certainly have no desire to see human nature forced into channels which are alien to it. On the contrary, what I have in mind is the realization of possibilities which have hitherto been neglected. Our educational system not only steers intellectual development into the wrong channels, but it also plasters over the intellect with a phony cult of emotionality. I shall return to this point later. . . .

Life in a modern society can, in the long run, only be mastered by a highly intellectual type of person.

1. The composite nature of the contemporary social world requires a highly developed mind on the part of the individual

[2]   Mannheim, *Man and Society*, p. 70.

living in it. He moves, day in, day out, in a field of social groups and reference systems in which he must be able to find his way about at all times and without hesitation. In each of the constantly changing social situations he enacts some membership role, now of this social unit, now of that one. In each of these situations he finds himself confronted by an entirely or partially different assortment of partners, and to each situation there corresponds a particular kind of conduct, dictated by custom and convention. "Social tact"—by virtue of which one acts, reacts, and does the right thing at all times in accordance with the given situation—is by no means to be attributed to instinctive assurance alone. Self-observation may seem to indicate that our conduct in a given instance is not the result of conscious deliberation, but rather that we adapt to the situation and the atmosphere "automatically." Granted that in actual practice this adaptation comes about subconsciously and instinctively; nevertheless the acquisition and exercise of this instinctive activity presupposes a high capacity for abstraction. Those who are less gifted and intellectually underdeveloped do not possess that natural self-assurance which one needs in order to move without difficulty in a highly heterogeneous social milieu. It is also evident that the less educated segments of the population generally move in more closely circumscribed and less heterogeneous social fields. In the case of children, it is significant that entry into the complicated society of the adults occurs simultaneously with the growth of the capacity for abstract conceptual thought, i.e., at about twelve years of age.

Orientation in the social field becomes a problem for the intellect because of the individual's freedom to move about between the social units of his environment. He has to find his equilibrium between them by himself, that is, he must bring them into a functional relationship within his social field in order to give it structure. This problem is not faced by people in a hierarchical-corporative or other form of stable social order. In such *monocentrically* organized societies the functional relationships of the various social units are fixed and determined in advance. By the fact of birth into a family and clan, more is defined than just the individual's social field and range of movement. Between his position in society on the one hand, and the objectively given functional relationships between the various social units on the other hand, his connection to each of these is also clearly established. It is entirely different in the case of the *polycentrical* (or centerless) modern society. Since the numerous groups and other units within the loose fabric of this society are not organized into a specific pattern of vertical and horizontal interrelationships, the connection of the individual to each of these and his position at the intersection of a multitude of social circles are not fixed in advance, but are largely left up to his own choice and the course of fate.

2. The above remarks bring us to another aspect. The actual social field (i.e., the real associations) of the individual never involve more than a small portion of the total fabric of the society, and one might expect that even simpler souls should be able to grasp such a limited area. Indeed, people are usually quite able to find their way around in their limited social fields. The social field of each individual is, however, only one segment of a total social context of gigantic proportions. Social processes which originate and evolve far away from that social field in which the individual feels at home never cease to affect him and interfere with his life. They restrict his freedom of action, influence the way he is treated by his associates, and lead to changes in his material living conditions. In short: these distant occurrences have repercussions across the sea of society in the form of waves or ripples finally reaching the shore of the individual. For the comprehension of *these* social relationships the average person is not adequately equipped, either in terms of knowledge or intellectual abilities.

Relationships which are too complex for the common man to grasp are found, however, in every society which has advanced beyond the most primitive stage of development. But in former times this never constituted a particular problem. If one compares our era with the Middle Ages, the essential difference is found in the fact that the lay population formerly regarded the order of the extensive social whole as ordained by God and humbly submitted to their fate. In a hierarchical-corporatively organized society the individual did not have any deeper insight into the complex ramifications, but, on the other hand, neither did he directly and actively participate in the larger social units. In contemporary society, however, the individual is directly implicated in these wider relationships, and is even called upon to cooperate in the democratic management of them. That undoubtedly requires, in view of the complex structure of our society, a considerable amount of intellectual ability. The only ones who will claim that today's average citizens are equal to these tasks are those who consider it democratic to flatter the masses. . . .

3. In the above discussion regarding the difficulties of grasping social interrelations we established that the complex interaction of numerous functions and processes exceeds the horizons of individual experience. Incomprehensible in another sense, however, are the various larger units within the modern society. It was mentioned above that nations, classes, churches, interest groups, and other associations are inaccessible to the direct sensory perception of their members. The individual is not able to conceive of such a large unit as a particular number of persons with whom he is united, but thinks of it as an abstract entity. If, moreover, one stops to consider that the majority of these larger units play a functionally limited part in the life of the individual, and that their formal apparatus is developed to the highest degree, then there can be no doubt that that sector of social life which is the province of the secondary groups presupposes the capacity for conceptual abstraction and an essentially intellectual attitude.

At this point it also becomes apparent that more is involved than merely raising the average intellectual level. In the present context the intellectual attitude appears as the antithesis of affectivity. Where the large-scale secondary groups operate, feelings and emotions must be subordinated to an intellectual attitude. Intellectualization in the truest sense is needed, i.e., a fundamental reorientation of attitudes and motives. The large-scale social units—and also certain less sizeable but highly specialized groups—do not entail the living together of persons, but are rather objectively founded systems of coordination, organization, and functional specialization. They are not based upon sympathetic affinities, but on a rational order. In this sector of social life and activity, therefore, the *homo intellectualis* has the last word, the *homo sentimentalis* must remain silent. . . .

There is a gaping disparity between man's mental nature and his external apparatus of existence, including the structure and organization of his society. Expressed in the language of Turgot and Comte, this would mean that the society, with respect to its structure, has reached the "positive stage of development," whereas man himself is still in the "metaphysical stage." Only an intellectualization of man can overcome this disparity. Unfortunately, the very word "intellectualization" will probably make many readers shy away. They sense the threat of a crippling of the emotions, an inner impoverishment, a kind of barbarization.

It must therefore be pointed out with the greatest of emphasis that intellectualization, as I understand it, means exactly the opposite. Man should by no means be weaned away from his emotions. What an absurd idea, by the way! The role of emotions and irrational ideas in social life will, however, be submitted to a critique. This role will be judged positively as well as negatively, depending on whether emotions and irrationalities contribute to amicable harmony or to disruptive antagonism, whether they are constructive or destructive.

Collective emotions are of two kinds. I will call the first *community feeling*. It is an affective sense of solidarity among individuals. It is the cement binding primary groups together, where a limited number of specific persons meet and live together. An entire sector of the society is hence the legitimate realm for collective emotion, where it may peacefully contribute to the profit and advantage of those whom it unites. That applies to the intimate, personal groups and relationships, that entire realm of social life in which the individual associates with others whose names and faces are familiar to him. . . .

On the other hand it was demonstrated above that another sector of the society has no place for collective emotions of this kind, but is by virtue of its entire structure geared to another kind of sociability: the "mass society" and the functionally specific groups. This is not refuted by the fact that community feelings are talked about in this connection as well, and that preachers of social devotion, grossly miscalculating the span of human sympathies, exhort to brotherhood and love between millions. Such efforts to "idyllicize" social life may be well-meant, but they remain nevertheless nothing but false sentimentality.

Can it really be that community feelings have no place in mass society and in functionally specific associations? Must not these forms of social life also be infused and supported by a spirit of fellowship and Christian love? The most absurd of all the precepts of Christian teaching is its main one: "Love thy neighbor!" Other people are not (except for a fairly limited circle) my neighbors, but strangers. I do not love the other person, but at best respect and preserve his integrity. For his part, he neither expects nor desires to be loved by me; he is quite contented if I let him go his own way. He does not care for a brotherly love which, as a rule, is manifested by someone wanting to convert him to some kind of "true faith." None of the Christian precepts is therefore so seldom followed as that of the brotherly love. It is a topic for the Sunday sermon, but no rule for daily conduct. I may be called cynical, but I cannot see any sense in propagating wonderful norms which nobody follows—the priestly guardian of the norm no more than his flock. Should the norm, even if not realized by any living person, nevertheless serve the purpose of providing some distant goal to be approached gradually? There is nothing to indicate that during the last two thousand years the capacity and will of man to embrace the whole of humanity, regardless of how personally near or remote, in a feeling of brotherly love has made even the slightest progress. The believers, under the skilled leadership of their clergy, were far too busy trying to decide by murder and violence in the name of which god they should love their neighbor. It rather seems as if Christianity, via that cult of emotional life, that contempt for the intellect which it has in common with other religions, has thus far made us unfit for an advanced form of social life in which men can live together in peace and compatibility—and that for the simple reason that no one demands of them that they should "love one another." . . .

It is true, however, that emotions play an extremely important part in mass-units as well, but these emotions are of a completely different nature. One is deceiving himself and others when he tries to represent them as interpersonal feelings of affinity. In the larger units one is not directly united with other persons, but stands in rank and file with a mass of others. Affective ties can only bind me to specific other persons, not to an indiscriminate mass of others. I can, however, easily harbor feelings for a cause which is also a matter of great importance to a mass of others. In this case I have no direct relationship to the others as specific persons, but rather an indirect one to them in their entirety as followers of a cause to which I too am dedicated. This kind of collective emotion is not affinity for others, but *pathos* for a common cause. Therein is rooted the *heroic* social attitude, as the antithesis of the idyllic attitude may be called.

Collective emotions of this kind do exist and sometimes attain a high degree of intensity. In a theoretical analysis of society, this must be recognized and accepted as a given fact. Pragmatic social criticism, on the other hand, cannot be denied the right to agitate against this state of affairs, and social policy-making may then devise means for changing it. . . .

3

NATIONAL FEELING AND
CLASS CONSCIOUSNESS

LIKE THE SYMPATHETIC community feeling, pathos for a common cause also acts as social cement. But with an important difference: the cohesiveness of persons in primary groups based on the sympathetic community feeling is not directed antagonistically toward the outside world. Such groups are inwardly oriented and in a certain sense, self-sufficient. Even when a number of people are bound together by mutual affinities (i.e., sympathy), it does not follow that they harbor any aversion or antagonism toward third parties. Sympathy for one person does not necessarily imply antipathy for someone else; it is, on the contrary, a positive feeling which distinguishes my relationship to certain persons from my indifference toward others. The Schulz family feels closely united, without therefore being on bad terms with families Miller or Wernicke. Only in the defensive do primary groups become belligerent. When such a group feels threatened from the outside, or when an outsider makes trouble for one of its members, its solidarity assumes a belligerent character.

The situation is entirely different in the case of secondary groups which are based on pathos for a common cause. This pathos binds the individual with strong ties to the group, creating at the same time a schism between him and all of those whose pathos is devoted to another "cause." The reasons will be given in greater detail below why this is so. First, however, we will describe the fact itself, using national feeling and class consciousness as examples.

It is impossible to define the nation adequately without making use of the concept "state." If the state is ignored, the concept of nation is left entirely without any substance of reality. As an actual phenomenon the nation consists of millions of people owing allegiance to a sovereign prince or president, being ruled by one government, following the same laws (to the extent that they do not violate them), and paying taxes to the same department (to the extent that they do not evade taxes). The nation is an organized body of individuals. Beyond this the concept has no tangible substance.

There is, however, such a thing as a national feeling, a national consciousness; no one will deny that. But that is not a matter of interpersonal sympathy.[1] May the flame of national feeling burn ever so brightly, it can never embrace the millions of unknown, anonymous compatriots as persons, but only the nation as a whole. National feeling is pathos, the fervor for a cause—the national one. But what is this "national cause"? The substance of this cause, that which the national consciousness clings to is, when reduced to its basic elements, a body of symbols, living or dead: king, seal, flag, and anthem—behind them, however, an ideological mist, a ceremonious void.

Indeed, ideologies are in their own way realities, namely to the extent that people actually believe in them and are guided by them in their actions. That is, they are psychic realities; their substance is chimerical. And it must be asked whether such psychical realities should be preserved or picked to pieces. . . .

In daily speech the distinction is made between the praiseworthy demonstrations of national feeling or patriotism and the malignant ones of nationalism or chauvinism (jingoism). As far as I can see, there exist between these "good" and "evil"

---

[1]   In a preceding chapter, here omitted, Geiger analyzes the concepts "state" and "nation" to show that they refer to large-scale secondary groups, which—as already indicated in the earlier discussion—cannot be based on affective community feeling. People only delude themselves into believing that as members of the national "community" (*Volksgemeinschaft*) they are bound together by affective ties. The true substance of national cohesion is rational and impersonal rather than affective.—Ed.

attitudes and modes of behavior only vague differences of degree. No one has ever heard a chauvinist describe himself as such; he says he "loves his country." No nationalist refers to himself in these terms, but rather as a "good German," or Frenchman, or whatever. There is no basic difference between the good and evil forms, no standard by which to determine where the one ends and the other begins. Only one thing is certain: give the devil an inch and he'll take a mile. The good patriot with noble national feelings is at least potentially a nationalist—and will turn into one in the hour of temptation. We are told that the aggressive sentiments associated with nationalism, chauvinism, and jingoism clearly sets these apart from inwardly oriented, peace-loving national consciousness and patriotism. As Edith Cavell stood before the German firing squad, she is reputed by legend to have said: "Patiotism is not enough. I must have no hatred in my heart." Sentimental woman that she was, she did not realize that this is exactly what is impossible: to be a patriot without admitting any feelings of enmity into one's heart. They may be carefully hidden, disguised beyond recognition, deeply buried, but they are lying in wait for a "righteous occasion" which will unleash them.

National feeling cannot be content with simply being inwardly oriented. This would require the nation to be a directly perceptible circle of persons from the point of view of the individual. As a whole, the nation can only be grasped in terms of its boundaries, and therein lies the heart of the antithesis: a nation exists only by virtue of the political boundaries which separate it from other nations.

This is a highly unsatisfying situation for the emotional attitude. An intellectual position on the matter would simply be reconciled to the fact that the course of history has led to the creation of certain territorially limited entities. These limits are the result of past power struggles. As long as these organizational entities, called states, fulfill a social function and one is forced to belong to one of them, one loyally submits to his role within it.

The advocates of community feeling refuse to accept such

a sober attitude and have another explanation. The boundaries and what lies within them must have a more sublime significance, must be exalted to something holy. The feeling seeks an object of veneration, and since no such object is to be found in reality, a chimera is invented: the holy cause of the nation, the nation itself as the highest good. These ideologies prefer to ascribe their origins to an alleged *ésprit de la nation*, a *Volksgeist* or national character, the soul of a people, or the distinction of a nation. In self-admiration one contrasts his own character traits with that of the others, without regard for the fact that such differences are extremely vague and, if they exist at all, are to be found in a variety of a thousand shades. The own traits are raised to types, thus giving an image of *the* German (Dane, Italian, etc.), not as he is on the average, but of the "true" German (Dane, Italian, etc.). Such an idealized sum of traits, a national supra-ego, put into sharp relief by juxtaposition with corresponding, but less flattering stereotypes of other nations, is then glorified as "the German character." This idol is further attributed with the familiar way of life found in the national region and with allegedly typical national cultural achievements. The historical legend provides this conceptual amalgam with a precious plating. This national idol is the focus of the national feelings. The imaginary substance of the idol is produced by a hectic search for that which supposedly distinguishes "us" from "them," by taking an artificially distant approach to oneself. The idol originates as the negative of the image—just as artificial and exaggerated— which has been created of the neighboring peoples. . . .

The nation, then, is a conception without substance. Hence it can only come to life in an antagonistic relationship to an opponent, or at least to a vis-à-vis. Nationalism ranges foremost among the phenomena which Simmel had in mind when he spoke of "the negativity of social behavior."[2] The national idea originated in the struggle against the dynastic territorial state. The struggle against this adversary gave the nation life

[2]   Georg Simmel, *Soziologie* (Berlin, 3rd printing, 1923), pp. 359 ff.

and meaning. With the rise of the democratic nation-state, the nation lost the monarch and the privileged estates as its domestic adversaries. All of the aggressiveness, the life-giving strength of the nation, has now turned outward. Without a real or imagined adversary it cannot exist. Everywhere that true national community—brotherly solidarity in the positive sense and inwardly oriented—is put to the test, it fails. No love unites the members of the nation. But in enmity and hate, in outward aggression and defense, there is solidarity. Even where for the sake of national community warnings are uttered against internal dissension and class struggle, one often detects a covert purpose: a redoubling of efforts to unite the militant forces in order to deal an outward blow.

At this point we may devote a word to imperialism. Contrary to the (for many years almost unchallenged) dogma, according to which imperialism was supposedly a concomitant of capitalism, it today appears more and more to be a direct function of nationalism. Not only has it been demonstrated that capital interests do not profit by the imperialism of states, but these interests are even directly menaced and jeopardized by it. Every imperialistic war to date has weakened the position of capitalism. War always means a provisional restriction of economic freedom of action, and the recent past has shown that the state is little inclined to restore in times of peace those freedoms which have been suspended as a result of wartime measures. Even the excess profits which capital interests, particularly in the defense industry, allegedly make on war contracts are of a questionable nature. As a rule these profits are soon dissipated by the favored parties. That wars result in a significant *redistribution* of capital is beyond all doubt, but it has not been proven that they are generally advantageous to capital interests. The small and middle-sized savings investments will be wiped out, but what the major financial interests thus gain in the way of concentration, they lose many times over in terms of the consolidation of labor unions and increasing demands from that quarter. The most that can be said regarding the connection between imperialism and economic interests is this: Depending on the configuration of the historical situation, imperialism assumes various forms—and one of these, under certain circumstances, is economic imperialism. But neither the imperialism of Macedonia under Alexander, nor that of ancient Rome, nor the Swedish imperialism of the Wasa kings and the insane Charles XII can be explained and understood in terms of economics.[3]

Imperialism in its various historical and particularly its military consequences appears to be an outgrowth of pure power-lust, the craving for power for its own sake. The true agents of imperialism, therefore, are the political rulers and their attendants, cliques, or beneficiaries. They are only able to find support for their imperialistic aims among the general public if they are successful in awakening and maintaining a sentimental, lyrical nationalism and a fetishistic belief in "national honor."

Nothing is sillier than this talk about the "honor" and "greatness" of a nation as something of meaning or value for the people, as something which is worth making sacrifices for. We may recall Göring's speech in Hamburg, in which he stated that "butter only makes people fat, whereas iron makes it strong." Why should people have any desire to be "strong" in this sense? Or "great," be it in terms of warlike deeds or be it in terms of territory, numbers, and power? Such heroic clichés owe their effectiveness entirely to the sounding board of a national myth, in whose name the insatiably power hungry partly persuade, partly coerce the people to make sacrifices for a specious national honor. What's in it for the man in the street? Only the aftereffects of the intoxication: a hangover the next morning. As Linklater put in the novel *Private Angelo*: When the great nations fulfill their historical destiny, millions of simple lives collapse in ruins. . . .

---

[3]   Dr. Uli Hertz, of Uppsala, has communicated to me personally that his analysis of the struggle for influence in the Near East has shown with certainty that economic interests in oil were only the third determining factor, both political and strategic interests being of greater importance.

The same feature, the same aggressive spirit, is also to be encountered in the so-called class consciousness. This too is pathos for a cause, in many respects in contradiction to that of the nation—although in the Soviet world it has been converted into a national feeling. Here a process takes place similar to that occurring in the case of the revolutionary bourgeoisie. Bourgeois national consciousness is first directed inward against the dynasty and the privileged estates; because of its nebulous character, however, it can only be sustained by animosity and must hence turn outward when these adversaries have been eliminated. In the same way, the struggling proletariat has its inner adversary in the bourgeoisie. If, with the triumph of the revolution, the bourgeoisie disappears in the "classless society," class consciousness is refashioned into Soviet national consciousness. In this way it may continue to exist, sustained by its antithesis to the "capitalistic" nations even after it has lost its function as the consciousness of a struggling class.

The idea of antithesis is implicit in the concept of social class itself, since it can only be understood in connection with the concept of class society. "Class" in the singular is absurd. As a social unit it is only conceivable in contradistinction to its anti-class. We may speak of class antagonism wherever the members of two or more segments of the population, called classes, have differing, supposedly irreconcilable interests as a result of differences in their social position. If the class antagonism is based on a conflict of interests, this would appear to demonstrate that this animosity is not the product of pathos without a real object, but of hard facts. There is indeed a difference between national feeling and class consciousness, inasmuch as national feeling has no other substance than itself, whereas class consciousness, at least in its origins, is related to real conflicts. It will now be shown, however, how class pathos dissociates this animosity from its foundations in reality, transfers it into an ideal dimension, and intensifies it to a vehemence out of all proportion to its actual object.

It would be childish and naïve to assume a complete absence of internal tension and friction as the normal condition of society. As long as men live together, thousands of occasions will arise for dissension and disputes. It may be desirable, however, to limit conflicts to those instances in which something is involved which can be realistically disputed about. I now intend to show that the class struggle, up to a certain point, has a *something* as an object, but beyond that—a *nothing*.

The conflict of interests between classes apparently means that within a society based on the division of labor certain segments of the population will be dissatisfied with their living conditions and will aspire to better ones. This is the "interest" of these persons, and interests belong to those emotional realities which one must accept as given. When a number of people have interests which coincide, the desirability of union for the purpose of pursuing these common interests is obvious and expedient. The aim and intention of the union should be the improvement of one's own living conditions—presumably at the expense of other persons or groups.

The working class of modern times has pursued this goal with good results through its labor unions, which were effectively supported by the *Realpolitik* of the labor parties. The history of these disputes makes two things evident: (1) The class of the wage earners did not have completely coinciding interests, but partly diverse ones, and that they therefore formed numerous interest groups, between which frictions occasionally arose. From the standpoint of real interests a "proletarian" class does not exist, but only a plurality of interest blocs. (2) Conflicts of interest can be potentially resolved by amicable agreement and compromise. The history of the struggle over wages and working time is the story of a series of compromises between employers and employees. The workers achieved their greatest actual successes not in the fervid revolutionary periods of their class struggle, but in the phases characterized by negotiation and peaceful settlement. That is connected quite simply with the rational aspects of the interests in question. When someone has an interest in this or that thing, it is clearly an emotional matter. But if the object of the interest is something real, action will be guided by a rational consideration of the relationship between means and ends. Pure conflicts of interest are always conducted in accordance with considerations such as: What do I have to win? Are my resources sufficient? Which means promise the greatest success in proportion to the effort and expense? How much sacrifice and risk is the goal really worth? That means that a pure, rationally conducted conflict of interest only exposes the society as a whole to a minimum of shock and destructive side effects.

Seen as a whole, the working class (and its anti-class, the bourgeoisie, as well) has no common interests to defend, and hence it is not organized as a corporate whole. What supposedly welds together and unifies the entire class, in spite of and transcending these organizational schisms, is the so-called class consciousness. But the sole substance of this consciousness— the "sole" because every other is inconceivable—lies in the feeling of hostility toward the anti-class. The ostensibly positive common goal is an idol and a figment of the imagination: the socialist society of the future. This socialist society is nothing but the anti-idea of the existing bourgeois-liberal social reality. By negatively idealizing this reality in the bugbear of "capitalism," its obverse is raised to the positive ideal of socialism.

This is the goal of the class struggle. In its first phase the socialist society appears as that order of things which alone can provide the wage earner with tolerable conditions, whereas in the existing "capitalistic" society he must, because of its power structure, be forever underprivileged. In this phase of the struggle, therefore, the connection can still be seen between class interest and class ideal. The struggle for a socialist future determines the political ideology of the labor parties and the activity of other revolutionary organizations. The socialist order is depicted and extolled as "just." But since the evaluation as "just" cannot look for authority to any kind of objective and generally valid standard—such a thing does not exist—one can only regard it as an oratorical expression of the fact that this social order is the one most congenial to the interests and desires of the speaker.

With the label "just" and the password "social justice," an

ideology is created which imparts an air of holiness to the plain and sober interest. Since the idea of socialist society is the negation of the existing social reality, being otherwise of nebulous or at least of ambiguous content, this idea is able to enlist in its cause the great, dissatisfied masses of the population, in spite of the fact that their real interests differ considerably. The idealistic password is thus able to array a very broad, united front with a negative objective (i.e., destruction of the existing order), whereas if only realistic considerations and positive goals were involved, there would be an instable system of various interest blocs. Thus the conditions are created for a battle of far greater proportions, a battle far more fraught with serious consequences for the society as a whole, than could ever result from a mere conflict of interests. Moreover, the so-called "idealistic" goal encourages the spirit of battle. One does not wrangle for base selfish interests; one goes into battle as an idealist for the holy cause of mankind. One is not party to a power struggle, but a crusader for the highest values. A dispute over concrete interests does not exceed the limits of reasonable risk; idealism and hate, on the other hand, do not shrink from self-destruction.

Thus in the second phase of the class struggle the idea becomes separated from the real basis upon which it was founded, the interest. In its tactics and strategy the class struggle thus gets out of proportion to its original objective: improving the living conditions of the struggling class. First one strives for the socialist social order as the only one capable of putting an end to the misery of the wage earner—as the means to an end. Soon, however, the means become an ideal end in itself. It is now no longer primarily a matter of what socialism, when realized, can offer the worker, but rather that the worker must make sacrifices for the realization of socialism. *Realpolitik* creates better, even unexpectedly favorable living conditions *within* the existing social order. The demagogues are not pleased with this situation. On the contrary, such successes are a thorn in their side. They attempt to deny them, explain them away, occasionally even obstructing voluntary reform measures on the part of the bourgeois anti-class on the grounds that every improvement in the standard of living threatens to dampen the militant zeal of the masses. The anxiety is certainly exaggerated. At this stage of the movement, the masses are already so thoroughly fanaticized and blinded by doctrine that they can no longer see their practical goals through the haze of the idea. Those engaging in moderate *Realpolitik* are even attacked with the argument that the realization of the socialist social order is the vital objective, hence the material circumstances in which the people live are of secondary importance. It is betrayal of the class to be diverted from the strict line of the class struggle for the sake of mere material advantages. When the masses have once been intoxicated by certain catchword phrases and conceptions, the politician trading in ideals has a far greater chance of being heard than those practicing political realism.

Thus the concern for the happiness and prosperity of the members of the class is succeeded in the class struggle by an heroic enthusiasm for the holy cause of the class. The earlier struggle for concrete goals becomes a struggle for the chimerical, a struggle for its own sake. For "the cause" is an ideology —a *nothing* inflated to sublimity.

Community in pathos for a cause is always hostile and belligerent toward those who espouse another cause. The binding tie is not love for one another but hatred of the out-group. Put less trenchantly: the common cause always unites the circle of its followers by creating a gulf between them and the others. And the common cause draws its unifying power, and even its substance, only from this contrast to an antithetical cause. . . .

Collective emotions of this kind coincide, in a very general sense, with the heroic social attitude. The common cause transcends the persons who serve it. The individual is called upon to make sacrifices for it, even to the point of sacrificing himself—for the nation, the class, the faith, etc. People are enjoined for the sake of their cause to annihilate each other—be it in a figurative or a literal sense. It is an unfounded and absurd contention that men cannot live without a sublime purpose for which they can fight, sacrifice—and die. The demagogues have never asked us whether we prefer bread and peace or slogans and the sword. We have never had a free choice.

The following chapter will answer the question, why the community of pathos is necessarily of a belligerent nature, and will establish what actually constitutes the object of such a community.

4

THE EMPEROR'S BEARD:
VALUE COMMUNITY AND
VALUE CONFLICT

A "COMMON CAUSE" to which one is fervently devoted is usually described as a "good." A good is a real or alleged something which presumably partakes of, represents, or embodies a value. To be united in pathos hence means to hold certain value-conceptions in common. We therefore speak in this sense of value community. The persons who unanimously espouse the nation or socialism or some other cause as a good, together comprise a value community. As members of such a group they are not united directly by mutual feelings of sympathy, but indirectly by the value-conception and their common dedication to that which supposedly embodies or partakes of the value. What is the substance of the value-conception? How do such conceptions come into being?[1]. . .

Behind our value judgments lie our emotional and volitional relationships to the objects of our environment and the events which we observe or to which we are exposed, as well as attitudes toward situations which we wish to realize or prevent. We call such emotional attitudes of approval or disapproval concerning given or imagined realities *primary valuations*. Something may appeal to me, something else disgust me. The

---

[1]   In the original text there follows a detailed discussion of the nature and genesis of value judgments. This has been omitted except for a few paragraphs; the reader is referred to pp. 132–42 where the matter is treated extensively.—Ed.

primary valuations are made in and with such acts of emotion. Our daily life is an infinite series of such evaluative acts. They are behind every action, every choice we make between two or more alternatives. Without the motive force implicit in primary valuations life would come to a standstill. The primary valuation is the emotional reaction of a person to an object. That A is fond of strawberries but detests tobacco are his primary valuations of these things. Such valuations can be neither criticized nor discussed; they are simply psychic facts. . . .

But how does it happen that the emotion with which one reacts to an object is transferred to the object itself as one of its presumed characteristics? In this event what is intrinsically subjective becomes objectified, thus providing the opportunity to make allegedly valid statements about the (aesthetic, moral, etc.) value of the object. The explanation may lie in the fact that the emotional reaction regularly occurs together with the perception of the object, so that the observer *constantly* associates it with an objective phenomenon. Thus for those not trained in epistemology, the emotional reaction fuses with the factual observation and description of the object and itself assumes the form of a theoretical statement about the object. Since every time and without exception, whenever I see and smell putrid flesh, I experience a feeling of repulsion, putrid flesh assumes in my mind the quality of *being* repulsive. This connection between emotional reaction and object becomes especially close if the same emotional reaction is experienced as constant not only by myself but also *in general* by the people around me. My own emotional reaction to the object is then confirmed by the same reaction of others and its overt expression. The general consensus of emotional reactions feigns the existence of an objective fact. If *all* (i.e., most) of the people around me abhor the idea of sexual intercourse between brother and sister, this act appears to be bad per se. Such consensus of subjective reactions is especially to be found in connection with the moral, including the social and political, evaluations which are reinforced by social rewards and sanctions. The denial of objective validity for such value judgments therefore encounters much stronger resistance in the general public even today then the exposure of the subjectivity of sensual or aesthetic evaluations. The recognition that moral value judgments have no factual validity whatever first became possible only after the previously existing consensus in moral evaluations had disappeared. . . .

Disagreement in regard to primary valuations merely means that the likes and dislikes of people differ, that one person wishes one thing and another something else. No one would ascribe any other meaning to his own primary valuations than simply that his own emotional make-up causes him to react in one way and not another. If, however, ideal value-conceptions are superimposed upon the primary valuations—as is usually the case—the situation is completely changed. By conceiving it as an ideal value, the primary valuation is raised to the level of objectivity, i.e., it claims objective validity. Whoever evaluates differently than myself "is wrong"; he is either ignorant or deluded, or simply a knave. At the level of the primary valuation I find myself with no possibility of criticizing the unpleasant fact that others have desires and evaluations other than my own. At the level of the value-idea, on the other hand, I may criticize these evaluations and value-conceptions deviating from my own as unfounded, wrong, and reprehensible, inasmuch as I claim general validity for my own. At both levels, therefore, value conflicts *can* arise—but these differ with respect to their nature and their social effects.

Disagreement over primary valuations of sense or taste does not give cause for conflict. It is of no consequence for those about me whether I prefer roasted locusts or steamed snails, whether I prefer to take my vacation in the mountains or at the seashore. If such primary valuations were to be raised to the level of ideal value-conceptions, we might even encounter conflict at this stage; but we will ignore that possibility here. It seems that in primitive societies there are norms, or at least conventions, even with respect to matters of sense and taste which cannot be deviated from without arousing public displeasure. But only in *primitive* societies. It may be noted that the more primitive the society, the more likely it is that the social environment will interfere with the evaluational attitudes of the individual. Hence one may conclude that further development in the direction of more refined social conditions will see a concomitant decline of such interference.

Moral, legal, and political primary valuations, on the other hand, are of general significance. One cannot have private property *and* full nationalization, democracy for one part of the population and dictatorship for another. Here primary valuation corresponds to the subjective (individual or collective) wish to preserve or bring about this or that state of affairs, and he who has this wish will strive to see it realized. The fact that others have a contrary wish and work towards its realization is for him a real obstacle, just as in other cases the forces of nature may stand between him and the attainment of his desired goal. The conflict is purely objective; it is a conflict of opposing forces. I may complain about others having different evaluations and desires, but I cannot take offense as long as I —remaining at the level of the primary valuations—regard these as psychological facts not enjoying ideal status. Implicit in the value-ideas superimposed upon the primary valuations, however, lie pretensions to greater dignity. The value-idea is normative, is above man. By virtue of the moral, legal, or political value-conception, that which I desire becomes a value in itself; if it is something which I do not just *want* to see realized for my own sake, but which I myself am *obliged* to realize. Whoever bars my way is wrong. He is an enemy of the good. . . .

Social class and the nation were cited in the preceding chapter as illustrations of the fact that community in pathos for a cause is of a belligerent nature. It cannot be otherwise, it was contended, and therefore there is little point in preaching reconciliation between the classes and pacification of the nations. Community in pathos for a cause is rooted in value-conceptions, and all value communities are heroically belligerent. That lies in the nature of the value-idea per se and in the structure of thinking in terms thereof. The value-idea is dogmatic and precludes every other value-idea. To experience something as a value necessarily means to confront it with the negative value of its antithesis. The idea "good" is only conceivable as the opposite of "bad"; "beautiful" has meaning only as the negation of "ugly." The meaning of the concepts themselves postulates their antitheses as hypothetical possibilities. Nothing could be called good if it were not compared in the mind with the notion of something which is taken to be evil or bad. Value concepts are polar concepts, that is, they are meaningful only in antithetical dichotomies.

The immediate consequence thereof is that every union in collective pathos for a good, a value, takes a hostile attitude toward those who espouse an opposite value-conception and hence hold something else for a good, a value. One cannot be enthusiastic about democracy without hating fascism; one cannot espouse the socialist order without damning the capitalistic one—whatever people may associate with these nebulous terms. Common advocacy of a good enveloped by pathos is the unanimous negation of everything which contradicts this good.

The motive of antagonism, the hostile rejection of other value-conceptions is implicit in the value-idea itself. Thus the conditions of social existence are undermined when a population occupying the same territory splits into opposed camps over values. Toleration of values would be betrayal of what is most holy. A value implies the normative demand for conformity, for realization in the world. If groups holding different values are separated by geographical boundaries, it is at least conceivable that each will cultivate and realize its social values in its own territory and let those on the other side of the border be happy after their own fashion. But if one population under a common organization and occupying the same territory becomes split over values, and to the extent that there is a balance of power, each of the value communities makes it impossible for the others' values to be realized within the same milieu. Thus everyone will be dissatisfied. If one value community is more powerful, it will coerce the others into a way of life con-

tradictory to their values: one set of values violates the opposing ideals. Even complete value-chaos—a situation in which
each individual adheres to his own particular values—would
be preferable to this. It would be harmless by comparison, since
no one could even think of trying to enforce his own values
against all the others. Conflict over values becomes more disastrous for the society as a whole the more it leads to the formation of fixed fronts, especially if these fronts are few and
extensive and large masses thus stand behind the opposing
value-conceptions. . . .

But when seen from a loftier point of view, are not such
battles of ideas, as senseless and murderous as they may appear,
necessary? Is not every new social development motivated by
a value-idea which has found a following? Without a struggle
for value-ideas, therefore, would there be any development of
the society? The question must be allowed whether "development" is an end in itself. What is the sense of a development
which is not one for the better? But every development, every
change, is obviously "for the better"—before it has occurred,
as long as it exists only in the imagination of its advocates. From
any value-idea whatever the most wonderful utopias may be
derived. But has such a utopia ever been realized? Only in the
form of a travesty of itself! On the other hand I would suggest
that those changes "for the better" which actually come to pass
are not the fruits of, but rather are effected in spite of, the battle
of ideas. Unvarnished conflict of interest and sober compromise
would lead to the same result—and at a lower cost to society.

Value community is a community about nothing, since the
value itself is imaginary. The reality behind the value-idea is
the primary valuation; the value as an ideal reality is a castle
in the air. Is this not, however, merely a semantic problem?
Does it make any difference whether the basis of a given collective relationship is described, correctly, as a unanimity in
the evaluation or, incorrectly, as a community sharing a value?
Does it have any practical significance that the so-called value
community is nothing but a matter of those who share the same
evaluation finding each other, and that common evaluation, the

concurring emotional relationship of a number of persons to the same object, only subsequently acquires the superstructure of an imaginary value? No, it would make no difference at all if these persons *really* concurred in their primary valuations. Value community as such is belligerent, but that we could bear if only the controversy had an object, if the members of the value community were at least really united in something, even if it then be: united against others! But the conflict has no object, the unity no substance. The value community is nothing but a pitiful self-deception.

What really happens is most peculiar. Pseudo-objective value-ideas first appear in the form of a superstructure for subjective emotional relationships. Then, however, these imaginary value-ideas become themselves the objects of secondary emotions. First we describe a mode of behavior as good because it appeals to us, whereupon we become enthusiastic about the idea of "good" or sermonize about "justice." The emotions are diverted from their original object in the world of reality and transferred to the value-idea, even though this is nothing but a pseudo-objective interpretation of the primary, evaluating emotion. These secondary, derived emotional relationships to the conception of value, to the value-idea, can be described as *value-feelings*. This enthusiasm for the value-idea is therefore an emotional commitment to deceptively objectified emotions; it is a narcissism of the emotions.

Collective pathos for a value-idea offers no guarantee that there is any concurring primary valuation of certain realities underlying it. And the same thing applies to goods which one fights for, assuming the good to be the realization of the value-idea. . . .

The value community is a community of the catchword slogan without intelligible meaning. Hence the tremendous importance in our society of words and symbols, insignia and emblems.

Words supposedly express value-conceptions, symbols represent them. The people who espouse socialism or democracy, who worship the Christian God or the nation, who are dedicated to freedom or justice, are by no means of one mind about the value-conceptions subsumed under the respective verbal formulae. Nor is it simply a matter of minor differences in the interpretation of a value. The most fundamental aspects of the value, the determinants of the value-experience, are at issue. This becomes evident every time that a movement based on ideas is ruptured and broken into factions by an internal conflict over values—and that eventually happens to every movement in the course of its struggle for the realization of its idea. The value-experience, and the value-idea which is supposedly its substance, are highly subtle miasmas. It is entirely impossible to communicate their total meaning to others and thus achieve true agreement with respect to the idea.

What actually happens, therefore, when a multitude of individuals come to be "bearers of the socialist idea"? Each of them associates the word "socialism" with certain conceptions which appeal to him, often very complex and unclear conceptions, which even waver and fluctuate in his own mind. How should he be able to make them absolutely clear to others? Such ideas assume countless different forms in the minds of different individuals. In any case it is impossible to establish how much consensus there is in the conceptions themselves. Max Stirner was painfully conscious of this incommunicability of individual conceptions: "What I say I don't mean—and what I mean cannot be said." The often cited value community is neither agreement on the value-idea nor on its underlying evaluations. It is at best the collective worship of a word. The word does not express a collective value-idea; a common word merely conceals the diversity of evaluations. The word is a monstrance before which millions kneel, each worshiping a different god or idol.

The value community is a community of word fetishists. A word—only a word—unites them. For the sake of the word they are prepared to do battle with those who worship other words. If however they approach the materialization of their word fetish there will be a falling out, since they were only united in the word, never in its meaning.

And what of the symbols? The symbol is supposedly a visible representation of the value and of its followers. The value is something ideal, a conception, and is inaccessible to direct, sensual perception. The mass of those who subscribe to the value is likewise not perceptible as a whole. The value community therefore needs the symbol as a rallying sign, representing to the individual the idea itself and the community of its followers. Without a unifying, admonishing symbol, the living community would crumble and wither away. So we are told. But only the last sentence is true. Its truth was experienced by Protestantism. A great refinement of religiosity lay in the rejection of the Catholic cult of symbols—of relics and images, of rituals and ceremonial spectacles. God, not God's image, shalt thou worship! But Catholicism had succeeded in uniting millions of persons in a cult of symbols, under which the *essentia Dei* was buried. Protestantism abolished the archaic cult of symbols, with the result that the church disintegrated. In God men are divided, and that in which they could be united, the symbol, has been taken from them. Catholicism creates a union not in faith, but in superstition. Protestantism is contemptuous of a union in superstition and still pursues, after four hundred years, the chimera of a community in faith. People can be taught to worship one image, but they will always have a thousand gods.

If the value-idea could bring about a living community, if people really felt united in the idea, then they would have no need for symbols. The symbol is not the material representation of the idea, but replaces it. It is the painted scenery in front of a gaping void. It symbolizes—nothing. . . .

"And even if men really worshiped only words, even if their community in the value *were* self-deception, that still does not alter the fact that an emotion actually unites them. Here too, therefore, the emotion proves to be a force which creates community." This is essentially the reasoning of the social irrationalists, and even Karl Mannheim follows in their tracks: ". . . the irrational is not always harmful but, on the contrary, it is among the most valuable powers in man's possession when it acts as a driving force towards rational and objective ends or when it creates cultural values through sublimation, or when, as pure élan, it heightens the joy of living without breaking up the social order by lack of planning."[2] It is not clear from the context which irrational phenomena Mannheim had in mind. Of course it would be foolish to reject and combat every irrational impulse. All emotions are irrational, and no one can or will "eliminate emotional life." No intellectualization can ever eliminate parental love; on the other hand no cultivation of the irrational will ever lead people to love other children as much as their own. Emotions as vital relationships of persons to other persons or things are inevitable, irrational phenomena, and emotional ties which bind us to others are socially constructive. All the arts are irrational. Aesthetic emotions find expression in artistic creativity, and the work of art releases aesthetic emotions in the contemplator. Both enhance and enrich life— and why should they be detrimental to society?

But what about the "irrational driving force towards rational and objective ends"? Inasmuch as every driving force, every choice of a goal necessarily belongs to the realm of the irrational, this sentence, taken literally, would be sheer nonsense. Mannheim apparently means something else however. In a given social situation, certain measures must be taken for the attainment of a proposed end. The individuals are possibly for the most part agreed in their primary valuations of the objective. But the ways and means available for the attainment of the end are unpopular. The masses do not want to listen to a rational argument. On the other hand it may be possible to convince them of the necessity of the measures by appealing to certain irrational value-conceptions. But that does not mean that "the irrational" in this case is socially constructive. It only means that in order to create a certain public opinion, one may take recourse to the irrational when reasonable arguments fail. It would undoubtedly be preferable if people were responsive to the rational insight into the connections between ends and means, i.e., if it were not necessary to appeal to their collective

[2]   Mannheim, *Man and Society*, p. 62.

pathos with value propaganda. In this instance the irrational is only socially "useful" because the intellect is not sufficiently awake. The invocation of collective value-emotions, however, militates against such an awakening. It can be demonstrated, by the way, that "the irrational way to a rational goal" is dangerous and often has bitter consequences.

With the "irrational in the service of rational ends" Mannheim himself does not seem to have been thinking only of irrational persuasion as a substitute for rational arguments. He actually believes, as may be inferred from many of his statements, in the rationality of certain objectives, as for instance when he ascribes to the social sciences the tasks of employing the critique of ideology to discover the "correct" policy by means of a synthesis of all current political ideologies.[3] Reason, however, can never govern the choice of an end. No objective can ever be "rational." Only the connection between a chosen end and appropriate means can be described as rational. Simply stated: reason never tells me what I should want, but only how I can achieve what I want or avoid what I don't want.

Returning to our starting point I will say this: I have nothing against the irrational as such—life is full of it—but only against one of the forms it takes, namely, the collective emotions associated with value-ideas. . . .

If however collective pathos, because of its belligerent nature, is a public menace, if aggressiveness is the direct and inevitable result of the intolerance inherent in every value-idea, then should not criticism be directed against value-thinking itself, instead of against the collective pathos which is only one of the forms it takes? . . . I think it can be shown that the collective cult of value presents a constant threat to society, whereas the devotion of the individual to value-conceptions remains relatively harmless.

The value-idea is intolerant, for it is the emphatic negation

[3] See Karl Mannheim, *Ideology and Utopia* (London, 1949), and my own detailed criticism of his view in Theodor Geiger, *Aufgaben und Stellung der Intelligenz in der Gesellschaft* (Stuttgart, 1949), pp. 61 ff.

of its anti-value. This remains the same, whether the value-idea is espoused by one or by many. Every value worshiper is an "idealist," and this honorary title seems to be a license for any kind of infamy. Every idealist is potentially dangerous to society. His value-idea is a condemnation of all contrary value-ideas; and since every ideal implicitly demands to be realized in the world of fact, the idealist is committed to stifling every attempt to realize contrary value-ideas and to destroying the forces acting in the service of the anti-values. Value-toleration is an internal contradiction. The idealist is ipso facto intolerant. Since the value is a highest good, the toleration of its anti-value can only be a betrayal and desecration of the holy of holies. If, however, the idea of tolerance itself is the value to which he subscribes, then he must persecute with redoubled intolerance those who are intolerant and seek to obliterate them from the earth for the sake of mankind.

Nevertheless, the individual cult of value is relatively innocuous. The individual idealist and worshiper of a value, may his intentions be ever so fanatical, does not have the power and means of doing any great damage. With respect to society as a whole, the individuals' cult of a value means only that they differ in their value-experiences, i.e., in the dream world. The unification of idealists into a front is a first step, leading unavoidably to the next, the antagonistic collision of such fronts—which in reality fight not for the sake of the value-ideas, but for the magical words.

Unfortunately all belief in values, all idealism, tends toward a collective cult. The believer seeks others who share his faith. This is an immediate consequence of all value-ideas and an unmistakable sign of their vanity. It is the nature of value-ideas to elude all rational explanation. The value-idea which is only believed in by a single individual is a "crazy idea," laughed at by others. Only when he finds others who share his blind faith can he vindicate himself. In the company of others it is easier to bear the ridicule of the world. Being confirmed by others frees me from being responsible for the absurdity of my belief. The product of imagination which is only believed by one person is gibberish. The gibberish to which many have been converted is a religion. That is why all worshipers of values are so interested in proselytizing, and that is why the more followers a faith has to begin with, the better its prospects of gaining more. The nonsense which is subscribed to by millions is truer than any demonstrable thruth. And if millions support the faith, they can use their power and the weight of their numbers, if not for the realization of the idea, then at least for the extermination of the heretics. . . .

Propaganda for ideas and collective cults of value and belief are almost as old as human society itself. Why should they be more problematic, more dangerous today than in the past? . . . The voluminous literature on mass psychology seeks to make the urban way of life responsible for those unrestrained outbreaks infused with irrational pathos, which are so characteristic of the contemporary social system. "Mass man" is supposedly especially responsive to suggestions and casy to fanaticize.[4] But this conclusion is ill-founded and based on an inexact use of the concept of mass. The mass, which can be proven with relative certainty to be especially suggestible, has a very special structure. It is a great number of persons in a specific state, characterized by (1) close physical agglomeration and (2) psychic concentration on a center of attention and experience. A political rally, a crowd of demonstrators, or a mob are examplcs. There is a heated atmosphere and an emotional tension present from the beginning. A suggestion which is consonant with the existing mood of the mass has the prospect of finding acceptance and enthusiasm. What is generally referred to as urban mass existence, however, is of a completely different nature. When many live crowded together in a small area, the mere density of population is something entirely different from the actual local congestion of the mass. And the urban population is anything but psychically concentrated on a common center of attention. *In these respects*, therefore, there are no grounds for supposing that the city dweller is especially sug-

---

[4]   This view is also expressed by Karl Mannheim, *Man and Society*, pp. 60 ff.

gestible. A statement which is justified with regard to "masses" in one particular sense is here misused to insinuate a judgment about the "masses" in an entirely different sense.

In another respect, however, the city does have a peculiar feature. Thanks to the anonymity of the urban milieu, the diversity and lively competition of intellectual activity, a large part of the urban population has no stable relationship to any given irrational conceptions, including value-ideas. Urban man is not *more* suggestible, but is rather less predetermined with regard to the *kind* of suggestions to which he is responsive, and hence unpredictable and easily swayed.

This puts a new light on Mannheim's contention that the irrational susceptibility of persons is especially dangerous in the urban mass society because of the uncontrolled emotional outbursts occurring in this milieu. In a society firmly structured in terms of clearly delineated groups, irrational impulses would be guided into established channels and directed toward objectives and goals which are desirable from the standpoint of the group. That is of course true, but it will not check the destructive effects of the emotions. What is a desirable goal for one group can very easily be disastrous for the society as a whole.

This brings another aspect of the question into view. The locally accumulated mass is responsive to a suggestion having a bearing on the object of its momentary attention. The same high degree of susceptibility is also found, however, without any actual local congregation in every value community based on pathos. A swarm of patriots is whipped into hysterical fervor by a national catchword, the followers of a sect ardently respond to a religious call to arms.

The increased menace of propaganda for ideas has nothing to do with the structure and attitude of the urban population, but is rather a matter of the technical means and organizational possibilities of the propaganda itself. The communications media—the dissemination of the printed word, the radio, the press, the modern propaganda industry—make it possible by incessant repetition to effectively mobilize great numbers of people in a very short time. These publics become dangerous by virtue of their sheer size because, once fanaticized, they easily slip out of the control of their hidden manipulators. The contemporary form of large-scale organization makes it possible to transform widely dispersed masses, mesmerized by irrational slogans, into efficient cadres under a centralized leadership. If it then comes to a conflict of arms in the form of war or civil strife, technical means of such devastating effectiveness are available to make the earth tremble in its very foundations under the impact of the encounter. . . .

The progress of technology cannot be turned back. Hence only one way remains open to us: to make the individual equal to his technology and to his instrumental apparatus through intellectualization. Whoever wishes to see neither the permanent war of competing value-ideas, nor its elimination within a society through stupefying regimentation (coinciding with redoubled fanatization directed toward the outside) must choose the third way: the education of the individual to abstinence from collective pathos through intellectualization.

5

THE BONDS OF

LARGE-SCALE SOCIETY

TOLERANCE of the values of others is insufficient, even if it were possible. The tolerant person is in any case of the opinion that whatever must be tolerated is somehow "wrong." Tolerance is to him a virtue, not something to be taken for granted. All tolerance has its limit where even permissiveness finds that "that is going too far." The only attitude appropriate for life in secondary groups is *emotional asceticism* and *value abstinence.*

These words alone are an outright provocation to the prophets of community emotionalism. Should the last traces of human warmth really disappear from our relationships with fellow men and society be turned into an unfeeling wasteland? After all that has been said, the reader will know by now that such intentions are completely foreign to me. No one would think of inhibiting the development of warm human relations— where they are able to develop. They can do so in the direct, personal relationships of the primary group, and there they should and will continue to thrive in the future—to the joy of us all. In secondary groups, however, the prerequisites of such relations are not given. It is futile to encourage them artificially, and it is foolish and dangerous to stir up surrogate emotions. . . .

Social interdependence means two things. First, that people are dependent on one another for the maintenance of their phy-sial existence, and second, that they have a psychological need for social intercourse with their own kind. In the following we will distinguish accordingly between *external* and *internal inter-*

dependence. The first is manifested in orderly cooperation, the other in emotional community. External interdependence assumes the form of the united effort of a number of persons for the satisfaction of various kinds of needs. Internal interdependence manifests itself in sympathetic relationships between persons; one could almost say, as spiritual communion. The ego of the one is interwoven with the egos of others. He more or less identifies himself with them, in extreme cases to the point of complete surrender of the self and total fusion. He cannot separate himself from the others or be torn from them without experiencing it as a kind of spiritual mutilation.

In societies with very primitive structures, one and the same social unit is held together by external as well as internal interdependence. Each accompanies, complements, and strengthens the other. Civilization and culture, however, develop separately. Technological devices and methods for the satisfaction of needs are improved. The division of labor becomes more specialized and extensive, and the circle of active persons united in external interdependence becomes ever greater. At the same time the standard of living rises and demands for the benefits of material existence increase. This process, which the social economists describe as the succession from the household to the municipal, national, continental, and finally to the international economy, has its counterpart in all fields of human activity and reaches its zenith in the global culture. This social evolution, however, is accompanied by an individual one. With the development of his intellect, especially the capacity for abstraction and conceptual thinking, man changes from a herdbound animal to an individual personality. The inner life of the individual gains independence, not in the sense that he retires from the community with others, but rather that he learns to distinguish between being-by-himself and being-with-others as two different modes of life and experience, between which he alternates according to situational circumstances.

As a result of this double course of evolution, the concrete forms assumed by external and internal interdependence become fairly well differentiated. The development of technical instruments and methods produces a rationally organized apparatus of material existence. The collective operation of this apparatus, i.e., the sum of devices and institutions by means of which we are able to master life, requires a rational organization of those cooperatively engaged. The circles of interdependent persons thus gradually become so extensive that sympathetic community with so many exceeds man's span of affectivity. But the moment that cooperation in external interdependence is no longer guaranteed by a community of feeling in internal interdependence, objective order must step into the breach. People learn—but unfortunately have only learned insufficiently—to join forces even without feelings of mutual sympathy. . . .

While the primary groups continue on the basis of internal interdependence, the secondary groups are only held together by external interdependence. That is the society of which Kant was speaking when he said that the individual would prefer to withdraw from it, but could not get along without it. Here people are linked with others, not because they are attracted to each other, but because of a mutual need for one another.

The conditions under which this external interdependence can be effective are the behavioral order and intellectual cultivation, basically the same thing seen from two sides, the objective and the personal. The order is that system of organs and that regularity of action which enable the social unit to fulfill its functions. Intellectual cultivation is that attitude of the individual enabling him to fit into the existing order.

Readers of an idyllic or lyric turn of mind may indignantly reject a society based on "cold calculation and self-interest," and will rebuke the author for being a hard-bitten cynic. His cynicism, however, consists in the simple observation that calculation and self-interest are social forces—and who would attempt to deny that? Would this fact become any more palatable if sweetened with the rhetorical romanticism of the community? Calculation and self-interest are, by the way, completely legitimate motives—solemnly condemned by a poorly understood Christian love-ethic, but never tamed and by no means abolished, least of all among its believers and prophets. Finally, however, the terms "cold calculation" and "self-interest" are negatively biased expressions for the fact of external interdependence. While correcting this bias we shall have an opportunity of explaining more fully: Why *intellectual* discipline? Or put the other way around: Why not a refinement of *morality?* . . .

If morality is called a social phenomenon, it means that "the isolated individual" knows no moral norms and needs none. Like law, custom, mores, and convention, morality is an order of interpersonal behavior. The distinction between these various orders is, however, a relatively late product. In the "First Morality" they are indistinguishably combined. It is *the* social order of behavior in primitive social groups, and is thus simply the *technique of social interdependence.* . . .

It would lead too far if we were here to go into a detailed account of all the transformations which lie between the moral situation of that time and ours. Taken as a whole, the process may be represented as a divergent development of morality and law as two separate, if interconnected, norm systems, as a progressive spiritualization and internalization of morality and, in the other direction, as an institutionalization and externalization of law. What interests us here above all is the development which morality has taken.

The spiritualization of morality occurs in the following main stages, which can only be alluded to here. The primary valuations of modes of behavior, finding expression in collective applause and displeasure, are first objectified as characteristics of the actions themselves (good and evil), upon which magico-religious conceptions (taboos) are superimposed. The moral authority is transferred from the collective self to a supernatural divine instance. With the evolution of abstract thought, the qualities Good and Evil presumably inherent in the concrete modes of behavior become generalized as a result of conceptual realism and elevated to value-ideas. The actual collective behavioral order becomes a morality of values. It is not necessary to repeat here in detail which psychological mechanisms are involved in this transformation. The value-idea of Good then becomes an object of ethical speculation. First there are attempts to define the substance of the allegedly real value-idea, and then to derive a code of norms from this definition. Up to this point, therefore, a system of merely habitual, value-free rules of behavior become, as the result of the attribution of primary values, a traditional morality, followed by (1) abstracting the value-idea Good from those modes of behavior regarded as being good, (2) moral speculation about the substance of this idea, and (3) deduction of dogmatic moral systems from it. The latter first appear in connection with religious revelation, and are therefore dogmatic theological value moralities, deriving their claim to general validity from revelation and faith. The profane, dogmatic philosophical value morality directly succeeded the traditional morality in ancient Greece (with Socrates). In post-medieval Europe, it succeeded the theological moral systems. With respect to the modern Western world, the schism of revelations and theological moral teachings was attributed by the emergent thought of the Enlightenment to human incompetence and superstition. By the correct use of moral reason it was thought possible to found a generally valid—because objective—moral system. These attempts of the moral philosophy of the Enlightenment were not quite new, inasmuch as the Scholastics had already developed by logical methods a "natural" morality of a lower order. Kant's work represents the climax of this search for an objectively founded and hence universally valid morality. At this point we will temporarily interrupt this train of thought and turn to the internalization of morality.

It was, I believe, Alfred Adler who described the conscience as social fear. When applied to the "First Morality" that is correct. The social group is here the moral lawgiver and judge at the same time. With the imposition of a religious superstructure upon the social behavior models, social fear (i.e., fear of social sanctions) was augmented by the fear of God, which remained the arbiter of moral conduct in the stage of dogmatic theological morality. Christianity still needs the omniscient

God, the all-seeing eye of God, that is, the belief in an instance superior to man to check his proclivity for "evil." Only with the advent of dogmatic philosophical morality was the judging authority finally imputed to the moral personality itself.

But this internalization process involves a change in the *object* of morality. The social group is mainly interested in the external conduct of its members, and this conduct is watched over by the respective "others." If moral judgment is first the function of the all-seeing God and then transferred to an inner voice, the *object* of the moral judgment is no longer merely the act, but also the idea, the temptation, the desire, the intent, the motive. That means, however, that the scope of morality goes beyond the vital interests of the social group. One has advanced from a morality of deeds to a morality of thoughts. In this respect, too, Kant represents a culmination point: the moral quality of action does not so much lie in the act itself as in whether or not the act was motivated by a sense of duty.

At this point we must briefly consider the law as a social order. The divergence of morality and law has a formal and a substantive source. As morality becomes increasingly spiritualized, i.e., related to a suprasocial authority (the Godhead, duty, a supreme value-idea), law becomes secularized, i.e., attributed to the mere temporal authority of the social group. Herein lies the formal differentiation between law and morality. The substantive one, however, lies in the fact that with the increasing internalization of morality, it exceeds that which can be subjected to interpersonal responsibility and controlled by society. Thus law becomes the sum total of the "enforceable moral norms," the unenforceable ones being relegated to the conscience of the individual.

Now we may return to the allegedly objective morality based on "moral reason." All appeals to moral reason have proven incapable of overcoming the moral schism, and attempts in this direction end by giving the moral value-idea of the good a substance which is general enough to insure it a wide reception. In this diluted form the value-idea is so vague that it becomes possible to derive a large variety of practical moral norms from it. The schism has only been transferred from the level of irrelevant discussions about the value-idea to the level of practical rules of conduct which could be derived from it, i.e., that level which alone has any interpersonal significance. . . .

The impossibility of resolving the schism between the dogmatic moralities, especially the impossibility of objectively founding a practical morality on rational principles, led inevitably to ethical relativism and subjectivism, to an ultimate dilution, even evaporation of value morality. The value of the good is retained as an ideal entity, but it is left up to the individual himself to provide this value-idea with substance. The internalization of morality thus reaches its climax as the moral personality becomes not only its own moral arbiter (conscience), but its own moral lawgiver as well.

The schism between the dogmatic moralities already makes morality a social order of dubious certainty. To the extent that moral value-ideas, and hence the behavioral norms derived from them, significantly deviate from one another, the members of the society cannot live together in compatibility and security on the basis of morality, but will instead become embroiled in quarrels about *which* moral principles should insure their compatible coexistence. With its subjectification or relativization, morality loses all power to regulate social life. In principle one may be tolerant, that is, each may concede the other the right to follow his own conscience. But in practice there is no tolerance, for to act according to one's own moral judgment is to violate someone else's moral value-conceptions.

Everyone knows that people in general do not make any use of the autonomy which has been granted to them by ethical subjectivism. Subjectivism, especially in ethics, has therefore not led to the anarchy of individual moralities, a general chaos. Its social significance lies more in the *legitimation of conflicts between group moralities*. As long as the philosophical belief in the objective general validity of a morality is maintained, the schism between the dogmatic moralities merely means that in matters of morality the one side is right and the other is wrong. And in the practice of social life the side which is right is naturally the one which has superior power. Ethical subjectivism nullifies this easy solution.

The historical sequence of philosophical theories of morality, closely interconnected with the history of thought in other fields, is also directly related to the history of the social structure. In the post-classical European world an essential feature of this development appears to be that small and undifferentiated social units grow into vertically differentiated large units, whereupon the double process previously referred to begins to occur: the personality becomes more and more emancipated as an independent singular entity, whereas the society becomes a complex system of organized units, composed of mobile individuals. The latter is what is usually called "mass society."

The emancipation of the personality as the basic unit of the society corresponds closely to the internalization of morality described above. The traditional or dogmatic theological morality corresponds essentially to a corporatively structured society. The control of moral conduct here lies in part with the conscience of the individual, but at the same time it is most effectively supervised by the other members of the group. The individual owes his position and standing within the society at large to his place in one of the component groups. He is bound to it and subject to its law. Here too there is a moral plurality, not in the sense of a schism, but rather in the form of variants. Knights, artisans, peasants, clergy are all Christian in different ways, but they are all Christians, and the various forms of their Christianity together constitute "Christianity" as a form of social life. The "value community" embracing them all is only the philosophical expression for the stable, centrally oriented social structure which comprises them. The deviant is an outsider and his value-conceptions are criminal heresy.

It is not of consequence here whether budding aspirations of the personality undermined this social structure or, vice versa, whether the crumbling of the social structure opened the way for individual emancipation. Presumably both tendencies mutually favored and strengthened each other. In any case the social structure has become less rigid since the fifteenth century. Intrasocial tensions grew into antagonisms between fronts. Slowly the vertical structure gave way to a horizontal stratification. That took place in connection with the decisive changes in external living conditions, growing prosperity, urbanization of the culture, enlargement of the world view through the major discoveries, overthrow of the cosmology, etc. Simultaneously, deviant moral philosophy ceased to be mere social maladjustment of isolated individuals and became a mass phenomenon. With the Reformation the schism of value-thinking in Europe became final.

The bourgeois era which began with the Renaissance and Reformation, came of age under Absolutism, and culminated in the Great Revolution, apparently tended to create temporarily once more a comprehensive value community in the interest of the national idea. Below the surface however the disintegration of value-thinking continued, encouraged by the social effects of industrialism and the intellectual effects of the critical, positivistic, and empirical schools of philosophy. At the turn of the last century this process had for the most part run its course.

Mass relocations in the social strata, mass migrations from the village to the city, and a general reshuffling brought about by industrialism and population growth ruptured traditional social ties and knocked the pedestal out from under the icons of the past, forcing the individual to find a new equilibrium in a new environment. After belief in authoritative dogmas had been shattered by the rationalism of the Enlightenment, this new orientation in value-thinking, free from the inhibitions of faith, was determined by impulses emanating from the social milieu.

The teachings of enlightened Liberalism, in the meantime, propagated a social world view based on the model of the dynamic equilibrium. In this image there is no unifying, harmonizing superstructure. The parts are held in balance automatically by the mutual neutralization of opposing forces. The antagonism itself becomes, in other words, the structural principle of the society. The schism of theological or philosophical moral dogmas is no longer decisive for value-thinking, but rather the antagonism of class moralities created by the social structure itself. Bourgeois and proletarian morality may serve as an example. (Aristocratic and bourgeois morality would not have been any less suitable.)

Since the Reformation, the bourgeoisie has evolved a form of estate morality with Christian overtones and superimposed this on its social living conditions and conceptions of society. The nucleus of this morality are the bourgeois virtues of industry, thrift, loyalty to contractual obligations, respect for property, and family responsibility. But moral standards do not remain in effect much longer than it is possible to conform to them, at least approximately. The enumerated virtues, however, were for the worker of the pre-interventionalistic industrial society either pointless or impossible. As long as the individual worker experiences his incapacity to meet the generally accepted standards of bourgeois virtue as his personal fate, he feels himself inferior and an outcast. But if the common fate he shares with others leads to an integration of the class, the impossibility of meeting the bourgeois standards will be experienced as a collective, class fate. As a result the so-called class consciousness gives rise to a new set of anti-values and a corresponding anti-bourgeois morality. The class morality is one component of the total class ideology.

The moral schism of the confessions and the psychological personality types—quietist and activist, religious or political man, personalist or institutionalist—is thus compounded by the moral schism of the classes and other strata. Peasant and urbanite, businessman and scholar, worker and employer, each have their typical value-conceptions and codes of value and correspondingly diverse, often sharply contradictory (property law!) moral concepts. Progressive social differentiation removes these groups ever farther from one another and alienates them in spite of democratic efforts to neutralize discrepancies. As the general (though conventional) religious convictions lost their influence, moral conceptions become increasingly the product of the diversity of social milieus and perspectives.

What does all this have to do with ethical subjectivism?

Nothing directly, but indirectly a great deal. If the moral value-idea has no *objectively* definable substance, then its subjective interpretations enjoy equal rights before the bar of philosophy, just as the social strata underlying these various moral ideologies enjoy equal rights in the democratic state. The theory of value subjectivism legitimizes the schism of the group and class moralities. In other words, we can in good conscience no longer demand from others, or even expect, that they will act according to our own moral value-conceptions.

At this ultimate stage of internalization, morality has lost all power to regulate social life. Seen as a *social* order, value morality has been led ad absurdum by its own development. We can, platonically, allow each other the personal autonomy of moral principles, but we cannot live together in one world according to different moral principles. "Law can't be made for individuals, as individuals. There can't be a law for you, and a law for me, except in our minds. There has to be one law covering both of us, like a blanket. Maybe our feet will stick out, but. . . ."[1] If the value-ideas of the individuals or the subgroups within a territorially circumscribed society are divergent, the requirements of social interdependence cannot be fulfilled by an order based upon value-ideas. Nor by a legal order, to the extent that it appeals to moral (or other) value-ideas. One may argue that there is still basic agreement on the moral value-conceptions underlying social life; that our social order is principally based upon a classical stoic and Christian heritage of moral conceptions which, in spite of many deviations in particulars, we all have in common. But that is not true; it is pious self-deception. We are today divided on the most fundamental moral conceptions—not only differing but diametrically opposed. Think of the property morality of the capitalist member of the middle class and of the socialist laborer; the work morality of the wage earner and of those who are economically independent; the achievement morality of the scholar or free-lance professional and the businessman; the evaluation of human life

[1]   This comes from an American detective story, but is nevertheless correctly and impressively formulated.

on the part of the pacifist and the power politician and his following. Each of these pairs represents two different worlds, and the clefts between them grow constantly deeper.

The philosophy of value nihilism itself is a theoretical counterpart of this social situation characterized by the divisions of value-thinking. That is not to say that value nihilism is a mere ideology, only valid in the context of the present state of value-disunity. It is a newly discovered, generally valid truth. But it was the disunity of value-thinking which occasioned the discovery. General consensus on values concealed the unreal nature of the values.

If we can no longer get along with one another on the basis of moral value-conceptions, then we must find a basis for compromise apart from them. The "Last Morality," the only one which is today feasible, must therefore resemble the "First Morality" in that it is value-free. Social life requires now as ever, that everyone be able to anticipate with relative certainty how everyone else will act and react in certain typical situations. Compared with this certainty of expectation, the specific kind of behavior which is customary in situations of a certain type and hence generally expected, is of secondary importance. In the name of a value morality I can only act according to the dictates of my *own* value judgment. And it must outrage my moral consciousness if in the name of moral value-ideas I am treated by others in a way other than what seems moral to me. But I will be even more outraged if society as such, in the name of moral value-ideas, forces me to behave in a way which, according to my own value judgment, is immoral.

But some kind of modus vivendi we must have. And indeed, we have one: habit, tradition, social pressures of various kinds, but above all the legal order, supported by the constellation of power in the society, provide us with rules of conduct insofar as it affects others. That these orders today appear either inadequate, or that they at any rate can only effect external compliance in the face of tenacious inner resistance, thereby creating bitter feelings of moral violation—that is the consequence of their claiming to possess the validity of values.

Social interdependence imperiously demands an interpersonal order which is generally complied with. Since we have been divided in our value morality, even shaken in our convictions regarding the validity of values, the sole motive for compliance with an interpersonal order of conduct is the recognition of its vital importance; in other words, rational insight into social interdependence itself.

I know what objection will be made: "Every social order will always run counter to the wishes and opinions of some social group or other. Nothing is gained by removing it from the level of values, which means to found it on sheer power. Resistance will not be slighter, it will even be encouraged." Now, in the first place, it is not the ideas developed here which found our social order on power. It is founded on power, but the power camouflages itself. The decision as to which value-conceptions will dominate the social milieu does not depend on the sublimity of those conceptions, but on the power of the groups espousing them. In the second place, inner resistance will actually be reduced. It is annoying and perhaps oppressive to comply with norms one dislikes. But it will be felt an outrage to be urged to comply with certain modes of behavior which are contradictory to one's own value-conceptions on the grounds of their moral value. If the social group renounces its appeal to value as a motive for obedience, it becomes easier for the citizen to suspend his own value judgments in actual social behavior.

Conformity to the existing social order (while reserving the right to strive for changes in it), based on the realization that social interdependence is a plain necessity of life, is certainly also a morality. But it is a morality other than in the usual, value-ethical sense. It stands and falls directly with the practical renunciation of value judgments. It is intellectual discipline. It is a social morality implying a high level of intellectual development.

In this sense I wish to contradict the popular proposition that man is not morally equal to his civilization. He is not equal to it intellectually. It is absurd to expect social recovery from a heightening of value morality after the pluralism of value moralities has been recognized. What makes today's world a nightmare is this very struggle of value-ideas, especially those of morality, seeking to be accepted as generally valid. Inasmuch as this dispute cannot be decided by intellectual weapons, it is conducted with iron ones.

We will now consider how the "morality in its final form," the intellectual discipline described above, will work in actual practice.

The individual may inwardly rebel against the fact that he is implicated in a gigantic system of interpenetrating, interdependent relationships, but he will not change it. He himself as well as the general public will be better off if he bows with good grace to the inevitable. However, as has been mentioned several times already, this system cannot be directly perceived and grasped by the individual. As a highly complex composite whole, it can only be grasped conceptually, and that requires an intellectual attitude.

When one has correctly understood the type of coherence of contemporary society, he will also assume an appropriate attitude toward it. He who approaches the complicated mechanism of the society with an instinctive or affective attitude, must necessarily feel his dependence on it as an unbearable, external coercion. But if he approaches it with an intellectual attitude, he will consider submission to the external interdependence represented by this society not so much as an oppressive force, but rather as a recognized social necessity. A certain, rationally founded solidarity will then take effect, i.e., the realization that one is, after all, in the same boat with others and that he must stay afloat with them or all will go down together. Even if one could transfer to another boat, the new circle would also subject him to the exigencies of external interdependence. The specific demands would of course be different, but who knows if in the long run the new yoke would really be lighter than the former one, with which he is at least familiar. . . .

However, I by no means suggest intellectual cultivation to be a quietistic finding-oneself-in-everything, the source of a paradiselike, frictionless state of society. Whereas the citizen recognizes the necessity of fitting into the external social interdependence, he can very easily criticize the various demands which are made of him. He may be of the opinion that the social order currently representing this interdependence should provide him with a more favorable position, and can accordingly strive for social changes. But since his relationship to the order of external interdependence and his attitude toward it are controlled by intelligent deliberation, his opposition will not be expressed in irresponsible squabbling, snarling obstruction, or hysterical, destructive rages, but rather in purposeful acts of interest. That is of greater benefit to him and does less harm to the public at large. Nothing makes a social class so blind to its material advantages as emotional reactions, embellished with idle value-ideas, directed against the existing state of society. Deliberate interest struggles, regardless from which quarter they originate, do not threaten the society with disintegration, but are, on the contrary, one of those forms of active participation in the management of society which today is so gravely missed by all friends of democracy.

Intellectual discipline means still more, however, namely the capacity to adopt one's attitude to the situation. In the present context that means the ability to give vent to one's feelings within the primary groups and to control them in secondary groups. It would be an unseemly request to ask that we feel affection and sympathy for all those with whom we are joined together in society and that we should love them as our brothers. No one does it. Instead of preaching a utopian brotherhood, one would do better to teach people to leave their feelings at home when they move into the sphere of public life. One does not need to feel any personal liking for those with whom one works or pursues a common end, and—figuratively speaking—with whom one eats at the same table. Of course, this may be accomplished without personal liking only if these relationships can be maintained in complete affective neutrality. Otherwise one may suffer having to cooperate with people one is indifferent to, or perhaps can't stand.

In the large-scale society and its relationships, loyalty takes the place of love.

Much greater demands are made by another form of emotional abstinence—the renunciation of collective cults of value and the search for confirmation of one's own value-conceptions by joining with others presumably of the same mind. This kind of emotional abstinence requires that one recognize that value-ideas, by their very nature, are unsuitable objects for collective emotions. This insight may be gained from two sources. One is the so-called *value nihilism*, the philosophical exposure of the value-idea as an illusion. The value nihilist of course also makes primary valuations, but since he does not impose a superstructure of value-ideas upon them, he is never tempted to seek confirmation in a value-community with others. He knows that his primary valuations are subjective emotional relationships and as such neither need confirmation nor are capable of it; his emotional relationships to things are entirely and irrevocably his own and he ridicules their objectification in value-ideas as the superstition which they are.

The other way is less radical. One subscribes to value-ideas himself, but regards them from the standpoint of *value subjectivism* as personal ideals which can be expressed in words only with great lack of precision and intelligibility. The value subjectivist does not recognize the value-idea to be meaningless as such, but does hold the community of value-thinking for a self-deception. He individualizes his value-experience by realizing that it is not enhanced by concentration in words and symbols, but can only be dragged down into a bubbling morass of phrases.

Such discipline and asceticism of the emotions is only conceivable on the basis of an essentially intellectual attitude. The comprehension of the relations of interdependence in the large-scale society is itself an achievement of the intellect. Only an intellectually self-controlled personality is in a position to keep two diametrically opposed social attitudes apart and to alternate between them: the affective and the rational. Only with an intellectual approach is one in a position to endure inner seclusion in the social sphere. Only a good portion of intellectual self-discipline can save us from trying to ascribe general objective validity to our own evaluations, and then together with others of a like mind wanting to shape the world in this image. Intellectual self-control alone enables us not only to "tolerate" the deviating value-conceptions of others in the relationships of external interdependence, but to remain undisturbed and untouched by them, since they are not our affair.

Selected Bibliography

1. "Zur Statistik der Unehelichen." *Allgemeines statistisches Archiv* 11 (1919): 212–20.
2. *Das uneheliche Kind und seine Mutter im Recht des neuen Staates: Ein Versuch auf der Basis kritischer Rechtsvergleichung.* Munich, Berlin, Leipzig, 1920.
3. "Adult Education in Finland." *Bulletin 25, The World Association for Adult Education,* 1925.
4. *Die Masse und ihre Aktion: Ein Beitrag zur Soziologie der Revolution.* Stuttgart, 1926.
5. "Die Gruppe und die Kategorien Gemeinschaft und Gesellschaft." *Archiv für Sozialwissenschaften und Sozialpolitik,* 58 (1927): 338–74.
6. *Die Gestalten der Gesellung.* Karlsruhe, 1928.
7. "Soziologie der Industriearbeit und des Betriebes." *Die Arbeit: Zeitschrift für Gewerkschaftspolitik und Wirtschaftskunde* 6, no. 11 (1929): 673–89, 766–81. Reprinted Soziologische Texte, vol. 1. Neuwied, 1959.
8. "Erziehung als Gegenstand der Soziologie." *Die Erziehung* 5, no. 7 (1930): 405–27.
9. "Klassenlage, Klassenbewusstsein und öffentliche Schule." *Die Arbeit: Zeitschrift für Gewerkschaftspolitik und Wirtschaftskunde* 7 (1930): 260–66, 331–40.
10. "Panik im Mittelstand." *Ibid.*: 637–54.
11. "Sozialpolitik im Betriebe." *Ibid.*: 831–40.
12. "Zur Theorie des Klassenbegriffs und der proletarischen Klasse." *Schmollers Jahrbuch für Gesetzgebung, Verwaltung und Volkswirtschaft* 54 (1930): 185–236.
13. "Die Mittelschichten und die Sozialdemokratie." *Die Arbeit: Zeit-*

schrift für Gewerkschaftspolitik und Wirtschaftskunde 8 (1931): 617–35.

14. "Formen der Vereinsamung." Kölner Vierteljahreshefte für Soziologie 10 (1931): 220–39, 355–63.

15. Die soziale Schichtung des deutschen Volkes: Soziographischer Versuch auf statistischer Grundlage. Stuttgart, 1932.

16. "Klasse." In Internationales Handbuch des Gewerkschaftswesens, pp. 947–50. Berlin, 1932.

17. "Natürliche Auslese, soziale Schichtung und das Problem der Generationen." Kölner Vierteljahreshefte für Soziologie 12 (1933):

18. "Soziale Gliederung der deutschen Arbeitnehmer." Archiv für Sozialwissenschaft und Sozialpolitik 68 (1933): 151–88.

19. "Statistische Analyse der wirtschaftlich Selbständigen." Ibid.: 407–39.

20. "Nationalsocialismens Fremtidsbillede." Socialt Tidsskrift 10 (1935): 245–57.

21. Sociologi, Grundrids og Hovedproblemer. Copenhagen, 1939.

22. Kritik af Reklamen. Copenhagen, 1943.

23. Intelligensen. Stockholm, 1944.

24. "Rettens Emancipation fra Moralen." Statsvetenskaplig Tidsskrift för politik, statistik, ekonomi, 1945, pp. 195–212.

25. Debat med Uppsala om Moral og Ret. Lund, 1946.

26. "Om intellektuel humanisme." Ord och Bild, 1946, pp. 458–65.

27. Vorstudien zu einer Soziologie des Rechts. Acta Jutlandica 19, no. 2. Copenhagen, 1947.

28. Klassesamfundet i Støbegryden. Copenhagen, 1948.

29. "Soziometrik und ihre Grenzen." Kölner Zeitschrift für Soziologie 1 (1948/49): 292–302.

30. Den Danske intelligens fra reformationen til nutiden: En studie i empirisk kultursociologi. Acta Jutlandica 21. Aarhus, 1949.

31. Aufgaben und Stellung der Intelligenz in der Gesellschaft. Stuttgart, 1949. (German edition of Intelligensen.)

32. Die Klassengesellschaft im Schmelztiegel. Cologne, Hagen, 1949. (German edition of Klassesamfundet i Støbegryden.)

33. "Kritische Bemerkungen zum Begriffe der Ideologie." In Gegenwartsprobleme der Soziologie: Alfred Vierkandt zum 80. Geburtstag, edited by G. Eisermann. Potsdam, 1949.

34. Den Danske Studenters Sociale Oprindelse. In collaboration with Torben Agersnap. Nordiske Studier i Sociologi 2. Copenhagen, 1950.

35. "An Historical Study of the Origins and Structure of the Danish Intelligentsia." *British Journal of Sociology* 1: 209–20.
36. "Methods of Studies on the Intelligentsia." *Explorations in Entrepreneurial History* 3, no. 2 (1950).
37. "A Radio Test of Musical Taste." *Public Opinion Quarterly* 14 (1950): 453–60.
38. "Some Reflections on Sociometry and Its Limitations." *Theoria*, 1950, pp. 36–48.
39. *Soziale Umschichtungen in einer dänischen Mittelstadt.* Acta Jutlandica 33. Aarhus, 1951.
40. "Die Legende von der Massengesellschaft." *Archiv für Rechts-und Sozialphilosophie*, 1951, pp. 305–23.
41. "Preliminary National Report for the First International Working Conference on Social Stratification and Social Mobility." In *Preliminary Papers and Proposals*, edited by Rinde and Rokkan. Oslo, 1951.
42. With David Glass. "Circular Letter Addressed to Participants in the First Working Conference." *Ibid.*
43. "Notes Concerning the ISA Programme of Research on Social Stratification and Social Mobility." *Ibid.*
44. With David Glass. "Survey of Existing Material Relating to Social Stratification and Social Mobility." *Ibid.*
45. With David Glass. "Discussion Paper for Conference." *Ibid.*
46. "Human Society and Scientific Law." *Canadian Journal of Economics and Political Science* 18, no. 2 (1952): 184–94.
47. Über dynamische Analyse sozialer Umschichtungen." In *Soziologische Forschung in unserer Zeit: Festschrift für Leopold von Wiese zum 75. Geburtstag*, edited by K. G. Specht. Cologne, Opladen, 1952.
48. *Ideologie und Wahrheit: Eine soziologische Kritik des Denkens.* Stuttgart, Vienna, 1953.
49. "Sociology and Democracy." *Acta Sociologica* 1, fasc. 1 (1954): 10–13.
50. "Social Sciences and Their Method." *Ibid.*: 14–17.
51. "Evaluational Nihilism." *Ibid.*: 18–25.
52. "A Dynamic Analysis of Social Mobility." *Ibid.*: 26–38.
53. "Recruitment of University Students." *Ibid.*: 39–48.
54. "Intelligentsia." *Ibid.*: 49–61.

55. "Der Intellektuelle in der europäischen Gesellschaft von heute." *Ibid.*: 62–74.

56. "Die Legende von der Massengesellschaft." *Ibid.*: 75–79.

57. "Bemerkungen zur Soziologie des Denkens." *Archiv für Rechts-und Sozialphilosophie* 45, no. 1 (1959): 23–53.

58. *Die Gesellschaft zwischen Pathos und Nüchternheit.* Acta Jutlandica 32, no. 1. Copenhagen, 1960.

59. *Arbeiten zur Soziologie: Methode; Moderne Großgesellschaft; Rechtssoziologie; Ideologiekritik.* Selected and introduced by Paul Trappe. Soziologische Texte, vol. 7. Neuwied, Berlin, 1962.